Wines of the Loire

Roger Voss is one of Britain's leading wine and food writers. He has written widely in many national newspapers, including the *European* and *Sunday Telegraph*, as well as for magazines such as *Wine*, *Decanter* and *House and Garden*. For four years he was editor of the *Which? Wine Guide*. His books include guides to the wines of the Loire, Alsace and the Rhône, fortified wines, Chardonnay and Cabernet Sauvignon wines, and most recently a full-colour, illustrated book on French food and wine *France: A Feast of Food and Wine*.

FABER BOOKS ON WINE
General Editor: Julian Jeffs

Bordeaux (new edition) by David Peppercorn
Burgundy (new edition) by Anthony Hanson
French Country Wines by Rosemary George
German Wines by Ian Jamieson
Haut-Brion by Asa Briggs
Italian Wines (new edition) by Philip Dallas
Port (new edition) by George Robertson
Sherry (new edition) by Julian Jeffs
The Wines of Alsace by Tom Stevenson
The Wines of Australia (new edition) by Oliver Mayo
The Wines of Greece by Miles Lambert-Gocs
The Wines of the Rhône (new edition) by John Livingstone-Learmonth

WINES
OF THE LOIRE

ROGER VOSS

faber and faber
LONDON · BOSTON

First published in 1995
by Faber and Faber Limited
3 Queen Square London WC1N 3AU

Phototypeset by Intype, London

Printed in England by Clays Ltd, St Ives Plc

Maps compiled by Soo Ware and designed
by Claire Bicknell, Stylo Graphics

A CIP record for this book
is available from the British Library

ISBN 0 571 164854 (cased)
0 571 164862 (pbk)

2 4 6 8 10 9 7 5 3 1

Contents

List of Maps — vii

Introduction — ix

1 Geography and history — 1
2 How wine is made and sold — 9
3 The wines of the mountains — 18
4 Sancerre and Menetou-Salon — 25
5 The wines of Pouilly-sur-Loire — 45
6 Reuilly, Quincy and the lesser *appellations* of the Centre — 57
7 Touraine and the wines of the Loir — 68
8 The wines of Vouvray — 92
9 The wines of Montlouis — 110
10 The great red wines of Touraine: Chinon, Bourgueil and Saint-Nicolas — 119
11 Sparkling wines of the Loire — 136
12 The still wines of Saumur and Saumur-Champigny — 147
13 The wines of Anjou — 158
14 The wines of Muscadet and the Pays Nantais — 179
15 The wines of Poitou and the Vendée, and *vins de pays* — 194
16 The food of the Loire — 200

Appendix 1. The *appellations* of the Loire — 205
Appendix 2. Production figures by *appellation* — 219
Appendix 3. Loire vintages as at autumn 1993 — 222
Appendix 4. Major producers and their addresses — 230
Appendix 5. Useful addresses in the Loire Valley — 239
Appendix 6. Where to eat and stay in the Loire — 242

Appendix 7. Table: Areas under vine on the Loire 247

Bibliography 248

List of Maps

France, showing the vineyard areas of the Loire   viii

The main viticultural regions of the Loire Valley   2–3

The vineyards of the Upper Loire   20

The vineyards of Sancerre and Pouilly-sur-Loire   26

The vineyards of central France   58–9

The vineyards of Touraine and the Valley of the Loir   70–1

The vineyards of Vouvray and Montlouis   94

The red wine vineyards of western Touraine   120

The vineyards of Saumur and Saumur-Champigny   148

The vineyards of Anjou and Saumur   160

The vineyards of Anjou Villages and the Layon Valley   161

The vineyards of the Pays Nantais   180–1

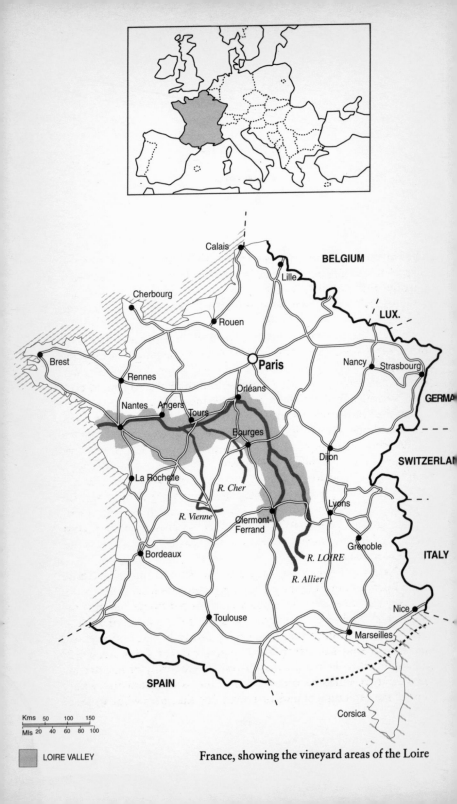

France, showing the vineyard areas of the Loire

LOIRE VALLEY

Introduction

The wines of the Loire have been curiously neglected in wine literature. While Bordeaux, Burgundy and Champagne have been frequently and variously worshipped and recorded, the Loire has received only occasional recognition, or has been passed over in silence.

Perhaps this is because the Loire has none of the star-studded cast of the other wine areas. There are none of the fireworks, the world-beating wines, the great names of showmanship. Loire wines are often understated, aiming to please rather than overwhelm, to provide enjoyment rather than imperishable memories.

Yet the Loire produces wines as fine as any in France. It has given the world one of its most fashionable wine styles – the dry whites made from Sauvignon Blanc. It produces what was until very recently the most popular inexpensive white wine – Muscadet. It can offer sweet whites, fine reds, enjoyable sparkling wines. If not all of what is sold from the Loire is of acceptable quality, that is no less true of other wine regions as well; but somehow, the lake of undistinguished Bordeaux gets forgotten when measured against the Crus Classés, while the Loire is not so easily forgiven a second-rate Anjou Blanc.

Perhaps Loire wines are harder to understand fully than those from Bordeaux or Burgundy. Their apparent simplicity is deceptive. It's very easy to enjoy a fine Pouilly Fumé or red from Chinon at the superficial level of pleasant fruit, and not to appreciate that these are wines that can age into something altogether exceptional. We have been told sufficiently often that great red Bordeaux needs ageing for it to be readily understood; we are only at the starting point of perceiving the same for some Loire wines. Similarly, we are just at the beginning of understanding that the sweet white wines of the Layon Valley need just as much maturity – perhaps more – to be really appreciated as Sauternes do.

This is one thing I learnt as I researched this book. Another was that just as the wines grow on you, so does the landscape. If the wines are understated, so is the region itself. Apart from the isolated vineyards of the upper reaches of the river in the Massif Central, the Loire landscape is gentle. The countryside rolls softly, with trees rather than hills or mountains the punctuation on the horizon. There is none of the drama of the estuary of the Gironde in Bordeaux or the slopes of the Côte d'Or in Burgundy, none of the powerful mountain landscape of Alsace. The light is dappled rather than brilliant – the colours that go into Impressionist paintings. This is rich countryside, justly called the Garden of France, where vines take their place alongside many other fruits of the earth, where people traditionally have lived well, and where the nobles built their châteaux because they could be assured of plenty on their tables.

I first visited the Loire many years ago. I stayed in Angers, travelling to Saumur to visit the cellars of the sparkling wine producers. Our road took us alongside a wide expanse of shallow, slow-moving river, dotted with sand banks and wooded islands. This first sight of the Loire was disappointing: wide, yes, but with none of the sense of power found in the Rhône or the Rhine. It was a surprisingly empty riverscape – occasional small rowing boats were all that moved. It was only afterwards I was told that, as a result of silting, the Loire's waters are today so shallow that any viable navigation is impossible.

That has had advantages. It has meant that the Loire's landscape has not been damaged by heavy industry in the way that the Rhône between Lyon and Valence has been so heavily polluted. It has meant that the cities along the river have looked away from its waters for their means of transport – to the railways and then the motorways – and have developed links which go north and south rather than east and west along the course of the river. There is still no decent road following the line of the river between Orléans and Angers. It has meant that the countryside has remained relatively unspoilt, still mainly agricultural, despite its central position in France.

Since that first visit, of course, I have been back frequently, especially in the last few years as I worked on this book. I have come to enjoy the approachability of the landscape, the way towns and châteaux appear through trees, the way the great forests with which this part of France is blessed give way to meadows and vineyards, the great vistas of rolling country that can be seen from the tops of castle towers or from the plateau land that stretches from the cliffs bordering the river in Touraine. I have also learned to appreciate and respect the immense distances involved in travelling the length of the Loire.

Wine plays a part in most regions of the Loire. Alongside its initial course in the mountains, the vineyards are tiny and scattered. They were destroyed by phylloxera, but their economic viability disappeared with the development of transport systems, such as railways, which could take wine around the country, replacing the lightweight products of the mountains with the robust wines of the south of France, and leaving the vineyards of the Auvergne, Forez, Roanne, isolated.

From the twin vineyards of Sancerre and Pouilly onwards, though, wine becomes increasingly important. In Touraine and Anjou, the heartland of the Loire, vines are found in every *commune* that is in some way connected with the Loire itself or one of its tributaries, themselves great rivers. The rivers provide the right microclimate, the extra degrees of warmth needed to ripen grapes at this northerly latitude in France. In Muscadet, the Pays Nantais, is to be found the greatest concentration of vineyards in France outside parts of Languedoc or Bordeaux.

It is much easier to talk about the diversity of Loire wines than about their similarities. There is apparently little in common between the Gamays of Côtes du Forez, produced on a level with the great red wines of the northern Rhône only a few kilometres away, and the white wines of Muscadet, apart from the fact that both are grown on the same river. And yet those Gamays share more characteristics with Muscadet than with Rhône wines: their lightness and acidity for a start, their cool climate fruit flavours rather than robust power. Even the richest wines of the Loire – the reds of Chinon and Bourgueil, the sweet whites of Quarts de Chaume and Bonnezeaux – rely as much on elegance as weight, on balance as much as on power. That is their charm, their accessibility, and also the reason for their relative obscurity in a world where wines seem designed to dominate rather than flatter.

In this book I have aimed to present a general portrait, embellished with detail, of the wines of the Loire region. I have described the landscape, the wine styles of each area, topping up the general with specific statistics. And I have offered pictures of some of the people who make the wine, not necessarily the most important producers, but those whom I think are producing the most interesting, perhaps innovatory, wines – perhaps wines that respect the best of the local traditions. There are too many producers in any area for more than a tiny selection to be covered, but they have been chosen to represent different approaches and styles.

For readers who relish greater detail, I have deliberately taken out the essential statistics and put them into appendices. These are the reference section of what is otherwise a book which I hope can be read as much as dipped into for facts and figures. And for those who feel inspired to find out more by travelling to the Loire, I have listed major producers and their addresses and – more important – places to stay and eat that I enjoyed while I was engaged on what became a much larger work than I had ever anticipated.

The amount of research needed explains why I delivered the copy to Faber and Faber two years late. My initial wild optimism rapidly changed to a belief that the work would never be finished. And if I offer my thanks to Sarah Gleadell and Belinda Matthews of Faber and to Julian Jeffs, the book's editor, for their patience and understanding, I suspect that I am following in a line of other authors in this series of books who have become so enthralled by their subject they have found it difficult to know when to stop.

Other acknowledgements are due and are gratefully given. My first must be to Charles and Philippa Sydney, who have established themselves in the heart of Touraine, from where they search out fine wines for export to Britain. Through them I met many of the producers profiled in this book, and with them I was able to enjoy unfailing and charming hospitality. In addition, they have contributed the vintage notes to be found in Appendix 3. Also to Tom Stevenson, author of *Sotheby's World Wine Encyclopedia* (Dorling Kindersley, 1988).

The French wine organizations have been especially helpful and patient with continuing requests for information and the arrangement of visits to producers. In London, Catherine Manac'h and Sophie Vallejo in the offices of Sopexa, the French agricultural export organization, have been a constant source of information, help and advice. In France, François Midavaine and Roselyne

Delaunay of the Comité Interprofessionel des Vins de Nantes; Claire Duchêne of Conseil Interprofessionel des Vins d'Anjou et de Saumur; M. Chabirand and Nathalie Royer of Comité Interprofessionel des Vins de Touraine Val de Loire; M. Masson of the Commission de Promotions des Vins de Pouilly and himself a wine producer; Jean-Max Roger, President of the growers in Sancerre; Claude Lafond in Reuilly. All have organized, helped, offered hospitality and information for which I am extremely grateful.

There is one further acknowledgement and a dedication. When I started work on the book, I was talking to Peter Hallgarten, wine importer, creator of flavoursome liqueurs and a mine of information. From him I learnt that his father Fritz, then only recently dead, had himself planned a book on the Loire. For that purpose, he had accumulated quantities of papers, books, notes and copies of articles. I was offered the chance to go through this wealth of information, which did not just provide a starting point for my researches but an inspiration as well. Therefore I dedicate this book to the memory of Fritz Hallgarten, with the hope that he would have approved of the book that finally came out of his researches.

I

Geography and history

The geography of the Loire

The river system of the Loire is the largest in France. Together with its tributaries – the Allier, the Cher, the Indre, the Vienne, the Creuse, the Maine and its tributaries the Sarthe and the Loir, the Sèvre Nantaise – it covers all the land north of Limoges, west of Vézelay, south of Le Mans and east of the ocean. The Loire itself, from its source close to the 1,551-metre volcanic peak of the Gerbier de Jonc in the Massif Central south-east of Le Puy, travels over a thousand kilometres to the Atlantic Ocean, the first half from south to north, the second half from east to west.

Given the extent of the land covered by the Loire system, it is no surprise that geographically and geologically, it is not a distinct entity. Geographically, the land traversed by the Loire encompasses the mountains of south central France in the Auvergne and Limousin, the cereal-growing plains of the north centre in Berry, the verdant pastures of Touraine and Anjou, and the flat lands of the Pays Nantais and the Vendée. The rivers pass through some of France's most ancient and beautiful cities – Nevers, Orléans, Blois, Tours, Saumur – and some of its poorest and most remote regions.

This diversity of landscape is a reflection of the different soil types to be found in the Loire region. From the volcanic soils of the Puy de Dôme at its source, the river flows north, emerging from the mountains to the calcareous and siliceous Kimmeridgean soils of Sancerre and Pouilly-sur-Loire, themselves extensions of the chalk hills of Champagne and Chablis.

From Orléans, at the half-way point of the river's journey to the sea, where from flowing north it turns almost a right angle and flows west, the soil type changes again. The tufa, a soft, almost white stone which forms the bedrock of the soil, with chalk and gravel on top, is almost ubiquitous. For centuries it has been used to

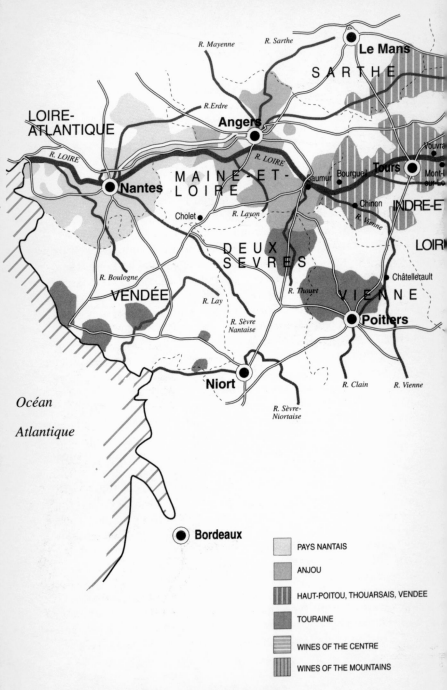

The main viticultural regions of the Loire Valley

R. Loir

LOIRET

Orléans

...OIRE

R. Beuvron

Blois

Gien

ET-CHER

CHER

Sancerre

Valençay

Pouilly-sur-Loire

Quincy

Bourges

Nevers

Reuilly

INDRE

R. Cher

Châteauroux

Château-
meillant

R. Indre

ALLIER

Saint-Pourçain-
sur-Sioule

R. Arnon

PUY DE-

Roanne

LOIRE

R. Sioule

Clermont-
Ferrand

Montbrison

DOME

R. Dore

R. Allier

R. LOIRE

10   20
5   10   15

build the local houses, and today the cliffs forming the main river banks are peppered with caves which provide natural storage for the wines. Vines grow on the slopes leading up from the river and on the tops of the cliffs along all the rivers in Touraine and the Saumurrois.

The landscape changes again in western Anjou. The small river Aubance marks a transition from chalk to schist, gneiss and granite. This western extension of the Massif Armoricain of Brittany forms the bedrock of the vineyards of Anjou itself and of the Pays Nantais.

Climatically, the Loire region exhibits a gradual shift from east to west, from the continental climate of hot summers and freezing winters in Sancerre (ideally suited to the fast-ripening Sauvignon Blanc) to the milder weather of western Anjou and the Pays Nantais, influenced by the Atlantic Ocean. The cooler summers of the west are often mitigated by warm, dry autumns. Some of the warmest parts of the whole viticultural area are found at the midway point, in Touraine and particularly in the sheltered vineyards of Chinon, Bourgueil and Saumur-Champigny, the source, unsurprisingly, of the best red wines.

The Loire itself forms a climatic boundary between northern and southern France. It is at the limits of viticulture: there is little wine produced to the north of the river except in privileged pockets such as Bourgueil and Savennières and the isolated vineyards of the Loir. Indeed, it would be fair to say that without the Loire and its tributaries, vines would not grow so successfully this far north in France. The effect of the rivers is similar to that of the rivers Rhine and Mosel in Germany – of raising the ambient temperature just those few vital degrees, enough to make the difference between viable viticulture and a severe struggle. Even so, ripeness can often be a problem in cooler years.

This means that vineyards are planted to obtain maximum benefit from long exposure to the sun. A classic example is Savennières, whose steep vineyard slopes face south and west, deriving benefit not only from the heat coming from the river, but gaining as many sunshine hours as possible. This need for sunshine and for heat from the river is particularly important towards the western end of the Loire; in the eastern vineyards of Sancerre and Pouilly, the greater heat of the summer means vines can be planted further from the river, although the exposure of slopes remains vital.

4

The history of viticulture in the Loire

The story of viticulture in the Loire region is as long as the history of viticulture in France. It was first the Greeks and Phoenicians, and later the Romans, who brought the vine to what was then Gaul. As the Romans pushed up the Rhône Valley, they planted vines as they went, hoping to recreate in the remote and hostile north at least some of the pleasures of the life they had left behind.

Legend then says that the Romans brought the vine to the Loire as they moved to occupy the whole country. There are certainly relics of them in place-names – the Porte César in Sancerre is named, so they say, after Julius Caesar, who certainly passed that way. Pouilly-sur-Loire was originally Paulica Villa, the villa of Paulus. Then there is the Roman name for Champigny, the red wine *appellation* of Saumur-Champigny: Campus Ignis, field of fire, a reference, it is supposed, to the especially beneficial microclimate that has allowed successful viticulture there.

Viticulture gradually moved northwards with the Romans' thirst. From the Burgundian vineyards of the Côte d'Or, which were planted early in the Christian era, it was not a long jump to planting vines on especially propitious, well-exposed chalk hillsides such as Sancerre. From there, by the fourth century, the eastern half of the Loire valley was being planted. At the same time, from Bordeaux, vines reached the western end of the Loire. Whether the different origins of the first vine plantings – one from Bordeaux, the other from Burgundy – explain the different allegiances of today's grapes on the Loire (those on the west close to Bordeaux, those in the east closer to Burgundy) is hard to say; at that early period, it is unlikely that the grape varieties being planted bore much resemblance to what is found today. But it is certainly true that the Loire still divides its viticultural origins conveniently down the middle.

The centuries following the collapse of the Roman Empire were as chaotic on the Loire as they were anywhere else in Western Europe. As elsewhere, it was the Church and its newly-created offshoots, the monasteries, which sheltered what civilization there was left, a civilization that always had a place for the fruit of the vine.

Certain names keep cropping up in connection with viticulture in the Loire region at this time. Saint Martin of Tours, one of the city's earliest bishops, is perhaps the most formidable. He lived in the fourth century and is credited with having planted vines at some time or another in most of Touraine. Both Montlouis and Vouvray claim intimate links with him, as does Azay-le-Rideau. Saint Gregory, a later bishop of Tours, is similarly credited with having inspired much vine planting within his bishopric. Over in Reuilly, it was the monks of the abbey of Saint-Denis in Paris who encouraged viticulture, while in Sancerre, wine production was stimulated by the proximity of the monks of Saint-Satur.

As the civil authorities gradually gained greater power, they too became involved in viticulture. In the Middle Ages there seems to have been something of a contest between rival lords – along the lines of those between Old World and New World wine producers – as to whose wine was best. It was all started by the Dukes of Burgundy, who used wine as a major export and diplomatic weapon. Not to be outdone, the rulers of Anjou and Touraine (who for at least a century were also the kings of England) promoted their wine, encouraging exports to England and the Low Countries, using the Loire as a river route at a time when boats could still use its shallow waters. Thus it was that, again, the Loire was divided: the wines of the east looking to Burgundy and being exported to Paris; those of the west looking to the ocean.

In addition, of course, Loire wines found a captive local market with the arrival of the age of the châteaux. Marking a convenient border between the realms of the French kings in the Île de France and the rest of France, which was normally at loggerheads with the king and likely to be invaded at any moment by the English, the Loire has its great medieval fortresses: the towering donjons of Angers, Langeais and Chinon are formidable edifices even today. The arrival of more peaceful times and a more leisured aristocracy changed the nature of the château from castle to palace. The fantasies of Chambord, Chenonceaux, Ussé (the original palace of Sleeping Beauty) testify to the wealth of the rulers of France from the sixteenth century onwards. They bought local wines – from Vouvray, from Montlouis, from Orléans, from Vendôme. Some wines gained sufficient notoriety for kings to go in search of them: Louis XIV is supposed to have journeyed to taste Savennières, although there is no record of him having arrived, so bad were the roads.

Vast quantities of wine were shipped on the river on flat-bottomed barges. Around fifty barges a day travelled along the Loire in

Touraine in the 1830s, all of them carrying at least some wine. Some was going up-river to Orléans, the closest river port on the Loire to Paris. Some was going down-river to Nantes, to be shipped to England and the Netherlands – always big customers of Loire wines – or later to the French colonies in the West Indies.

By the end of the Middle Ages some of the more recognizable grape varieties had arrived in their present homes on the Loire. The Cabernet Franc, the grape of the red wines of Touraine and Anjou, arrived from Bordeaux, thanks to the links through the English crown. Known as the Breton, most probably because it was used for the red wines sold to Brittany, it soon established itself in much of Anjou and Touraine. The Chenin Blanc's origins are somewhat more mysterious. The most recent theory, propounded by Pierre Bréjoux and endorsed by Jancis Robinson, is that it is a mutation of a native wild vine found in Anjou and called the Pineau d'Aunis, after a village near Saumur. This pale, red-berried vine still makes rosé wine in Touraine. By selection, it yielded the white Chenin Blanc, also called the Pineau de la Loire and sometimes Pineau d'Anjou. It has certainly been recorded since the fifteenth century, and may possibly have been extant as early as the ninth century.

The Sauvignon Blanc is a relative of the Cabernet Sauvignon, and has its origins, like its other close connection the Cabernet Franc, in Bordeaux. It was widely planted in the sixteenth and seventeenth centuries in the regions of Berry and Nevers where it is encountered today: Sancerre, Pouilly-sur-Loire, Reuilly and Quincy among others. Then, for some unknown reason, it was largely abandoned in favour of higher-yielding vines, such as the Chasselas, before regaining its place after phylloxera at the end of the nineteenth century.

The other major grape varieties of the Loire – the Pinot Noir and Gamay at one end and the Melon de Bourgogne at the other – are both imports. The Melon arrived in the seventeenth century as a result of a frost which destroyed the plantings of red vines in Muscadet. The local growers were persuaded by their best customers, the Dutch, who used the wine for distillation, to import white grape varieties which were most suitable for the end product. The Melon de Bourgogne was found to be the most resistant to frost, and duly took over as the major vine of the Pays Nantais, under the name of Muscadet which it had adopted by the eighteenth century.

The time of arrival of the Pinot Noir and the Gamay, even more direct imports from Burgundy, is more uncertain. The Pinot Noir, one of the most ancient vines, was already planted in Burgundy in Roman times, and could well have arrived in the Loire not long after, quite possibly in its local spiritual home at Sancerre. Gamay, popular in Burgundy even before the Middle Ages, could well have followed the same venerable route, but is more likely to have arrived in the nineteenth century in the Touraine regions where it is now most popular.

Phylloxera, the aphid that attacks the roots of the vine, was just as much of a scourge in the Loire, where it arrived in the 1850s, as it was everywhere else in the wine world. In some regions, it literally wiped out the wine business. It particularly affected the trade of the vineyards of the upper and central reaches of the river: Roanne, Auvergne, Gien, the Orléanais. Many of the vineyards in the mountains at the edge of the Massif Central, in the upper Loire Valley and its tributaries, have never recovered. From 60,000 hectares before phylloxera, the Côtes d'Auvergne has a mere 1,200 hectares today. The total plantings in the whole Loire region, including tributaries, are only a little over a half of the 200,000 hectares they were before phylloxera, and despite increases in certain areas such as Sancerre and Pouilly and in Anjou and Muscadet, are unlikely to get any larger as peripheral areas continue to decline.

2

How the wine is made and sold

Wine-making in the Loire vineyards differs little in principle from wine-making in other parts of France. It is organized in much the same way, and follows most of the same basic rules. A few years ago, it would have been possible to say that the Loire had been slow to move into the modern era of wine-making, with its emphasis on hygiene, on the health of the grapes, and on the need to ensure that wine is treated as rigorously as any other food product. To a large extent, though, that has changed, as outside influences and wider knowledge have filtered through to even the smallest cellar and poorest *vigneron*.

The vineyards of the Loire are organized on strict hierarchical principles. Where the vineyard is, its exposure to the sun, its soil, its microclimate, what grapes are grown in it, what yields the grower gets from his vines (expressed in hectolitres per hectare), and how the vines are pruned and trained (vines are normally trained on wires arranged in such a way as to allow maximum exposure of the bunches of grapes to the sun): on these will depend what level in the hierarchy the vineyard attains and, consequently, how the grower can describe his wines.

At the most basic level, a vineyard will be classified simply as *vin de table*. There are few, if any, vineyards in the Loire which fit into this basic category; any that did will long since have disappeared, when they became uneconomic to run because of the low price the grapes or wine could fetch. You can still find small strips of vines, backyard plots, which are there just to make wine for the farmer; these may be, legally speaking, *vins de table*, but will never be seen on the market.

On the next level in the hierarchy are the *vins de pays*. These are, technically speaking, *vins de table* but with some regional characteristics. The description is often used for wines which do not fit into the truly local, more tightly-classified styles of wine which are found at the top of the hierarchy. *Vin de pays* is equally used to describe wines made from grape varieties which are not indigenous to an area but which, nevertheless, are of high quality. In the Loire the main *vin de pays* – the Vin de Pays du Jardin de la France – is used, for example, to produce Chardonnay wines from areas where Chardonnay is not indigenous, or from vineyards which lie outside the main traditional areas.

Traditional wines from the heartland of the Loire vineyards occupy the top two levels of the hierarchy. They can be *Vins Délimités de Qualité Supérieure* (VDQS), generally wines from areas where there are only small numbers of vineyards, or which are aspiring to higher quality. However, they do possess as much regional character as the other major category, *Appellation d'Origine Contrôlée* (AC or AOC). All the Loire's important wine areas are covered by ACs. A map of an *appellation* is a complex affair: every individual vineyard, even portion of a vineyard, is considered for inclusion or exclusion in the AC. Its inclusion will depend on whether it satisfies all the criteria mentioned above. Even after all that, the subsequent wine will be judged by tasting panels to determine whether it is worthy – and, more important, typical enough – to bear the *appellation contrôlée*.

One of the problems with this system, certainly as far as the Loire is concerned, is the complexity of the vineyard divisions. The boundary between different *appellations* especially in Touraine and Anjou, can seem tortuous, almost arbitrary. A vineyard can sometimes be allowed more than one *appellation*, depending on how the grapes are vinified; for example, in parts of Anjou, whether a white wine is dry or sweet, and the way the grapes are picked, can determine whether it gets the *appellation* Anjou Blanc or the *appellation* Coteaux du Layon. The vines may be the same, but the climate of that year and the decision of the grower will decide the final style, and therefore the *appellation*. Vouvray is even more complicated: a grower can make two wines from the same patch of vines, both labelled Vouvray, one of which may be medium sweet, the other dry.

Just as there is a hierarchy of *appellations* in the vineyard, so there is a hierarchy in the wine trade. At the most basic level of vine-growing is the *viticulteur*. He grows grapes and then sells them, perhaps to his local co-operative, of which he will be a member; he will be paid according to the quality, the potential alcohol and the quantity. What then happens to those grapes is determined by the co-operative, not the *viticulteur*. The same thing happens if a grower decides to sell his grapes to a *négociant*. These are firms who buy grapes (they may also own a few vineyards, but not sufficient to supply all their sales needs) and then vinify the wines according to their own blends and styles. Again, the decisions are those of the *négociant*, not the grower.

Alternatively, a grower may decide that he will get more money for his grapes if he also vinifies them. He can then sell the finished wine to a *négociant*, or he can bottle and sell it himself. With few exceptions, the finest Loire wines are those made and bottled by *vignerons*. However, because these are often made in small quantities, they can be more expensive than wines bearing the same *appellation* but made in larger batches by co-operatives or *négociants*.

Because of the Loire's northerly position in France, the vineyards can have an irregular growing season. This means that vines are susceptible both to adverse climatic conditions and to the consequent diseases. Climatically, there are three periods during the year that can pose a threat to the production of a large, healthy crop of grapes.

The first is in the spring, as the vines begin to shoot, bud and flower. Spring frost can damage the vines at this tender stage, killing off the year's growth and preventing any grapes being produced at all. Some growers try to prevent this by lighting fires in the vineyard on nights when there is a risk of frost, or by having a system of water sprinklers which can spray the young shoots, enveloping them in pellets of frozen water but preventing them from suffering from even lower temperatures. However, both these systems are expensive, and most growers simply cannot afford them.

The second period of risk is during high summer. The centre of France is prone to severe summer storms, accompanied by heavy rain and often hail, which can damage the crop in a vineyard, perhaps even destroy it. Even more than with the spring frosts, there is little that can be done – except to pray to *le bon Dieu* that the hail falls on your neighbour's vineyard!

The third period of great anxiety for the grower is from the beginning of September. Every day he watches his grapes, to monitor their ripeness and maturity, and he watches the skies, hoping that the rains will not come. A wet harvest-time is not only thoroughly unpleasant for picking, but can also lower the sugar – and therefore the potential alcohol – in the grapes in a matter of hours. Low-sugar grapes mean either low payments at the co-operative or *négociant*, or thin wines which will need heavy bolster-ing – called chaptalizing – with added sugar (a device permitted within certain limits).

If he survives all these climatic threats, a *vigneron* will still need to ensure that his grapes are free of disease at harvest-time. He will need to watch for fungal diseases, for plagues of insects, for endemic problems, all of which need to be monitored and, if neces-sary, rectified by spraying. While the latest thinking in viticulture is that minimal sprays are better than the practice which has grown up since the war of heavy spraying with more and more vicious chemicals, there is still a need, especially in cooler, damper areas like the Loire, to keep problems at bay with the safe, ever-popular *bouille Bordelaise*, 'Bordeaux mixture', based on copper sulphate.

There is, of course, no letting up once the grapes have been harvested. There are just as many pitfalls in making wine as in growing grapes; the only difference is that they are more control-lable, provided the *vigneron* knows what he is doing. Until very recently, wine-making in the Loire was more a question of follow-ing tradition – 'what my grandfather did is good enough for me' – than realizing that methods have reasons. More and more, how-ever, a new generation is taking over, one that has been to university to study wine-making – oenology as it is called. They all understand the science of producing wine: if they are good, they will also understand that wine production is not just a science but also an art, in which they can influence and encourage the expression of the land and the fruit of the land.

Modern technology in the cellar is particularly important where white wine is concerned. To produce wines that are in the modern idiom of fruity, fresh flavours requires clean juice before fermen-tation and controlled temperatures during fermentation (it is gener-ally agreed that 20°C is a maximum temperature for white wine fermentation). Fermentation is more easily controlled in tanks, which are made nowadays of stainless steel, but fermenting certain styles of wine – generally Chardonnay, occasionally Chenin Blanc or Sauvignon Blanc – in wooden barrels, while harder to control, is considered to give the wine an extra dimension of flavour from the taste of the wood. While grapes will often be pressed as quickly as possible before fermentation so that only clean juice is fermented, more innovative techniques allow the juice to remain in contact with the skins for some hours to give the wine more flavour – called *maceration pelliculaire* or skin contact. With rosé wines, also made nowadays in stainless steel tanks, the skins will be left in contact with the juice for up to 24 hours, maybe two days, to impart some of the pigmentation of the skins of the black grapes to the juice.

While the dead yeast cells (the lees) are normally removed from the wine after fermentation, traditional practice in the Muscadet region is for the lees to remain with the wine over the winter period in order to preserve the freshness and the vivacity of the wine before bottling. Similarly, wines fermented in wood will sometimes be left with the lees, again to impart greater complexity and flavour.

The making of red wine has changed less than that of white or rosé wines. Colour is important – and in the Loire, which has cooler weather than more southerly vineyards, getting colour and tannin from the skins is vital, and harder. Treading grapes by foot is time-honoured and is still seen as one of the best ways of extracting colour, but it is labour-intensive and therefore expensive, unless the treaders happen to be the *vigneron*'s family. More normal today is to use a system which keeps the skins in constant contact with the juice by stirring the two together; this can be done by pumping the juice around and over the cap of skins that forms on top of the juice, or in a technique perfected in Australia, having rotating fermenters which keep the juice and skins regularly mixed together.

A technique now widely practised in the Loire, especially where the Gamay grape is concerned, is carbonic maceration. Whole bunches of grapes are put into a closed tank full of carbon monoxide, and fermentation takes place inside the grapes. The results are soft red wines with good colour but low tannins, meaning they can be drunk young. The classic example of this technique in France is Beaujolais Nouveau, a style which has been copied in the Loire with Touraine Primeur.

After the first, alcoholic fermentation, a wine can go through a second fermentation, called the malolactic fermentation, which converts the harsh malic acid (the tartness of apples) into softer lactic acid, thereby lowering the perceived acidity of a wine. All red wines go through this process, and on the Loire, where grapes have a high natural acidity, so do most white wines.

The ageing of red wines in wood after fermentation depends on the style of wine that is being made. Wines intended for early consumption will be kept in tanks and bottled in the spring following the harvest. Those intended as *vins de garde* – for keeping – such as the red wines of Chinon and Bourgueil, will be put into wood for ageing. The wines acquire greater complexity through the taste of the wood transferring to the wine. The effect is also to give the wine some gentle and beneficial oxidation through contact with air through the wood. After ageing, wines will be fined or lightly filtered to remove any deposits before bottling.

At some stage in the wine-making process a producer has to decide, depending on its quality, on the destination of a wine in a particular tank or barrel. He may have decided already when the grapes were picked, by the vineyard or the quality of the grapes. He may decide by regular tasting, or he may not decide until right at the bottling stage. According to his decisions, the wine will be blended with wine in other tanks or barrels, or if it is very special, may be kept as a top *cuvée* to be sold only in small quantities. He will not, however, be allowed to sell the wine under an *appellation contrôlée* until it has been approved in a blind tasting (the origin of the wine is concealed) by the local regulatory authority.

Two other wine styles are produced in the Loire. The *appellation contrôlée* sparkling wines are made by the traditional method also used in Champagne. Fermented wine is bottled with yet more yeast and goes through a second fermentation in the bottle in which it will be sold. The fact that the bottle remains closed means that the carbon dioxide from the fermentation cannot escape, but remains in the wine to form the bubbles when it is finally opened.

Sweet wines, produced mainly in the Layon valley of Anjou and also in Vouvray and Montlouis, are made from grapes which are naturally very high in sugar. If the climatic conditions at harvest-time are right – misty mornings and warm, sunny afternoons – a natural fungus will grow on the grapes (called noble rot, *pourriture noble* or *botrytis cinerea*) which has the effect of shrivelling the berries, removing the water and concentrating the sugar. These shrivelled berries are pressed and the small amount of juice ferments slowly over many months, never fermenting dry because the amount of sugar is too great for the yeast, and leaving rich, sweet wines.

Small holdings and large *négociants*

The Loire is a region of small holdings. Many vine growers are peasant farmers for whom vines represent only a small part of their produce. Others, dedicated to the vine, have larger plots of land, often scattered, rarely one unified estate. The small size of the vineyard holdings has meant that much of the Loire wine trade is controlled either by co-operatives or *négociants*. Only in recent years has the contribution of the grower who also bottles his own wine increased in importance, just as it has done in Burgundy, in Champagne and to a lesser extent in Alsace.

It's worth taking two famous names, one from each end of the river – Sancerre and Muscadet – and looking at them in greater detail. In the 2,138 hectares of productive vineyard in Sancerre, there are 442 growers in total (a figure which includes both the vineyard holdings of larger firms and small, part-time growers). Of these, 164 (37 per cent) own fewer than 1.5 hectares and 178 (40 per cent) own between 1.5 and 5 hectares. This means that 77 per cent of all growers own less than 5 hectares. Only 2 per cent – four growers – own more than 20 hectares, all of them both growers and *négociants*. The average holding therefore works out at 4.8 hectares. Given these figures, it is amazing how much of the wine in Sancerre is actually produced and sold in bottle by growers: 48 per cent. Local *négociants* sell 29 per cent, the local co-operative sells 6 per cent, while the remaining 17 per cent is taken by *négociants* from outside Sancerre – some in Pouilly, but others from as far afield as Saumur and Muscadet.

Turning to Muscadet, the picture is somewhat different. In 1989, the last year for which statistics were available from the local Chambre d'Agriculture, there were 1,540 different holdings in the Muscadet region (that includes both Muscadet Sèvre et Maine and Muscadet: for more details on *appellations*, see Appendix 1). In the same year, the total area of land under vine was 10,987 hectares – which means that the average land holding was 7 hectares, considerably more than in Sancerre. However, the structure of the trade is quite different. Here in the Pays Nantais only 18 per cent of wine is sold in bottle by growers. Two per cent is sold by the region's one co-operative. A massive 80 per cent is sold by *négociants*, most of whom are based locally, others in Saumur.

What does this stark difference between Sancerre and Muscadet tell us? Principally that Muscadet is dominated by big firms whose primary concern is to supply large volumes of wine at a price (there are, of course, honourable exceptions to this). That is why the frosts of 1991, when Muscadet was in short supply, caused tanker-loads of white wine to arrive from the south of France into the cellars of *négociants* in the Pays Nantais (which was then sold as *vin de table*, of course). They had contracts to fulfil and the source of wine was immaterial, as was the state of the Muscadet market.

In the case of Sancerre, where in the past decade the balance has changed in favour of the growers, we learn that there is now a greater emphasis on local character, on quality, on presentation. Again, some of the local *négociants* in Sancerre (who are generally vineyard owners as well, unlike some of the *négociants* of the western Loire) are as concerned as the growers for the reputation of the *appellation*.

The story of Muscadet, with its domination by big *négociant* firms, is instructive for much of the Loire. Take another *appellation* – Vouvray – whose reputation, poor even five years ago, has risen remarkably. Again we learn that in the years 1983–4 only 8.8 per cent of wine was sold by growers in bottle. By 1991–2 that percentage had risen remarkably to 65 per cent. I do not think it can be just coincidence that the quality of Vouvray has risen at the same time as the proportion of wine sold by *négociants* has fallen.

Another criticism has often been made of the quality of Loire wines. That is the question of the yield, or *rendement*, from the vines. Yields are in theory controlled by the *appellation contrôlée*. But the basic limits set out under individual ACs are often pretty high; 60 to 70 hectolitres per hectare is normal, and yields like that can only come from relatively dilute, watery grapes. Added to that are two curious French sleights of hand. The first is called the *Rendement Annuel*, which adjusts the basic *rendement* according to the climatic conditions of the year. In theory the adjustment could be downwards, but it is almost invariably upwards. A further adjustment can also be made, again upwards. Called the *Plafond Limité de Classement* (PLC to the trade), this allows a further increase of up to 20 per cent, provided the resultant wine is accepted after an obligatory tasting; if it is refused, the entire production has to go for distillation. If both adjustments are made, the final yield can be at least 30 per cent higher than the (already high) basic yield laid down in the *appellation*.

That higher yields adversely affect wine quality is generally accepted, especially if the final product is to be still table wine (sparkling wines can survive on higher yields). Good growers know this and work hard to keep their yields down, even going so far as to thin the bunches of grapes during the ripening season (the so-called 'green harvest') to allow the remaining bunches to gain greater ripeness. They will also cut away excess growth in the vine to allow the bunches the best exposure to the sun. Less conscientious growers – generally, but not always, those who sell grapes to co-operatives and *négociants* – will aim for as high a yield as the system permits, believing that in this way they will maximize their income.

If this part of the book reads like an attack on *négociants*, then it will have succeeded in its aim. *Négociants* have a vital place in the market of any wine area. They can produce large quantities of reliable, good-value wines, the sort of wine that can then be sold in supermarkets at exceptionally low prices. They can show the way forward in new wine styles, in marketing, in giving *viticulteurs* with only small vineyard holdings a living. But they can also affect the reputation of an area: their dominance of the market in Muscadet has done the image of that wine no end of harm, an image that the growers struggle hard to improve. The fact that the cellars of many *négociants* are hundreds of kilometres from the vineyards from which they draw their grapes (the *négociants* of Saumur buy grapes, or more likely wine, from all corners of the Loire vineyard) means they have to rely on sometimes biased local knowledge to source the product they need.

If any *négociants* read these pages, I suggest that they ask themselves one basic question. Is what you are doing likely to enhance the image, the value and the quality of the *appellations* of the Loire? If they can answer yes – and there are *négociants*, some mentioned in the following chapters, who can honestly do so – then they are the ones who are able to think long-term rather than from year to year. If they answer no, I suggest they change their ways before an increasingly quality-conscious drinking public, able to buy better cheap wine from other parts of the world, passes them by. The Loire, I believe, can only survive by continually improving quality.

3

The wines of the mountains

Along the upper reaches of the Loire and its tributary the Allier, among the foothills of the Massif Central, there are tiny pockets of wine production which are ghosts of their former selves. Looking in two directions, east towards the nearby Beaujolais, and north to the main regions of Loire wine production, they have suffered from an identity crisis which has meant they have never recovered from the ravages of phylloxera in the early years of the century.

What it takes to move a vineyard area forward is quality, which is not easy to take for granted in these small areas. Much of what is made could never stand up in the wind of competition, and relies heavily on local trade and passing tourists for its consumption. But in at least three of the four areas – the exception being the Côte Roannaise – there are producers (or local co-operatives) which are leading the way forward through investment and through bringing in knowledge and experience from the great wine world outside.

Côtes d'Auvergne

It was a lovely sunny morning, still fresh enough to be pleasant, but promising great heat later in the day, even storms. The mountains and hills of the Puy de Dôme, the region of ancient volcanoes, were lushly green, and the small villages to the north and south of the ugly industrial sprawl of Clermont-Ferrand had a distinct air of the langour of southern France.

From the ramparts and hillside streets around the castle of Châteaugay I looked down on to the valley of Allier and the huge mass of the Michelin tyre factory. Up here, though, the nearest view was of the vines. For even here in the Côtes d'Auvergne, remote as I was from the Loire in its infant valley more than 100 kilometres away, they make wines that not only technically (since the Allier is a tributary of the Loire) but also in style are much closer to other Loire wines than to the much nearer wines of the Rhône.

It is strange to think that about 100 years ago the Puy de Dôme was the third most prolific viticultural *département* in France. From the high point in those days of 60,000 hectares of vines, there are today a mere 1,240, of which only 440 are within the VDQS region of Côtes d'Auvergne – the rest being Vin de Pays d'Urfé.

The Côtes d'Auvergne is a widely-scattered area north, south and west of Clermont-Ferrand. Activity centres on the five *crus villages* of Madargues, near the town of Riom, Chanturgue, which is in the western suburbs of Clermont-Ferrand, Corent and Boudes south of the city, and Châteaugay, just on the edge of the northern suburbs. Together they make 60 per cent of the Côtes d'Auvergne wines, the rest coming from tiny parcels around the region.

Of the five, Corent with 42 hectares of vines and Châteaugay with 58 hectares are the most active wine villages. Corent is near the home of the regional co-operative, Cave Saint-Verny (named after the local patron saint of *vignerons*), at Veyre-Monton, now undergoing extensive renovations, with the installation of stainless-steel tanks for the 1993 harvest, and aiming, according to its commercial director Patricia Couturaud, to increase the proportion of wine it bottles.

It was in Mme Couturaud's office that I learned a little about the grape varieties and soil of the Côtes d'Auvergne. The soil is mainly volcanic, with some clay and limestone. The main grape of the region is Gamay, a special clone called the Gamay d'Auvergne which, compared with the Gamay in Beaujolais, has much more open bunches of grapes making it much less susceptible to mildew. Gamay occupies 95 per cent of the vineyard, while two other varieties – Pinot Noir and Chardonnay – make up the rest.

From the co-operative I went to visit the man whom many rate as the best producer in the Côtes d'Auvergne. Roland Rougeyron and his father Michel have 11 hectares of vines in the village of Châteaugay, in vineyards which drop precipitously in terraces down the hillside towards the Allier valley. The soil, black and volcanic, is rich and well-drained. The Rougeyrons have no Pinot Noir, and only a tiny amount of Chardonnay.

The Châteaugay vineyard is a hotchpotch of well-tended and neglected plots, all tiny. Among these the Rougeyron vines stand

The vineyards of the Upper Loi

out, well-pruned, their foliage trimmed for the summer and the ground well-turned. It's a good augury for the cellars, which like most in Châteaugay are carved out of the rocky hillsides. But inside there is something different from the old cement tanks most producers still have here: the Rougeyrons installed stainless-steel tanks before the 1988 vintage, fitting them into niches in the cave, and the effect of this modern equipment on the wines is very apparent in their freshness and fruit.

They make only three wines – a red, a rosé and a white – all under their brand name of Bousset d'Or. They are, like all Côtes d'Auvergne, light and fresh, but unlike the wines of the co-operative which I had tasted earlier (and which will, one hopes, be improved once the stainless steel is installed), these are wines with clean, intense flavour. The rosé particularly, with its salmon pink colour, is deliciously refreshing, the red full of raspberry fruit, the white a soft, creamy wine.

The Côtes d'Auvergne could easily become more prosperous, and the vineyards could increase. The *vignerons* have applied for an *appellation contrôlée* to replace their VDQS status, and believe this will do much for their reputation. The wines they make, with their typically crisp, mountain acidity, are mainly consumed locally by local people and tourists, which means there is never any problem in selling what they produce. If other producers followed the route the Rougeyrons have taken and improved their sometimes primitive equipment (some still have ancient open stone fermentation tanks), then the Côtes d'Auvergne could produce some attractive, light-weight and refreshing wines.

Côtes du Forez

Later the same day I drove east from Clermont-Ferrand, through the beautiful wooded Monts du Forez, to visit the vineyards of the Côtes du Forez. Strictly speaking, this is the most southerly of the Loire wine areas. And unlike the remote Côtes d'Auvergne, it is much closer in style to the wines of southern France, and especially to its close neighbour Beaujolais, just across the Monts du Lyonnais. The vineyards for the VDQS of Côtes du Forez, covering a mere 200 hectares, are on the eastern slopes of the Monts du Forez, facing east across the Loire Valley, around twenty-two villages north of Montbrison, of which the most important are Boën-sur-Lignon and Marcilly.

There is only one grape variety, the Gamay Noir à Jus Blanc of Beaujolais, and only two styles of wine made, red and rosé. Virtually all the grapes go to the local co-operative, Les Vignerons Foreziens at Trélins, in the suburbs of Boën-sur-Lignon. Here they make a wide variety of tailor-made *cuvées* which often bear the labels of restaurants or wine shops and are mainly sold locally. The style is very much in the Beaujolais mould: wines made to be drunk young, with a slight prickle and a light, raspberry taste.

The vinification plant at Les Vignerons Foreziens is modern, full of stainless steel and efficiently run. They make a *primeur* for sale, like Beaujolais Nouveau, within a few weeks of the harvest. Rosé wine is made either by pressing the grapes lightly or by leaving the skins in contact with the must for 24 hours. They also make a somewhat yeasty pink sparkler. Chardonnay has been planted for white wines in the future.

Côte Roannaise

Down the Loire from the Côtes du Forez is the Côte Roannaise. The vineyards, on the slopes of the Monts de la Madeleine and centred on the town of Renaison-de-la-Tache, are only a shadow of their former selves. Even at the beginning of this century, an average of 800,000 hectolitres of wine was produced every year. Today, with 5,000 hectolitres and 100 hectares, it is rare to find signs of wine production locally, let alone bottles of wine.

Of all the Upper Loire areas, this seems to be the least organized and the least prepared for the future. The Côte Roannaise is a VDQS and would like to become an AC, but that is less likely than with the Côtes d'Auvergne.

As with other Upper Loire *appellations*, Gamay is the grape of the region, with a local clone, the Gamay Romain. Some Pinot Noir is planted, but results are not entirely successful. There are no white wines produced under the VDQS, although there are some Chardonnay plantings making Vin de Pays d'Urfé. The vineyards, on steep granite slopes, are sometimes terraced.

Techniques are still primitive here, and the taste of the wines shows it. I tried some young Gamay Côte Roannaise, made to compete with Beaujolais Nouveau. It was frankly an uninspiring wine, lacking the essential fruitiness of Beaujolais or even of Côtes du Forez. The one Pinot Noir I tasted, with its heavily woody, dry taste, was even less exciting.

Saint-Pourçain-sur-Sioule

Of the four mountain vineyards of the Upper Loire, that of Saint-Pourçain, sixty-five kilometres north of Clermont-Ferrand and twenty kilometres north of Vichy, is by far the most exciting. A delightful market town on the Sioule – not far from the famous gorges which are one of the major sites of the Auvergne – Saint-Pourçain has a long history of wine-making, dating back, so the locals claim, to the Phoenicians, although Roman origins are more likely.

Nineteen villages make up the *appellation*, of which Saulcet is the most important. The vineyards are spread out thinly along the banks of the Sioule and the Bouble, both tributaries of the Allier, and on the western slope of the Allier valley. They lie among an intensely rural landscape: small fields with cows or cereals are dominated by the huge forest of the Tronçais.

While Gamay is yet again the dominant grape variety, Saint-Pourçain is already at one remove from the influence of the Beau-jolais, already looking much more directly towards the main vine-yard areas of the Loire, as well as taking a side glance towards Burgundy. The white grapes show this most obviously: Sauvignon Blanc and Chardonnay are increasingly popular, but the most typi-cal white grape of the region is the Tresallier, the local name for the Sacy of Chablis.

The Tresallier is a difficult grape to grow, barely ripening in some years and only achieving good maturity once or twice in a decade. When it does, it makes a very acid, low-alcohol wine that is ideal for sparkling wines – of which there are now an increasing number – but also, when blended with Chardonnay or Sauvignon, lending a fragrance which certainly sets the whites of Saint-Pourçain apart. The proportion of Tresallier in the blends (which can be up to a maximum of 50 per cent) is being decreased as more Sauvignon and Chardonnay are planted; this is a pity, because the crisp, nutty taste of Tresallier is very attractive, not unlike a very crisp Muscadet.

Reds predominate though, accounting for three-quarters of the production of Saint-Pourçain. This is a recent trend, dating from since the Second World War. The standard red, made from Gamay, is not surprisingly a wine to be drunk young, and is occasionally sold as Nouveau. With Pinot Noir, the other red grape variety, there are still problems: whether to blend it with Gamay, whether to try to make a wine matured in wood and designed for ageing, and how, in the vineyard itself, to cope with its habit of attracting rot. At the moment, some *vignerons* and the Cave des Vignerons de Saint-Pourçain, the local co-operative, are experimenting with new wood ageing for Pinot Noir; what I tasted suggested that the new wood taste is too much for the light fruit. '

It is this willingness to experiment which shows that there is plenty of life in the Saint-Pourçain vineyards. When on my last night in the region, spent in Vichy, I had a half-bottle of fresh, fruity, strawberry-ripe Gamay 1991 from Joseph Laurent, it seemed to me that this was not just a wine to be drunk out of curiosity, but to be drunk with pleasure.

4

Sancerre and Menetou-Salon

Sancerre

The best way to approach Sancerre is from the south. As you drive up from Bourges, the flat plains and cereal fields give way to a range of hills, wooded on top, with vines on the south-facing slopes. Off to the left are the southern wine villages of the Sancerrois: Crézancy, Champtin, Bué, in small, narrow valleys surrounded entirely by slopes of vines. Just past the turn to Bué the road rises to a crest and there, through an avenue of trees and across vineyards, is the town of Sancerre, its red-tiled roofs tumbling down the slopes of a conical, 1,000-foot hill which dominates everything around it. For a moment, this could be Tuscany.

Sancerre is everything a wine town should be, I decided as I drove up the steep, twisting road to the central square, along tiny, narrow streets which occasionally gave glimpses of a huge semicircular panorama of vines. In the central Place des Halles, there are cafés and restaurants, with tables outside shaded by umbrellas; there are wine shops, and a bakery selling the local nougat biscuit speciality, *croquets de Sancerre* (a taste I can happily avoid, but one which is enthusiastically promoted throughout the town). Little streets lead perilously downhill, passing underground taverns, or more sedately uphill to the grounds of the local landmark, the Tour des Fiefs, all that is now left of the medieval castle. A short walk from the square leads out to the Esplanade de la Porte César.

Standing on this Esplanade on my first evening in Sancerre – a lovely balmy evening, with the light only just beginning to fade at ten o'clock – I joined the locals on a promenade looking out over one of the most spectacular views in the Loire Valley. Immediately down below were the vineyards and the village of Saint-Satur, above which runs a splendid road viaduct crossing from the hill of Sancerre to the hill north of Saint-Satur. Beyond the hill are the

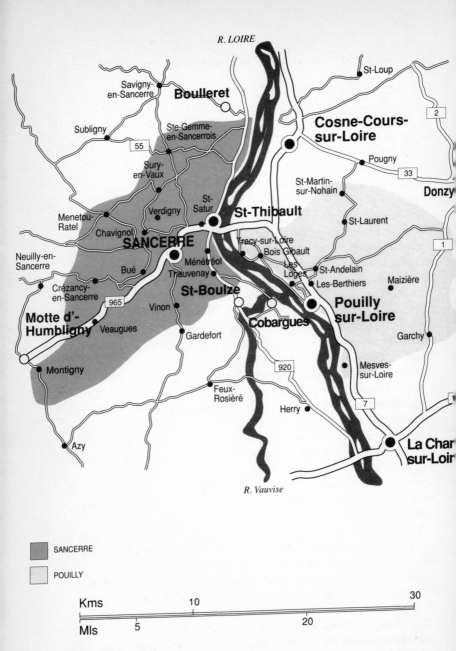

The vineyards of Sancerre and Pouilly-sur-Loire. Menetou-Salon is shown in the map on page 58.

cooling towers of the nuclear power station opposite Neuvy-sur-Loire.

To the right, at the foot of the hills, the Loire flows gloriously, majestically, its path broken, as always, by sand banks and small islands. Across the river are the vineyards of Pouilly-sur-Loire. In the far distance a thin line of mountains marks the Morvan, the remote forests of Burgundy. And in the imagination it is possible to see, on the furthest eastern slopes of those mountains, the vineyards of the Côte d'Or and the city of Dijon.

The Sancerre vineyards

The Sancerrois, the region of Sancerre, is on the eastern extremity of the *département* of Cher, which also marks the eastern edge of Berry. Pouilly, across the Loire, is already, administratively at least, in Burgundy. The sharply-inclined chalk hills mark Sancerre out from the surrounding soft, flat lands of the Loire valley. The vineyards, in the valleys which radiate north, west and south of the town, are much more closely packed, more intensively cultivated than in most areas of the Loire; the closest equivalents are Champagne or Chablis. Indeed, Sancerre is on the same band of Kimmeridgean chalk soil that runs from Châlons-sur-Marne in Champagne through Chablis to Bourges to the south.

At the time of the 1992 harvest, the vineyards occupied an area of 2,138 hectares out of a possible 3,627. Most of this, 1,684 hectares, was of Sauvignon Blanc and the remaining 454 hectares was of Pinot Noir, producing both red and rosé wines. The area of vineyards and the quantity of harvests have been steadily increasing (apart from the hiccup of the famous frost year of 1991) as worldwide demand for all styles of Sancerre – white, red and rosé – has increased.

There are sixteen villages within the *appellation* of Sancerre. The six largest – Bué, Chavignol, Crézancy, Sancerre itself, Sury-en-Vaux and Verdigny – between them account for 56 per cent of the total vineyard. The other, smaller villages are Amigny, Maimbray, Menetou-Ratel, Ménétréol-sous-Sancerre, Sainte-Gemme-en-Sancerrois, Saint-Satur, Thauvenay, Veaugues, Isoles and, smallest of all, Montigny. These villages cover two *appellations*: one, for Sancerre Blanc made only from Sauvignon Blanc, was created in 1936; the other, for reds and rosés made only from Pinot Noir, was not created until 1959, basically because there was still a lot of Gamay planted in the region in 1936 which some growers did not want included in the *appellation*.

Yields vary slightly from year to year. In 1992 the yields for Sauvignon Blanc were 67.4 hectolitres per hectare and for Pinot Noir 62 hectolitres per hectare. For 1993 the official *appellation* figures were dropped to 60 hl/ha for Sauvignon and 50 hl/ha for Pinot Noir, a welcome sign of a search for quality, even if it was dictated by a large increase in stocks.

All this, and much more, I learned on my first morning in the region sitting in the small office of Jean-Max Roger in Bué. An energetic, talkative man with a short beard, he is the president of the Syndicat des Viticulteurs, the wine-growers' organization, as well as being an important producer. Over a glass of his Sancerre Cuvée GC from the Grand Chemarin vineyard in Bué, we talked about the structure of the wine business in Sancerre. It is a region of small holdings. There are 442 growers in those 2,138 hectares, giving an average holding of 4.8 hectares. But when those figures are broken down, we find that 164 growers have 1.5 hectares or less, 178 have between 1.5 and 5 hectares, 72 have 5 to 10 hectares, and only 24 have 10 to 20 hectares, while above 20 hectares there are only 4 growers – of whom, incidentally, Jean-Max is one.

It is surprising therefore, given such small holdings, that 48 per cent of the wine made in Sancerre is actually bottled by the producer as *domaine* wine. The co-operative manages only 6 per cent of production. The rest, of course, goes to *négociants*, mostly local ones (including those in Pouilly), the majority of whom – again like Jean-Max – are also growers themselves. Only 17 per cent of the wine leaves the region for bottling elsewhere, but as so often with the Loire, it is that 17 per cent which has damaged the reputation of Sancerre, particularly on the export markets, leaving an image of wines made entirely to a price from high-yielding vines.

The yields are also a sign of the pressure on the producers of Sancerre, certainly until 1991–2. The huge demand from around the world for their wines could often only be satisfied by cutting corners, or planting more vines. The figures for vineyard plantings tell the tale: 1,252 hectares in 1978, 1,410 in 1982 and on up to today's figure of 2,138. In 1991–2 things changed: planting stopped, as producers of Sancerre pushed their prices to the limit and beyond to cope with the shortfall from the 1991 harvest, and as buyers, particularly in Britain (which has been the main export market) but also in other European countries, decided that there were other Sauvignon Blancs which were better value.

Upon which gloomy note, and to cheer ourselves up, we clambered into Jean-Max's little van for a tour of the vineyards. First we drove through Bué. Here is a wine village if ever there was one: there are thirty *vignerons* in the village, and out of 400 inhabitants, 350 are involved in wine, married to wine, or the children of wine. 'Everybody is in wine, apart from the baker, the post office, the garage, the cheese shop and a couple of restaurants – and of course the priest', Jean-Max told me. All along the long, narrow main street there are signs for *vignerons*, some attached to smart new cellars, others to small sheds which hardly look inhabited. Even in the main square, opposite the church, there are more cellars, up the little lanes leading into it.

At the top end of the village, the road runs past the Clos de la Poussie, an almost perfect amphitheatre of vines owned by the *domaine* of the same name (which I was due to visit later in the day), and up the slope to the top of the hill. From here it is possible to see how Bué is literally surrounded by its vineyards.

Here are some of the most famous vineyards in Sancerre: Chêne Marchand, Le Grand Chemarin, Clos de la Poussie. They are names which along with others, particularly in Chavignol, have over the years appeared on countless labels from different producers, all owning a small parcel of these precious vines. For the last ten years, however, the use of vineyard names has been in suspension, as the authorities work out the actual sizes and delimit them. Hence producers are forced to adopt stratagems – such as Jean-Max's Cuvée GC (for Grand Chemarin) – that will give cryptic clues to their customers.

From Bué we crossed the plateau. Here the vineyards stop and cereals – maize and wheat – take over. Only the slopes are in the *appellation*. We descended on rough tracks through the vineyard into Chavignol, famous not only for its wines but for its goat cheese, Crottin de Chavignol, one of the *appellation contrôlée* cheeses of France. Once, every farmer had a few goats and made cheese; today, wine has taken over completely and nearly all the Crottin is made in a co-operative which isn't even in Chavignol itself, but on the southern edge of the Sancerre *appellation*. Not that this stops Crottin being, as it always was, one of the best foods to go with Sancerre – a classic example of synergy between food and wine.

Chavignol's valley is even narrower than Bué's. All along the northern side – facing south – is the best-known vineyard of the village, Les Monts Damnés, an almost sheer wall of vines, showing how some of the best sites in Sancerre are as difficult to work as those in some of the great German vineyards of the Mosel. Hand operations, supplemented by a system of winches, will, it seems, never be replaced in vineyards like this.

The Chavignol valley debouches towards the high western edge of the hill of Sancerre. To the left, the land slopes down through Saint-Satur towards the Loire; but we drove to the right, through the outskirts of Sancerre and into the bowl of vines that belong to the *commune* of Sancerre itself. Cresting the southern edge of the bowl, we could see the open end of the valley of Bué once more, completing the circle.

The ever-expanding Jean-Max Roger
Then it was into Jean-Max's cellars. What with 24 hectares under vine (and another 4 hectares for white Menetou-Salon) and his purchases as a *négociant* of Pouilly Fumé and Menetou-Salon Rouge, the Roger family has run out of room in their home cellars. So a hundred yards away two anonymous farm sheds provide the space for stainless steel fermentation tanks, which is where we tasted the wines of the 1992 harvest.

Like many producers in Sancerre, Jean-Max vinifies his different parcels of land separately. Tasting them gave me the chance to see the differences between wines produced in the three different soils of Sancerre. The highest slopes of the vineyards, covering 40 per cent of the *appellation*, are of marl on the Kimmeridgean chalk, a combination known locally as *terres blanches*. This soil produces wines which develop well once bottled, and which can last at least a year or two, often longer if the producer is good. Lower down, covering another 40 per cent of the *appellation*, is *la caillotte*, dry limestone soil which makes wines for younger drinking. The third soil type, covering the remaining 20 per cent, is called *silex*, a more stony soil on the chalk sub-stratum, found mainly in the northern part of the *appellation* and making wines which are more austere, with a floral bouquet.

Certainly, from tasting the wines in Jean-Max's cellar I found that his wines from the *terres blanches* in the Grand Chemarin vineyard were steely, crisp and green, while those from *la caillotte* in the Chêne Marchand were rounder and already more balanced. We also tasted some red Pinot Noir, full of raspberry fruit flavours, of which half is aged in wood, never new, and then blended with wine matured in stainless steel.

Then it was back to the tasting room in his house for a look at a few bottles. We started with some Menetou-Salon – of which more in the appropriate section – and then tasted reds before whites, an approach which is sometimes found in Sancerre, the crispness of the whites happily replacing the roundness of the reds. In the classic year of 1990 Jean-Max made a special *cuvée* from old vines, which he aged fourteen months in wood and which has ended up tasting more like a Burgundy than normal red Sancerre. The 1991 red was more typical, rounded but with a hint of citrus and only the lightest of tannins.

The whites from 1991 and 1990 made a fascinating contrast of years. The 1991 Cuvée GC, from a year which (apart from the frosts) produced only average wines, was very steely, very flinty to taste, whereas the 1990 Vieilles Vignes was full, lemony, oozing with the flavour of exotic fruit.

From the cellars of Jean-Max Roger, it was only a matter of moments – and a pause in the local bar for a ham *baguette* and a beer – to the cellars of Domaine de la Poussie. Over my beer, I took the opportunity to swot up on the history of Sancerre.

Julius Caesar may have been here

It has been a long and, at times, bloodthirsty one. In a delightful pamphlet, *Les Vignerons du Sancerrois*, published in 1962, Monseigneur André Girard, who was Vicaire Général of Bourges, makes great play of the theory that the so-called Porte César in Sancerre means that the great Julius himself must have come this way, calling the town Cortona, and that vineyards surely followed. Effectively, though, it was the monks of the monastery of Saint-Satur who were responsible for the creation of the vineyard. In the early Middle Ages the town was ruled by the Counts of Champagne, and it was they who, recognizing the strategic value of a site with such a wide panoramic view, constructed the fortress which once stood on the hill.

Initially, Sancerre was better known for red wines than for white.

During the reign of King Philip Augustus at the turn of the thirteenth century, a poem called *The Battle of Wines* praised the wines of Sancerre as suitable for the royal table. Things were not, however, always so peaceful, and in 1573, during the religious wars in France, Sancerre, a Protestant stronghold, suffered a terrible siege of seven months. A further siege in 1621 finally brought about the destruction of the castle, save for the Tour des Fiefs which we see today.

White wines are mentioned for the first time in Sancerre literature when, in his 1816 *Topographie de Tous les Vignobles Connus*, Jullien wrote that, while Sancerre mainly produced red wines from Le Grand Noir and Le Pineau, it also gave 'quite the best white wine of the area', and that 'when young, they have a softness and poise, when old they keep their freshness and can be compared to the wines of Chablis'. The grapes used, says Jullien, were the Pinot Gris, the Sauvignon and the Melier – the last-named, possibly the Chasselas, being the most preferred. Chasselas was the predominant white grape until well into this century, and before the arrival of *appellation contrôlée* laws in 1936 much of the white wine of Sancerre was shipped to Champagne for blending.

Like all wine areas, Sancerre suffered from phylloxera, which arrived in 1885. The vineyards thereafter declined from their peak of 12,000 hectares. Even after the Second World War there were still only small amounts of Sauvignon – 175 hectares in the late 1940s. In fact, the whole of the Sancerre vineyard continued to decline until 1960, when there were only 600 hectares under vine and, by that time, hardly any Pinot Noir for reds or rosés. Then the fashion for dry white wines came in, with the wines of Sancerre and Pouilly jointly in the lead, followed in the late 1970s by a fashionable demand, fuelled by Paris restaurants, for rosés and, later, reds.

Amphitheatre of vines
The vineyard of the Clos de la Poussie is a paradigm of Sancerre's recent history. If it seems today that the Sancerre vineyard is divided into small holdings, the situation used to be worse, as the history of the Clos de la Poussie shows. Created by the monks of Bué, the Clos passed into the hands of the Crochet family, who are still prominent in Bué's affairs. With the devastation caused by phylloxera and the decline in the importance of wine in Sancerre, the then owner, Octave Crochet, abandoned the Clos and went to Paris, where he

ran a successful dairy business, returning only after the end of the Second World War.

Setting about the rebuilding of the vineyards, he found that he had to buy up 150 small plots of land to make a vineyard that would be viable to operate. This has been the problem throughout Sancerre – a problem due entirely to the French laws of inheritance, which insist that property is divided equally between children. Although fair in theory, these laws create vineyard holdings which consist of strips of vines all over the place.

Octave Crochet eventually put together the magnificent 6-hectare vineyard, a huge, terraced wall of vines, almost perpendicular in places, the name spelt out in enormous white letters, which acts as a full stop to the Bué valley. This is the Clos de la Poussie, now owned by the Cordier company of Bordeaux, who also have another 26 hectares mainly in the commune of Sancerre.

'Ring and enter' said the notice on the huge wooden doors to the ivy-encrusted, almost Alpine-looking residence which houses the Domaine de la Poussie. Once inside, I was confronted by a long avenue of cement wine tanks and by Mlle Bidon, the *régisseur* of the estate. She is young, and had obviously put on smart clothes for my visit, because I could not see her mucking about with tanks or barrels in the blouse she was wearing. She was, she told me, trained in oenology at Bordeaux and has been in Sancerre for two years.

Inevitably, we talked first about the Clos. Because of the steepness of the slopes, it is worked entirely by hand, save for spraying (and here's the modern touch), which is done by helicopter. Yields are kept deliberately low: 35 hectolitres per hectare compared with the norm of 60 hectolitres per hectare. She was well aware of the awkwardness of the name Poussie (which actually refers to the light dust of the soil) in Anglo-Saxon markets, so in the USA the wine is called Clos de Chailloux.

Wines from this vineyard go under the name of the Clos. Wines from other Cordier holdings in Sancerre are designated Domaine de la Poussie, a subtle distinction which I hope is registered by drinkers. Fermentation is mainly classic, using stainless steel and leaving some of the wines on their lees until bottling. Red wines macerate for fifteen days to three weeks, and at a high temperature for a short period. 'The problem with Sancerre Rouge,' said Mlle Bidon, more used to the colour of Bordeaux Rouge, 'is the colour.'

Rosé wines are left to macerate for twenty-four hours and then pressed.

There is one departure from normal Sancerre practice. For 10 per cent of the wines of the Clos, fermentation and maturation are in wood until bottling in the spring. Most producers prefer to retain freshness by using only stainless steel. I must admit that, when tasting the wine of the Clos, I was barely able to detect any wood taste, but the 1992 was certainly a subtle, elegant wine, still citrusy and young when tasted the following summer. It is designed as a wine for ageing, and I agree that it would be better eighteen months after the harvest.

It was also much more interesting than the other *domaine* wines. I have tasted the wines of the Domaine over the years, and apart from the wine of the Clos, they have always disappointed me. However, to be fair, I think they are better now than they have ever been: the red, and particularly the rosé, are classic Sancerre, with the hint of earthiness, the rosé perhaps slightly too soft and, seemingly, sweet. The white Domaine de la Poussie 1992, however, gave little indication of the taste of Sauvignon – it was a pleasant, refreshing wine which could almost have come from anywhere.

The most important Monsieur Crochet

It was perhaps fitting that I should move from the Domaine de la Poussie, now under the control of a Bordeaux *négociant* house, to the *domaine* of Lucien Crochet, a relative of Poussie's previous owner. There are some names which crop up time and again in Sancerre, such as Bailly, Reverdy, Fleuriet, Raimbault – and Crochet. There are eight in Bué, all making their own wine, so it pays to know their first names.

Lucien Crochet is perhaps the most important. He is certainly the busiest, and I was not able to see him on the day of my visit because he was in Paris. Instead, the diminutive Mme Crochet showed me around, and asked me to open the bottles because she found the corks too hard. It is an impressive, spotlessly clean and modern cellar, dug out of the hillside; 1,200 lorries were needed to remove all the earth displaced by excavating the huge, hangar-like bottling and storage hall. It is big because this is a big estate, 32 hectares in Bué, Sancerre, Crézancy and Vinon. A quarter of the production is of red and rosé, the rest of white.

The cellars are an extreme example of what has happened in

Sancerre in the last few years – even in the seven years since I had last been in the region. That is the arrival of new wine technology, closely following the boom in the wines of Sancerre. Where once there were cement tanks, old-fashioned hard hydraulic presses and hand-bottling, there is now gleaming stainless steel, modern soft pneumatic presses and smart, up-to-the-minute bottling lines. Everything gleams. The New World has arrived in Sancerre and, just as in New Zealand, where Sauvignon Blanc succeeds because it tastes so fruity, so in Sancerre it is fruit above all which is emphasized now. Maybe that is at the expense of more subtle flavours, but it is hard to blame the producers here who see consumers demanding fruit, fruit and more fruit. And it does mean that, in the right hands, the wines are tasting better and better.

Lucien Crochet's are certainly the right hands, because his wines are most impressive. In the tasting room, with computers humming away in the modern office through the glass doors, I first tasted the 1991 Sancerre Cuvée Le Chêne. It comes from the Chêne Marchand, but since the vineyard name cannot be used, there is a simple picture of an oak tree (*chêne*) on the label – 'to guide the consumer', as Mme Crochet put it delicately. Despite the only average quality of the year, this was a rich wine, packed with ripe, exotic fruits, very floral, which would not (a compliment this) have seemed out of place in New Zealand. It was more agreeable than the almost over-the-top 1990 Cuvée Le Chêne which, because it is from such a rich year, is very, very rich. Mme Crochet and I agreed that, fine as the wine is, it is not at all a typical Sancerre. In fact, 1989 seems to have produced better wines at M. Crochet's, for the Cuvée Prestige 1989 has delicious green herbaceous fruit in the classic Sauvignon style.

Those two years, 1989 and 1990, were so unusual that the Crochets managed to make a *vendange tardive*, a late-harvest wine, from bunches left on the vines until they became super-ripe. 'We decided to seize the opportunity, since it's a chance that might never occur again in our lifetimes,' said Mme Crochet. Both wines are named after their picking dates – the 1990 on 25 October, the 1989 on 26 October – and both are huge wines, high in alcohol, very tropical, rich rather than sweet, the 1989 more balanced than the 1990.

Reds are from the Clos du Roy vineyard in Crézancy, but once again the use of the vineyard name is side-stepped by calling the wines Croix du Roy. The 1991 is fresh and fruity, with an earthy, leaf-mould hint and delicious acidity. The 1990, like many reds from that year, tastes more like a light red Burgundy. The 1988, still with good tannin and fruit, and just perfectly ready to drink, proved that Sancerre Rouge can age.

Vacheron and the art of red Sancerre

Had I needed convincing about the ageing potential of Sancerre Rouge, my next visit should have dispelled any doubts. This was back in Sancerre itself, in the cellars of the Vacheron family. I had been there seven years before, and had memories of a warren of underground cellars and a slightly fusty air. Today, although the underground cellars have not changed – except for some further burrowing – the atmosphere has. Here again are the stainless steel and the pneumatic presses, the signs of the new technology of Sancerre. One thing, though, has remained the same: the rows of wooden barrels used for the red wines. For Vacheron are rare among Sancerre producers in that they concentrate their reputation more on reds than whites.

As I arrived in the narrow side-street that contains the entrance to their cellars, I found Denis Vacheron waiting for me. He is a slightly-built man, very energetic, very charming, who rushed me around the cellars pointing out what was new. He told me these were fifteenth-century cellars that had once belonged to a typical family of *vignerons*, with a staircase down into the cellar from the two-room house above – the sort of small cottage still to be found in villages and smaller towns in Berry. One room was for the people, the other room for the animals, and down below were the wines.

The Vacheron family have been in Sancerre for a mere three generations, but on the maternal side the Pinards (the local argot for wine) have been here for ever. Today there are two brothers, Denis and Jean-Louis, and two of their sons in the business. Theirs is an established presence in Sancerre, on the route for tourists, who buy either at the cellars ('on Saturdays, it is like the Metro', according to Denis) where there is an atmospheric corner with a tasting counter, or at the Vacheron shop on the edge of the town.

As we passed the stacks of bottled wine, Denis kept on pulling out bottles for tasting, handing some to me to carry. Eventually we tottered into the *cave privée* – 'this is the chapel', said Denis as we entered – an arched, low-ceilinged corner with an ecclesiastical grille as the entrance. We sat at the wide wooden table, surrounded by bottles behind more grilles, as Denis wrestled with a huge corkscrew with a vinewood handle.

Then we tasted. The Vacherons have 34 hectares of vines, all in the *commune* of Sancerre. Their whites – despite their keenness on reds, they still make more white – are attractively fruity, very ready to drink nine months after the harvest, but with a certain finesse from the blend of wines from *silex* and *caillotte* soils. We tasted the 1992 white and then a fresh, fragrant 1992 rosé, before moving to the serious matter, the reds. I knew it was serious because, with perfect timing, Jean-Louis, more thick-set than his brother, arrived to check out the extraordinary range of older bottles which were now being opened: a 1991, all matured in wood, beautifully perfumed; a 1981, with the developed, mature, earthy, rotting flavour that is so typical of mature red Burgundy, and then a 1986, full of cigar-box flavours and smells, dry but with spicy fruit. To finish we had a white from 1983, tasting of almonds or spice cakes, an almost ten-year-old wine which convincingly disproved the idea that white Sancerre needs to be drunk young.

As we talked, the discussion drifted satisfyingly into the nooks and crannies of local wine politics. There is, it seems, in Sancerre a simmering controversy between those who believe in wood for white wine and those who think it takes away from the fruity character. There is no wood used with a Vacheron white, and it is easy to tell that both brothers are against it. 'It is as if they wanted to make a Chardonnay rather than a Sauvignon,' said Denis.

Then suddenly I was being whisked away to see the Fault of Sancerre – not, as I at first thought, a big mistake, but a fault-line in the hills where it is possible to see a perfect division between *silex* and *caillotte* soil. Certainly, on one side was gravelly soil and on the other the white limestone. 'We have vines on both sides,' said Denis. 'Put the wines together and you have Vacheron.'

Mellot, the name you cannot escape

Back in the square of Sancerre, I found myself surrounded by reminders of the Mellot family. Theirs is the most prominent name in Sancerre, and Alphonse Mellot is not only a big landowner but a major *négociant* as well. But it was not so much the members of the family as their multitudinous shops which made it impossible to forget the name. Every other shop in the square seems to be owned by a Mellot. There is the Auberge Joseph Mellot, owned by a cousin: a rustic restaurant which has an open front to the square when times are warm, and at the opposite end a very smart tasting room and restaurant (which seemed, however, to be permanently shut while I was there). In a side-street just by the *auberge* there are two wine shops owned by Alphonse Mellot facing each other.

The wines of Alphonse Mellot are founded on a long family tradition, which perhaps explains the dominance of the name in the town. The name dates back at least to 1513, and even the first name Alphonse is now enshrined in tradition. His land holding goes under the name of Domaine la Moussière, and at 45 hectares is the largest in the Sancerrois. The Mellot cellars, like those of Vacheron, are in the heart of old Sancerre, just behind one of the shops; there, modern techniques rub shoulders with a regular use of wood for at least a percentage of the white wines, and for a high proportion of the prestige Cuvée Edmond, which Alphonse has produced since 1987 in memory of his father.

Paul Millerioux's spotless cellar

Another of the producers I had met seven years ago was Paul Millerioux. He is another who has invested his earnings from the boom years of Sancerre in his cellars. Occasionally, I visit cellars where I would, metaphorically at least, be happy to eat my dinner off the floor; his was one. The stainless-steel tanks were rectangular rather than round, a shape I found in both Sancerre and Pouilly but rarely elsewhere (it is more economical with floor space). From the shiny bottling line and tiled cellar continually being hosed down, we went to the reception rooms, curiously clinical and unused despite the antique wood and the old photographs and charts of Champtin, and then to a small bar in one corner of the cellar, where we tasted.

Millerioux is another well-known local name, and Paul has a family tradition in wine stretching back five or six generations. He is a tall, slightly stooping man, now in late middle age, who looks awkward in front of his computer screen in the front room of the spacious modern house which has been built above the cellars. His idea is to make a wine that pleases, one that tastes of the land of Sancerre rather than just of Sauvignon. He has 16 hectares of vines around his cellars in the hamlet of Champtin, part of the *commune* of Crézancy. With land on *caillotte* and *terre blanche* soils, he is typical of Sancerre in believing that a blend of the two styles of wine is best for his white wine.

Since it was now mid-morning, we both felt a snack to be in order. So Crottin de Chavignol appeared on small saucers to accompany the wines as we tasted. His 1992 Sancerre Clos du Roy, named after a vineyard in Champtin, shows just what M. Millerioux means by pleasure – it was fresh, young, eminently drinkable, just a shade too soft to finish, but very enjoyable, yes, pleasing. A second *cuvée* of 1992 was much crisper and drier and attractively green. The ripe year of 1989 had, by contrast, produced a white Clos du Roy which was almost too fat and was already beginning to taste old.

Reds go into old wood for six months, which certainly benefited the 1990, big, meaty and perfumed, and the 1989, soft, smooth, Burgundian in its richness, but was perhaps less suitable for the 1991, which was almost too tannic for the fruit. The 1992 red, however, restored the balance with its spicy fruit, typical of the lighter Sancerre red style.

I like M. Millerioux. He has made a success of his business, and it is perhaps sad that he has no children to whom he can leave it. His wife is from another of the famous wine families, the Reverdys, so there is no lack of contenders to take on the *domaine* when M. Millerioux retires.

Chavignol families

While Champtin has its Millerioux, Sancerre its Mellots and Vacherons, Chavignol has its Delaportes and its Bourgeois. The Delaportes live in a fine old courtyard house in the middle of Chavignol, and have 12 hectares of land, mainly in Chavignol itself but also in Amigny and Sancerre, of which two hectares are planted with Pinot Noir. It was *chez* Delaporte back in 1986 that I tasted the oldest Sancerre I have ever seen, a 1947 which was tasting more and more like the local goat cheese but was still eminently drinkable, with a distinct *nervosité* – that marvellous French word which epitomizes a wine poised on a knife-edge of elegance.

The Bourgeois name is even more noticeable in Chavignol than that of Delaporte. This is because every building at the top end of the village seems to be part of the rambling collection of cellars and shops that house their buoyant empire. Jean-Marie is the patriarch of the family, a busy, bustling man, but I was to be shown round by

Arnaud, the grandson of Henri Bourgeois, whose name the family company still bears.

We started at the top (of the village, that is) with the huge, cathedral-like cellar carved out of the hillside. First, though, a glance across the narrow valley at the vineyard of Les Monts Damnés. I had realized it was steep, but when Arnaud told me that each year they have to put back the soil that has eroded from the vineyard – a job that has to be done by hand – I wondered whether the effort was worthwhile. 'Wait until you taste the wine,' I was told. But it seems that many other *vignerons* have also asked – and answered – my question about this appropriately-named vineyard, since only about a third of it is now planted.

Once inside the cellar, and out of the rain that had decided to blot out my view of Les Monts Damnés, I realized that, as well as being scattered through the village, this was a very big business. The huge hall was humming like a palace to the Nibelungs with bottling lines, pumps and air conditioning. At harvest-time, with fruit coming into the three modern pneumatic presses from their 48 hectares of vines and from the grapes they buy in from other *vignerons*, the noise must be deafening.

Amongst all this high tech, some interesting traditional techniques are used. Whites are left on their lees for up to six months to give extra concentration of flavour; with the partly wood-fermented prestige *cuvée* Étienne Henri, the lees are stirred in the barrel. Different yeasts are used to allow the *terroir*, the individual vineyard, to speak. All the reds go into some wood, especially the Vieilles Vignes *cuvée*.

The ties with tradition were reinforced as we wandered back down the hill into the village. Each Bourgeois property represents a sign of expansion. As Arnaud said: 'Every time a new generation has come along, they have built a new cellar.' Since there have been ten generations so far, that makes for a lot of cellars. We looked into one building which is where the wood is stored, into another which is a shop run by Arnaud's mother, and into yet another where there is a tasting room.

Eventually we dived down some stairs into a tiny tasting room, where Arnaud was able to unload the metal basket, like a milk-bottle holder, which was full of bottles to taste. We started with rosés and reds. While the rosé was perhaps too obviously the result of all that high tech up the road – all soft fruit and not much character – the reds were better. They make two reds, one from their *domaine* and one from bought-in grapes, and their labelling is very careful to emphasize the different provenance of each, the *domaine* wine only being *mis en bouteille au domaine*. Both were from 1990; the *négociant* wine was soft, with plenty of colour but only light tannins, whereas the *domaine* wine, from young vines, was lighter in colour but with a better structure of tannin and acidity – a wine that will age.

Then on to the whites. There is quite a range, from the basic Grande Réserve, the 1992 creamy fresh, through 1992 Les Monts Damnés from thirty-year-old vines, crisp, concentrated, lemony and still very young, on to the top *cuvées*: La Bourgeoise from *domaine* vineyards of *silex* soil in Saint-Satur – the 1991 very flinty, steely, green, with a slight hint of wood and definitely in need of ageing – and the 100 per cent wood-fermented 1990 Cuvée Étienne Henri, full, rich, only just hinting at wood, more at power and tropical flavours.

As we finished tasting, a car roared up to the side door of the tasting room, which gave on to a dirt-track leading up the hillside, and Christophe Gadais put his head in. He is the manager of Domaine Laporte, owned by the Bourgeois family for the past seven years. Despite the fact that this was eating into everybody's lunch-hour, we piled into cars and drove to the Laporte cellars, ten minutes away outside Saint-Satur.

The Cave de la Cresle, as the cellars are called, are on a hillside and look totally out of place in Sancerre. Put this A-frame wooden structure into the middle of California and the effect would be happier.

There are 15 hectares of the Domaine Laporte, mainly on the *silex* soil of Saint-Satur. Other grapes are purchased. The labels are a good match for the building, very modernistic with lots of gold and vivid lines. The wines seem to follow the same approach, emphasizing fruit and, where it was used, bringing the taste of wood to the fore – perhaps the most New World of all the wines I had tasted in Sancerre. That was particularly true of the Clos de la Comtesse 1991, wine from a vineyard that is a continuation of the slope of Les Monts Damnés, giving concentrated, tropical fruit tastes from low-yielding vines. As a contrast in taste but not in style, there was the Domaine du Rochoy 1992, lean and flinty, from *silex* soil. Together, these two wines were the best possible exposition of the differences in taste between wines from *caillotte* and *silex* soils. Then there were the wood-dominated flavours of the Grand Domaine, matured for six months in oak from the local forest of Charne.

Tasting over, and lunch-time almost gone, there was time for a quick snack with Arnaud in the village restaurant of Chavignol. For once, restraint was the agreed order of the day, and we were able to survive most enjoyably on an omelette filled with Crottin de Chavignol and made with eggs from the hens who were happily scratching around in the yard behind, a succulent fresh salad, and a glass of the Sancerre of the house. And then it was time to make the short journey across the Loire to Pouilly-sur-Loire.

Menetou-Salon

The day before arriving in Sancerre I had stopped in Menetou-Salon. Of the three country cousins who exist in the shadow of Sancerre – Quincy and Reuilly are the other two (see Chapter 6) – Menetou-Salon now has the largest amount of land, 200 hectares under vine. But as recently as 1959 there were a mere 20 hectares, and for Pierre Bréjoux, writing his *Les Vins de Loire* in 1956, they did not rate even a mention.

Menetou's return from near-extinction is due as much to the fame of neighbouring Sancerre as it is to the wines themselves. It has fed on the success of Sauvignon Blanc and, to a lesser extent, on that of Pinot Noir red and rosé – aided by the fact that *négociants* and vineyard owners in Sancerre are buying fruit from, or now own land in, Menetou. But it has also been helped by the arrival of a new generation of growers who appear determined to keep the vineyard going, and by a co-operative whose standards encourage smaller growers to make the most of their vines.

The vineyard of Menetou is south-west of Sancerre, tenuously joined to the Sancerre *appellation* south of Crézancy. Here the high hills of the Sancerrois drop away, and the ridge on which most of Menetou's vineyards are planted offers a low slope down to the Loire Valley. But the soil is the same – the Kimmeridgean ridge which continues further south-west towards Bourges – even though it is richer here, and muddled in with the lesser Portlandian chalks.

Driving around the area, I at first had difficulty in finding any vines at all. If one arrives in the village of Menetou from the west, there are no signboards of *vignerons*, no offers of wine for sale or tasting. In fact, the only alcoholic beverage I could find advertised was a Belgian beer. The village, though, is quietly pretty, dominated by a wide, sloping boulevard with trees and grass down the centre and a few desultory shops and a café on the edges. At the top of the rise are the gates to the magnificent château constructed by Jacques Coeur, finance minister to Charles XII in the sixteenth century, who fell from grace when he became richer than the king. In the nineteenth century the huge building was bought and renovated by Prince Auguste d'Arenberg, president of the Suez Canal Company, the sort of entrepreneur Jacques Coeur would undoubtedly have been had he lived in later times.

It was only as I left the village that the vines appeared. Above the village the vista opens out, and the long ridge above the Loire starts. Vines tumble down the hillside in a narrow band, with cereal crops below and on the plateau above. The concentration gets greater as you arrive in the hamlet of Morogues, which in reality is more of a wine centre than Menetou. Here there are signs of *vignerons* – cellars, tractors with vineyard equipment blocking the road.

While Morogues is the main wine village in Menetou, there are nine others: Menetou-Salon itself, Humbligny, Aubinges, Saint-Céols, Parassy, Quantilly, Soulangis, Vignoux-sous-les-Aix and Pigny. The *appellation*, for red, rosé and white only, came into operation in 1959. The late date as compared with Sancerre was an indication of the sad state of viticulture up to that point, but AC status has subsequently acted as a spur to the development of the area.

Although it is easy to bracket Menetou with Sancerre, as simply a lesser, cheaper alternative, there are certain differences in style which make Menetou wines attractive in their own right. The whites tend to be more floral, more lively and less full than those of Sancerre; they are bottled earlier, around Easter, and also age more quickly. The reds, according to many observers, are of a higher general standard than those of Sancerre; although they are light, cherry-flavoured, they have excellent colour, good soft tannins and a more open style, which make them delicious early drinking one year to eighteen months after the harvest.

The most important producer in the *appellation*, Eric Pelle, is based in Morogues. His importance stems not only from his vines, but from his position as supplier of vines and rootstocks to other growers in Menetou. His father Henri worked on experiments in clonal selection. Eric, who trained in Beaune, now has 30 hectares of vines, planted about 60 per cent with Sauvignon Blanc, 40 per cent with Pinot Noir. They have mechanical harvesting machines, believing that with their relatively flat vineyards this is more practical than hand harvesting. Stainless-steel fermentation tanks and relatively low-temperature fermentation for the whites – at 17° C – all go towards making a fresh, modern style of Sauvignon.

Effectively they make two whites from their vineyards: a blended *cuvée* from different parcels of vines, and one from twenty-five-year-old vines in the Clos des Blanchais which is treated separately and makes a particularly floral wine. The red is very much in the fruity Menetou style, with good colour, light acidity and tannin, and plenty of red berry flavours.

The Clément family, of the Domaine de Chatenoy, is one of the most prominent wine families in Menetou. They can trace their wine-making activities back many generations, certainly to the eighteenth century and maybe even to the seventeenth. While in some ways they are quite traditional, in others – particularly with red wines – they are very much in the modern fashion, with their use of new and one-year-old wood (which works better in years like 1989 and 1990 than it does in leaner years like 1991). A wine like their 1990, very Burgundian in style, does suggest that red wine in Menetou is of much greater significance than it is in Sancerre.

5
The wines of Pouilly-sur-Loire

Standing on the ramparts of Sancerre, or on the hill above Thau-venay, it is easy to see the whole of the vineyards of Pouilly-sur-Loire. Across the Loire, as it describes one of its slow, lazy loops, is a low ridge which rises up from the river's edge. It stretches, with dips and undulations, from the hamlet of Tracy in the north down to Mesves-sur-Loire, a distance of about ten kilometres. In the centre of the ridge, the small town of Pouilly-sur-Loire faces out on to the river, presenting a placid, dull front to the world, a thousand miles away from the tourist spots and bustle of Sancerre.

The landscape is much less dramatic than the Sancerre *vignoble*, with its valleys and steep hillsides. Here in Pouilly things are soft, with gentle contours. It is, however, as heavily-dominated by the vine as Sancerre: from the slope that drops down to the river-bank up to the highest point of the vineyards, by the tall church spire of Saint-Andelain, it is all vines, divided right through the centre by Route Nationale 7, which once ran through the town of Pouilly but now has left it to its quiet life.

Pouilly itself is of Roman origin, deriving its name from Paulica Villa, 'the villa of Paulus', and vines were first planted during the Roman occupation of Gaul, taking advantage of the well-exposed south and south-west facing sites by the Loire. In the early Middle Ages this was feudal land, owned by a Baron Humbault, but by the twelfth century it was the property of the Benedictine monastery of Charité-sur-Loire, just to the south, and remained in monastic hands until the French Revolution six hundred years later.

Today the wine has lent its name to a style that is familiar around the world. To the Californian, for a Sauvignon Blanc wine to be called Fumé is to give it an air of grandeur, of weight, sometimes of wood maturing, certainly of ripe fruit; it is intended as a contrast to the flighty numbers which are emulations of Sancerre. Whether that contrast is fair or true – whether Pouilly Fumé wines are more 'serious' than those of Sancerre – is a matter for happy debate in the wine circles of this part of the Loire.

The origins of the term Fumé itself are open to discussion. The practical school of thought opines that it comes from the slightly smoky haze that occurs on the skins of Sauvignon Blanc grapes as they ripen. The more romantic view is that Fumé refers to the slightly smoky, mineral or gun-flint taste that a mature Pouilly Fumé can develop. Both could be true. Sufficient to say that Pouilly Fumé, or Blanc Fumé de Pouilly, is for many the supreme expression of Sauvignon Blanc on the Loire, purer even than Sancerre. Pierre Bréjoux, writing in the 1950s, called the wines 'stark naked' meaning, I imagine, that their virtues and vices cannot be concealed, and that they express the character of the Sauvignon Blanc in complete simplicity.

The Fumé wines of the Sauvignon Blanc have almost completely eclipsed the other wine that can be produced in Pouilly. The *appellation* of Pouilly-sur-Loire is dedicated to another white wine, made from the Chasselas grape. It was, until the replanting of the vineyards after phylloxera, the predominant grape variety, not just for wine but, more importantly, for the table grapes which used to be sent to Paris by train. Already, though, the superior quality of the Sauvignon Blanc for wines was recognized; Jullien wrote of the Sauvignon at Pouilly that it made wine with 'body, alcoholic strength, a slight flinty perfume and very pleasant flavour'. Referring to the Sauvignon, he compared it to the 'other wine districts of the area which produce wines which are known in the trade as Pouilly wines, although most of them are inferior in quality'.

In this century the plantings of Chasselas and the production of Pouilly-sur-Loire have declined, thanks to the popularity of the Sauvignon and the relative unreliability of the Chasselas harvest. Today there are 51 hectares, although the decline has stabilized as producers find that the Chasselas offers a distinctive style which has a niche market, and also makes a pleasantly simple sparkling wine.

The vineyards of Pouilly are relatively simple to encompass. At 945 hectares and 60,000 hectolitres in 1992, the *appellation* of Pouilly Fumé is about half the size of Sancerre. Those figures have grown dramatically in the past few years; in 1988 the vineyard area was only 635 hectares. It is a sign of the increased world demand for Pouilly Fumé wines that has brought much greater prosperity to the 152 different *vignerons* with vines in the seven *communes* that make up the Pouilly vineyard.

While it is possible to find a few vines in the four outlying *communes* – Mesves-sur-Loire, Garchy, Saint-Laurent and Saint-Martin-sur-Nohain – essentially Pouilly's vineyards are concentrated in the three *communes* nearest to the Loire: Saint-Andelain to the east of the RN7, Pouilly-sur-Loire and Tracy-sur-Loire between the RN7 and the river. Although it is theoretically possible to have as many as 1,800 hectares of vines planted for Pouilly Fumé, in climatic terms the riverside *communes* are the only ones where the annual risk of spring frosts is at a bearable minimum. Not even these, though, can escape from the regular summer threat of hail.

The range of soils in Pouilly is similar to that of Sancerre. The dominant ones are marls and Kimmeridgean chalk. But within these, there are differences. The *silex*, flint soils that can be found in parts of Saint-Andelain and Bois-Gibault in the *commune* of Tracy, are reckoned to produce the longest-lived Pouilly, while the more clay soils nearer the town of Pouilly and the hamlet of Les Loges make quicker-maturing wines.

By comparison even with Sancerre, the vineyard holdings of Pouilly are minute: of the 152 *vignerons*, 33 have under 1 hectare (and supply their grapes mainly to the co-operative), 117 farm less than 10 hectares, 146 have less than 20 hectares, while only one owner – Château du Nozet – has more than 60 hectares. Despite the small size of individual holdings, by far the greatest amount of Pouilly is now bottled and sold by the growers; in 1992 it was 75 per cent, compared with the 17 per cent that goes to the *négociants* and the mere 8 per cent that is processed by the co-operative.

The export markets are vital to Pouilly's success. Some 60 to 65 per cent of local production is exported, primarily to Britain, Belgium, Germany, the Netherlands, the USA and Japan. These overseas sales have obviously brought prosperity, even to the *vignerons* with tiny vineyards; all seem to have their smart cars, their comfortable houses and their well-equipped cellars. The problem in the early 1990s has been competition from the New World Sauvignon Blanc, and many times I was anxiously asked whether I thought their wines – generally higher-priced than most of the New World competition – were still appreciated in the export markets. I told them to keep their prices down, to which reply there was generally a Gallic shrug and a look of concern at the new car parked outside.

A tour of the Pouilly vineyard is quickly accomplished. I was taken by M. Masson, director of the Union Viticole – the association of growers – which seems to be the only body that represents Pouilly to the outside world. His cellars are in the centre of Pouilly, and his house is right on the most strategic corner of the village, allowing him to have a smart shop at the front as well as a fully-computerized office. We drove northwards up the main street of Pouilly, under the railway bridge and climbed up the hill to the RN7.

Across the main road and to the right are the vineyards of the largest estate in Pouilly, based around the nineteenth-century Château du Nozet owned by the de Ladoucette family. The road twists round through the vineyards of Saint-Andelain and Les Berthiers, the little hamlet that lies between Saint-Andelain and the main road. Both villages seem to live only for wine, Les Berthiers in particular appearing to be just a row of *vignerons'* cellars with smart new bungalows attached.

Back across the main road the vineyards spread out, facing the Loire. The little vineyard lane drops precipitously down into the hamlet of Les Loges, another settlement devoted entirely to wine, picturesque in an untidy sort of way, with tiny alleyways, hanging baskets of flowers outside seemingly-empty properties – and everywhere, at harvest time, the traffic jams of tractors and the hum of machinery from inside the cellars which, despite their tumble-down outward appearance, are stuffed full of the most modern equipment.

From Les Loges the road follows the river to the village of Bois-Gibault, with its tranquil, tree-shaded triangular square, and then goes on through woods to Tracy, passing the other château of Pouilly, the thirteenth-century Château de Tracy, in a most romantic setting at the bottom of a slight valley surrounded by its vineyards. This is the northern extremity of Pouilly vineyards; a short distance away is the road that crosses the Loire at Saint-Thibault into Sancerre.

The demanding Dagueneaux

In such a small, close area, it is hardly surprising that gossip and rivalries are rife, and that those who achieve success are envied by those who do not. Even worse, there are also internal family squabbles that seem unfathomable to the outsider. The Dagueneau family is a case in point: there are, I think (it is easy to lose count), three Dagueneaus making wine all in or around Les Berthiers and Saint-Andelain. The largest landowner is Jean-Claude, with 15 hectares of vines in Les Berthiers on clay and *silex* soil and in Les Loges on clay and limestone, but all within one kilometre of his cellars in the centre of Les Berthiers.

Just up the road from Jean-Claude is his cousin Serge, while up the hill in Saint-Andelain is Jean-Claude's son Didier. It is, so I am told, between Didier and Jean-Claude that the main rivalry exists, and having met both of these larger-than-life characters I do not find it surprising.

I visited Jean-Claude one warm, sunny afternoon. His cellars are next door to his large, comfortable eighteenth-century house, dripping with flowers and with a delightful walled garden attached. Jean-Claude, however, was firmly inside in his little wine-tasting area, cigarette in hand, glass of wine beside him, chatting to a local who had dropped in for a moment. He's a large, bearded man, with a comfortable, indeed ample, stomach. While I was with him it was obvious that no spitting-out of wine samples would be done, while any qualms I might have had about smoking during tastings arose not at all.

I could not quite work out at first if Jean-Claude was pleased, or even interested, to see me. Conversation was at the level of 'have another glass', rather than the passing-on of information about his vineyards. In short order, I tasted his 1992 Pouilly Fumé – which was more pepper than fruit and obviously suffering from recent bottling – learnt that the vineyard had been started by his grandmother's family after the First World War and that he had taken over in 1968, and that his *domaine* name is Domaine des Berthiers.

In addition to a standard Pouilly Fumé he makes prestige *cuvées*. His Domaine des Berthiers 1991, now maturing nicely, was full, round and complex, and lived up to Jean-Claude's reputation as one of the top *vignerons* of the *appellation*. I was then offered a glass of his Cuvée d'Ève 1990, made from forty-year-old vines and named after his wife Eveline. He told me that he had created this *cuvée* when one of his Parisian customers, wanting to get a prestige *cuvée* of Pouilly Fumé, had asked him to buy some Baron de L of Château du Nozet. Rather than do this, he had created his own prestige *cuvée*. It is a wine that does his wife a lot of justice: big, full, rounded, bursting with tropical fruit, from low yields (40 hecto-litres per hectare, compared with the normal 70 to 75 hectolitres per hectare) and destined for a good life. The 1989, developing well, was even more extraordinary: smelling exactly like the catty gooseberry bush often used as a description of Sauvignon Blanc, it had an enormous, explosive Sauvignon taste.

Suddenly, Jean-Claude mellowed and in a rapid trot we went round his rather austere cellars housed in the modern shed next to his house. As we left, I felt I must have passed the test, as I was handed a bottle of the 1992 Cuvée d'Ève – a bottle which I intend to put away for some years.

From Jean-Claude it may only be a five-minute drive up to Saint-Andelain and the cellars of Didier Dagueneau, but to do so is to enter another world. While Jean-Claude is relaxed about his wines, still – despite stainless steel – working in a traditional world of small, local horizons, for Didier the world of wine is as universal as it would be for an Australian or Californian.

When I first met Didier back in 1986, he was operating from a tiny, underground cellar in Les Berthiers. He had 6.5 hectares and we spent most of one freezing-cold evening sitting around the dinner table in his tiny cottage of a house before a huge log fire. It was obvious then that he was going to be different from other Pouilly *vignerons* – for a start, we drank white and red Burgundy with dinner – as we discussed the ageing of Pouilly and the use of wood in its fermentation. Both were ideas then being dismissed by all but a handful of producers in either Pouilly or Sancerre; the Sauvignon Blanc, so the gospel went, made wines that had to be drunk young and were best when fermented in the brand-new stain-less steel.

By 1993 Didier's reputation had grown enormously. He went through a stage where he was known as the Wild Man of Pouilly, not only because of his extremely hirsute appearance – long, curly hair and dramatic beard framing a face with a look of permanent intensity – but also because of his ideas. Now he is seen as some-thing much simpler: the best producer in the *appellation*, able to command prices for his top wines that rival those of Château du Nozet, for long seen as the showpiece of the region. He is still something of a revolutionary, though, to judge by the American Confederate flag which flies outside his house.

The showpiece cellar is no longer housed underground in Les

Berthiers. It is now in a spanking new building in Saint-Andelain, next to Didier's house, a cellar that is almost certainly as clean as anything you would find in the New World, where the hose is in constant use, where stainless-steel tanks are used in conjunction with a formidable array of new and almost-new *barriques*, and where the wood-ageing cellar is a smaller version of the smartest that Burgundy or Bordeaux could offer.

We tasted from different woods, from Tronçais, from Allier, wines made from different portions of his vineyard. He makes a number of different *cuvées*, each an expression of different parcels of his land. There was the lightly woody Cailloux, the new wood tastes of Buisson Menard, the hugely rich Pur Sang, which is in slightly larger Burgundy *pièces*, and finally the austerity overlying tropical richness of Silex. Meanwhile Didier talked: of his dislike of chaptalization (the addition of sugar to increase alcohol) because it changes the character of the Sauvignon, making it too herbaceous; of his belief that wine is as much a cultural event as a mere drink; of the fact that, in the old days, Pouilly Fumé wines were aged for as much as twenty years, a character he is trying to recreate with his use of wood; of his admiration for the wines from *silex* soil because of their longevity; of his belief in high-temperature fermentation, even for whites, because it brings out the tastes better.

Then it was into the car with Didier and his wife for a drive to lunch. As we drove up the little lane we passed the local school playground, where the Dagueneau children, a boy and a girl, were playing. The boy wanted to stay, but the girl was scooped up – how many schools in Britain would allow this? – and we shot, at more kilometres per hour than I cared to notice, over the Loire and up the hill to Sancerre; 'there are no decent restaurants in Pouilly', I was told firmly when I asked. Here we dined in splendour in Sancerre's best restaurant, the Restaurant de la Tour with its panoramic view of the Sancerre vineyards, tasting wines and discussing the world.

They are great wines by any standards. The question is whether they are Pouilly Fumé. They are less different from other Pouilly Fumé wines today than they were even seven years ago, when I first tasted them; the appreciation of greater fruit character and the ability of Pouilly to give this is now much more widespread. They also underline strongly the differences between Sancerre and Pouilly: the fact that Pouilly wines should be weightier, more rounded, with less *nervosité* (that apt French word used to describe a wine that is, as it were, walking a tightrope of balance) than Sancerre. The difference between Sancerre and Pouilly would be, in Burgundian terms, the difference between the white wines of Chablis and those of the Côte d'Or.

The châteaux of Pouilly

Didier Dagueneau is a hard act to follow. But his methods are only a spectacularly extreme example of the way the quality of Pouilly Fumé wines is improving. That the aim of quality was inspired by the success of Patrick de Ladoucette at Château du Nozet is accepted by all. His prestige *cuvée*, Baron de L, may be the priciest Pouilly Fumé on the market, but it has for long been seen as the best. It is the top *domaine*-produced wine from this 60-hectare vineyard which, both as estate producer and *négociant*, dominates Pouilly Fumé with its production of 1.5 million bottles and its tentacles which spread to Comte Lafond wines in Sancerre and Marc Brédif in Vouvray as well as to Albert Pic in Chablis.

The spectacular château building, created in 1850 by the architect Viollet-le-Duc for Comte Lafond, governor of the Bank of France and ancestor of M. de Ladoucette, lies in what the guidebooks might call a privileged position just off the RN7 in a glade of trees, surrounded, just as if it were in Bordeaux, with the bulk of its vineyard. Some of the vines in the individually-named plots are of great age: those of the 12-hectare Le Désert on *terre blanche* soil have an average age of forty-five years, while those of Le Calvaire, a 15-hectare plot near Saint-Andelain, average twenty-five to thirty years.

These plots are at the heart of Baron de L, which is a blended wine from different parts of the estate, assembled in the June following the harvest, and only in better years. It comes at the head of a range which has become even better in the few years since a brand-new cellar installation was inaugurated in 1989. The style is very rich – at Château du Nozet they like to call it Burgundian – and, like the wines of Didier Dagueneau, has this ability to age which gives the lie to the view that all Sauvignon Blanc should be drunk young.

There is a second château estate in Pouilly that has even greater claims to seniority in the area than Château du Nozet, and that is Château de Tracy. It has been home to the Estutt d'Assay family since the sixteenth century, a formidable time considering the changes in France over that span of time. The family was originally from Scotland, the Stutts of Lagan, and came to serve Charles VII against the English in the fifteenth century; they were rewarded with lands in Assay in Berry, later acquiring Château de Tracy through marriage.

Wine was certainly made here in the sixteenth century, and grape-growing – albeit mainly of Chasselas for sale as table grapes – continued until the advent of phylloxera, when the vineyard was abandoned. It fell to Alain, the late father of the present count Henri, to revive the vineyard in 1952, and now there are some 27 hectares of vines, including new plantations spread around Tracy and Bois-Gibault.

Comte Henri, a tall, thin man sporting a bright bow tie, lives in the château with his mother, wife and family, and is the only man I have yet met who can fondly dandle a baby son on one knee while opening a bottle of wine with one hand. We were sitting in the huge *salon* of the castle – a pleasant change from standing around in a cold cellar – while I tasted and we talked about the estate. His approach to making wine seems to be somewhere between the high-tech chemical approach and that of the ecologists and biodynamists. He keeps chemicals to a minimum, and is now developing techniques such as whole-bunch maceration and keeping the wine on the lees – both supposed to extract great flavour.

Certainly his 1991 Pouilly Fumé, which I tasted as we talked, is the epitome of elegance – much like the family of its producer. It is not in the designed-for-ageing league of some other producers in Pouilly, and reflects much more the character of Sancerre, whose hill can be glimpsed through the trees surrounding the château. We made a brief tour of the cellar, newly-equipped with stainless steel, to taste the 1992 – which was rounder than the 1991 and altogether bigger – and to admire the mural of the family with Bacchus which adorns the huge back wall of the *chai*.

Families with a long tradition

Another family which has been making wine in Pouilly for a long time is that of Masson-Blondelet. 'For six generations' says the cover of the publicity literature, which I picked up as I returned to their tasting room in the centre of Pouilly. There are now 16 hectares in this *domaine* (three of them in Sancerre), large by Pouilly standards and formed by an amalgamation of the family lands of Jean-Michel Masson and his wife Michelle, née Blondelet. They are an energetic, hard-working couple with one young daughter, all living literally behind their shop. Just up the road is their brand-new cellar, much of it excavated and underground. Jean-Michel and I literally tore up the road as the heavens opened and deposited several centimetres of rain – but luckily no hail – and we descended by lift to the fermentation cellar to taste, while I wondered, but did not like to ask, what would happen if there were a power cut.

The vines of the Domaine Masson-Blondelet are divided into as many as forty different parcels, which might make harvesting a headache but does cut down the risk of total loss from hail, which tends to be very localized. We first tasted a Pouilly-sur-Loire, the Chasselas wine, crisp with what I was told was a typical peppery background. M. Masson told me that there was increasing interest in France in the Chasselas wine – 'out of curiosity, if nothing else'. After a momentary taste of Sancerre, a particularly light and fresh example, we moved on to the real matter of the moment.

There are four Pouilly Fumé wines in the Masson-Blondelet range: Les Bascoins and Villa Paulus from vines on marl soil, Les Angelots from limestone soil, and Tradition Cullus which comes from old vines on *silex* soil and is partly vinified in new wood. The most immediately approachable is Les Angelots, the 1992 round and soft, with lemon flavours. By contrast, the 1992 Les Bascoins was more austere, more complex with higher initial acidity. The 1992 Villa Paulus was richer, sweeter, with ripe, soft, almost honeyed flavour. Finally, 1990 Tradition Cullus was perhaps almost too spicy from the wood, but was bearing its fruit well and obviously had a long way to develop to maturity.

An equally long tradition in Pouilly is that of Michel Redde. I must admit to having viewed his tasting cellar bang on the RN7 with some initial suspicion. It seemed too dominated by furniture carved from vinewood and general knick-knacks to be serious about making wine. I am delighted to say I was proved wrong within a matter of moments. Michel Redde and his son Thierry represent the seventh and eighth generations of the family firm which now owns 35 hectares of vines in Pouilly and also buys fruit from Sancerre. Their vines are planted on a mix of all three Pouilly soils, mainly in the *commune* of Saint-Andelain but also in Pouilly.

It was Thierry who showed me round the tasting room and cellars, built in 1980, after first letting me taste some of his wines.

La Moynerie, named after the monks who once farmed this land, is the name of the vineyard and also of their main *cuvée* of Pouilly Fumé. The 1992 vintage of this wine is classic Pouilly, rich, with the sweetness of tropical fruits and just a hint of honey, with a faint smoky, flinty character – everything these wines should be, overt and obviously ready to drink relatively rapidly. In the better years they make a prestige *cuvée*, Cuvée Majorum, meaning, I was told, 'the best' in Latin, and certainly a distinctive name; I tasted first the 1989, smelling of black and red currants, very dry but full, bursting with young fruit. The 1990 was much more floral, tasting of very ripe grapes, explained by the fact the grapes for this wine were harvested very late in the year.

We then toured the cellars, which are much larger than appears from the road, where all the visitor sees is the curious fake-château-like structure of the tasting room. It's stainless steel all round, new pneumatic presses providing a counterpoint to a thirteenth-century wooden press which is for show only. Thierry told me that his father started life with one tank for his wine, and now they have thirty. We tasted the 1992 wines from some of these tanks. They make individual *cuvées* from the different soils: the wine from the limestone and clay soils of Les Loges was already much fruitier, and also less complex, than the powerful, tight wine from the flinty *silex* soil, confirming – if any confirmation were needed – that these *silex* wines are wines to keep.

I discussed these soil differences later with Patrick Coulbois. He is best described as a strong, silent type, not given to many words, operating his 8.5 hectares on his own, living above his cellars in Les Berthiers in a smart, modern bungalow. He has vines in Saint-Andelain on *silex* soil and in Les Loges on limestone and clay. The wines of Les Loges, he said, are initially more powerful, while those from the *silex* of Saint-Andelain are firmer, eventually becoming finer, but needing time.

M. Coulbois is from yet another family of *vignerons* on both his father's and his mother's side. They have been making wine in Pouilly since at least the seventeenth century, and both came from Saint-Andelain. His father's business has now gone to his cousin, because Patrick does not want to get any bigger: 'I would have to employ people if I had more land, and I wouldn't make any more money.'

His cellar, modern, clean and spacious, is as straightforward as possible: a row of square, stainless-steel tanks and three *cuvées* of Pouilly Fumé, one from Les Loges and two from Saint-Andelain. I tasted first his Pouilly-sur-Loire, the Chasselas-based wine, very peppery to taste, low in acidity and alcohol and high in earthy character. Then it was on to Pouilly Fumé, the lighter, fruitier character of La Corneille from his Les Loges vineyards contrasting with the full, rich Les Coques and the very powerful La Charnoie, made from older vines in Saint-Andelain. Sadly, Patrick told me, he lost the 1992 crop from La Charnoie because of hail. I only hope he was insured.

After Patrick Coulbois I went to see another young *vigneron* whose family has been making wine in Pouilly for several generations. Unfortunately, personality differences meant that the two Bailly brothers, Michel and Jean-Louis, had to split the family land between them and go their separate ways. I visited Michel, who runs his vineyard of 13 hectares from a tiny, unpretentious shed on the slope above Les Loges. He is another taciturn type, seemingly in pain from a limp which, to judge by his build, he acquired in a rugby accident. He makes two *cuvées* of Pouilly Fumé, one for early drinking and one for ageing which he calls Cuvée MB.

The wines he makes are essentially fruity in the style of the lighter wines of Les Loges. The young 1992 early-drinking Pouilly Fumé was fat, round and full of currant fruits, very attractive nine months after harvest. Cuvée MB, which he has so far only made twice – in 1987 and 1989 – is rich, honeyed and nutty, a selection of fruit from young vines and from free-run juice. The 1987 is still young, crisper than the weighty 1989, and full of green, fresh fruit.

As I drove south down the RN7 from Pouilly I reflected on the small size and great influence of this region. It takes a passing traveller less than ten minutes to go from north to south of the Pouilly vineyards. Some of the names familiar to wine-drinkers are hardly more than prosperous peasant farmers. And yet with their wines, they have put this sleepy community with its long-established, sometimes warring, families on the map, and are producing to higher and higher standards what many see as the Loire's best white wine. Now all they need to do is keep their prices in perspective and realize that competition from the New World gets stronger every year.

6

Reuilly, Quincy and the lesser appellations *of the Centre*

Reuilly, a vineyard back from the brink

Reuilly is a rather sad little village on the boundary of the Indre *département*, facing across the River Arnon towards the Cher. Empty shops, a complete dearth of restaurants and thoroughly undistinguished architecture – and few, if any, signs of *vignerons* – hardly make for a welcoming wine town. That it once enjoyed more prosperous times is apparent in the large square, one Renaissance façade (above a seedy café) and church that are its only claims to interest.

Coming from the south, from Châteauroux and Issoudun, you pass through some of the dullest country in central France: flat cereal fields, open horizons, hardly any trees. As you approach Reuilly a low ridge appears to the left of the road, facing out to the rivers Théols and Arnon, and the first vines can be seen on the higher levels of the slope, around the hamlet of La Ferté, which seems to have a goodly collection of *vignerons*. To the north of the town too there are vines around the hamlet of Bois Saint-Denis, interspersed with more cereals. It was those cereals, and the fact that *vignerons* could make more money growing them than producing wine, which caused the precipitous decline of Reuilly's vineyards until, at the beginning of the 1980s, there were fewer than 50 hectares.

That today things are improving, and there are 120 hectares of vines, is down to two factors. One is the decline in the market for cereals and a simultaneous (but unconnected) increase in demand for wines made from the Sauvignon Blanc grape. The other is the arrival of a small group of exciting younger *vignerons* who want to bring about a renaissance of the area. At least ten new growers have

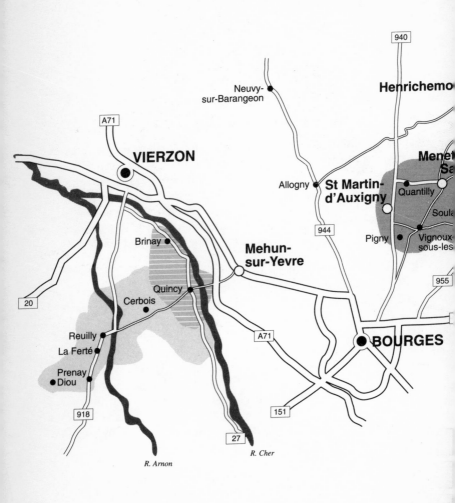

940

Neuvy-
sur-Barangeon

Henrichemo

VIERZON

A71

Allogny

St Martin-
d'Auxigny

Mene
Sa

Quantilly

Soula

Menet

944

Pigny

Vignoux-
sous-les

955

Brinay

Mehun-
sur-Yevre

Quincy

Cerbois

20

Reuilly

La Ferté

A71

BOURGES

Prenay
Diou

918

27

151

R. Arnon

R. Cher

Kms   10   30

Mls   5   20

The vineyards of central France

Cosne-Cours
sur-Loire

SANCERRE

Crézancy-en-Sancerre

Motte d'-
Humbligny

sy

Morogues

Aubinges

Les Aix
D'Angillon

Pouilly-sur-Loire

Mesves-
sur-Loire

La Charité-
sur-Loire

R. LOIRE

R. Vauvise

Baugy

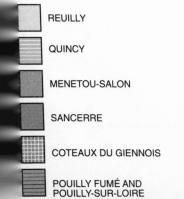

REUILLY

QUINCY

MENETOU-SALON

SANCERRE

COTEAUX DU GIENNOIS

POUILLY FUMÉ AND
POUILLY-SUR-LOIRE

appeared on the scene in the past two years, and in 1992 a co-operative was created by seven who did not have cellars – they now produce a third of the wine of the *appellation*.

The co-operative operates from the backyard of Claude Lafond, who is president of the local growers' syndicate. He is a quiet but efficient man who obviously wants to get things done. His cellars, in the hamlet of Bois Saint-Denis, are in sheds which surround three sides of a courtyard, the fourth being the family's brand-new bungalow which M. Lafond shares with his parents. With 15 hectares of land, he is certainly one of the most important growers in the area.

He has been behind attempts to stimulate quality with the creation of a Charte de Qualité, a name attached to prestige *cuvées* produced with low yields, using local strains of yeast, low chaptalization and clonal selection of the vines, and which have to be approved by a tasting panel (the way M. Lafond described it, the tasting sounded like a rather good party as well). The wines for these Charte de Qualité *cuvées* are held back from sale until May (the normal release date for Reuilly wines is March) and they are given special labels.

Reuilly can come in three colours. Whites are made from Sauvignon Blanc, rosés from Pinot Gris or Pinot Noir, and reds from Pinot Noir. There used to be Gamay as well for red wines, but this grape variety was not included in the *appellation* rules for reds and rosés which came in in 1961 (whites gained the *appellation* in 1937), and can therefore only be made into *vin de pays*.

Vines are scattered over seven *communes* in both the Indre and Cher *départements*, with the main concentrations in the *commune* of Reuilly above the River Arnon (Bois Saint-Denis and La Ferté) and in the *commune* of Preuilly, which is in Cher between Reuilly and Quincy. Growers have traditionally tried to have small parcels of vines in different parts of the *appellation* to minimize the problems of frost (which can occur on fifty days a year) and hail (three or four severe outbreaks a year). With such scattered vineyards, the soils are varied. There is sand and gravel soil near the river, and Kimmeridgean chalk soil on the higher ground west of Reuilly. This chalk soil, similar to that of Champagne, gives the region its name, La Champagne Berrichonne.

M. Lafond gave me a rapid tour of the vineyards in his battered van, dropping sharply down dirt tracks and through fields of cereals to get to the patches of viticulture, before depositing me at the local Syndicat d'Initiative, where I was given a fascinating tour of the small wine museum which has been created to show something of the history of viticulture in Reuilly.

As in many places in this part of France, vines came with the monks: those of Reuilly, who were tied to the abbey of Saint-Denis in Paris. They set out regulations for vine-growing and recommended the land which was suitable, advice which is still being followed to this day. The sale of Reuilly wines was controlled by the Duc de Berry in a charter of 1365, while in 1567 Nicolas de Nicolay in his general description of the Duchy of Berry heaped praise on the Reuilly wines.

Up to this point, I had still to taste my first Reuilly. And, in fact, when I did so I was already in neighbouring Quincy. That was because M. Lafond had arranged for me to join a tasting of white wines from the 1992 vintage of both Reuilly and Quincy at the Château de Brinay, organized for *sommeliers* – wine waiters – from some of the top restaurants of the Loire Valley. That there should be a tasting at all shows how the *vignerons* in both *appellations* realize the need to make two small, unknown names better known. The fact that this was a joint tasting of wines from two *appellations* was something very special for France, where local rivalries can be intense.

The Reuilly wines, of which there were eleven, seemed to fall into two distinct styles. There were some really concentrated, quite fat, full-bodied wines which could outshine many a *négociant* Sancerre. And there was a much smaller group of wines which obviously came from high-yielding vines and were therefore rather dilute. The star producers were, not surprisingly, in the first category: Gérard Bigonneau, full of blackcurrant fruit flavours, almost New World in its intensity; that of Bernard Aujard and Alain Mabillot with soft, restrained Sauvignon flavours; the lively, balanced, early-drinking style of Domaine Henri Beurdin; and a very full, fat contribution from Claude Lafond.

One producer whose white Reuilly I did not taste, but who has vines both in Reuilly and in Quincy, was Jean-Michel Sorbe. A large, fat, bearded man who would be the life and soul of any party, his wines were consistently good: his rosé Reuilly 1992 from Pinot Noir, made with light pressing to extract colour, had a delightful pale salmon-pink colour, a lift of acidity and some soft tannins, while his red 1988 had some soft, perfumed raspberry flavour and a light, sweet finish.

The reds and rosés of Reuilly appeared with the lunch at the local restaurant in Brinay which followed the tasting of the whites. The two styles of rosé – from Pinot Gris and Pinot Noir – were the ones that excited most comment among the assembled *sommeliers*. The producers of Pinot Gris are obviously in a minority among Reuilly producers; only Claude Lafond and Jacques Vincent (a shy, quiet man, owner of eight hectares, sitting next to me at table, who only produced his light, fresh Pinot Gris rosé and his soft Pinot Noir red after much prompting from those around him). The style of Pinot Gris, sometimes slightly peppery to taste, is certainly unique in this part of the Loire – the only other area to plant it is right at the other end of the river at Ancenis in the Pays Nantais. It needs good years, I was told, and it is this unreliability which makes it unpopular with the *vignerons*.

Although rosés from Pinot Noir are more conventional, they are certainly attractive enough. However, reds from Pinot Noir are perhaps the least successful wines in Reuilly; the climate is not conducive to colour extraction, and with light colour, almost non-existent tannins and sometimes high acidity, they really can only have local interest.

Quincy, a noble wine

While Reuilly makes all three colours of wine, Quincy only makes one. Whites from Sauvignon Blanc cover all 170 hectares of the *appellation*. Red and rosé vines – Pinot Noir, Pinot Gris and Gamay – do not have the *appellation* and are made into red Vin de Pays du Jardin de la France or the departmental Vin de Pays du Cher.

Quincy is a small village twelve miles west of Bourges, six miles east of Reuilly, on the banks of the River Cher. It is an attractive place built round a village green, with a small church and what looks like a thriving café facing each other across the grass. Unlike in Reuilly, there is plenty of evidence of viticulture here, with signs enticing the few cars that pass to taste and buy. Three miles further along the road, also on the banks of the Cher, is Brinay, the other *commune* in the Quincy *appellation*. This is a delightful village, its fifteenth-century château and church forming a small group in the trees well away from the main road.

The vineyards face south-east, stretching between the two villages on a low terrace above the Cher. The soil is mainly sand and gravel on a mix of flint and chalk, well-drained, and the land drops gently to the river. At around 30 hectolitres per hectare, yields are low because of the relative poverty of this soil.

As at Reuilly, it is the arrival of a new generation of *vignerons* which has breathed life into an old *appellation*. But it has never suffered in the same way as Reuilly from competition with cereal production for the available land, simply because the soil is too poor for anything but vines. It is near to Bourges, which gives it good local trade, and in history it was the favoured wine of the Dukes of Berry – hence the epithet 'Vin Noble' which bottles of Quincy bear to this day. In more modern times, its concentration on whites from Sauvignon Blanc has given it a good position as an alternative to more expensive wines from Sancerre.

The style of Quincy is more angular, crisper, than Reuilly – paralleling the contrast between the lightness of Sancerre and the greater weight of Pouilly Fumé. With their good acid balance, however, they can age well, and will develop a fascinating series of flavours, of herb infusions and honey. Tasting the Quincy wines with the *sommeliers* at Château de Brinay, there seemed to be a greater variation in quality between them than there was with the Reuilly wines at the same tasting. I was seven wines into the tasting before the star 1992 wine of Jean-Michel Sorbe (whose rosé and red Reuilly I was to enjoy at lunch later) appeared and gave me some idea of what Quincy can taste like: ripe, tropical fruit flavours balanced a streak of acidity to give an excellent food wine, with local fish dishes or with seafood. Two other wines came close to this standard: Domaine Jean Mardon and André Barbier. It was a pity that the wines of the largest *domaine* (25 hectares) in Quincy – Domaine de Maison Blanche – were not at the tasting: these are sold by the *négociant* firm of Albert Besombes, whose cellars are at Saumur.

Some of the wines I tasted had a definite *goût de terroir*, emphasized, I was told, by the fact that these 1992s had only recently been bottled; of that style, the wine of Claude Houssier at Domaine du Pressoir and the steely crisp style of René Marchais showed well. Some other wines showed many faults – excessive sulphur being the most common – which put them out of consideration, a view I shared with the *sommeliers* tasting around me.

Châteaumeillant – for local curiosity only

My visit to Châteaumeillant, made one Sunday, was necessarily brief. As far as I could see, the town – apart from one excellent restaurant – was closed. Lunch gave me the chance to drink one wine of the *appellation*, the first and probably the last time I will get a chance to taste a wine from what is the smallest eastern Loire *appellation*, and one that survives only on passing trade and curious voyagers like myself.

Châteaumeillant is just inside the *département* of Cher, seventeen kilometres east of La Châtre. If anybody wanted to encapsulate a French town at its most ordinary, here it is. A rather ragged main street with occasional shops, and a wide, tree-lined square-cum-car park with a few more ancient shops are about all that is on offer. There is a museum of Gallo-Roman remains, an impressively large police station (are there many criminals in this part of France?) and the pretty, pink-decorated restaurant of M. and Mme Piet-Finet, Le Piet à Terre.

There are signs of viticulture. As you enter the town from the west, there are roadside notices offering a chance to taste: one *vigneron*, Jean-Paul Bourdeau of the Domaine du Parc, has a modern cellar on the main road – closed on Sundays – while Paul Raffinat et Fils are down a side road among a housing estate. Coming the other way, the Cave Co-operative, with large fibre-glass tanks outside, offers sales but is also closed on Sundays. And in the middle of the town I found the timber-framed house of Maurice Landoix, who owns the Domaine de Feuillat.

Châteaumeillant, a *Vin Délimité de Qualité Supérieur* (VDQS) created in 1965, produces red and rosé wines only, either from Gamay alone or in a blend with one-third Pinot Noir, two-thirds Gamay. There are just under 75 hectares of land under vine. Legend relates that vines were first planted here by Gregory of Tours in 1220.

Before lunch I drove out of town to discover where the vines were. After much searching I discovered what I imagine is the total planting, along a low slope above the small valley of the Sinaise (a tributary of the Cher) which flows south-west of Châteaumeillant. The vines, mostly old and with little sign of new plantings, are on red, sandy soil, trained on three wires and widely-spaced. Looking at them in June, and judging by the number of bunches forming on them, it seemed that yields must be low.

I drank a half-bottle of the rosé from the Cave Co-operative with the salmon I had for lunch. As a thirst-quencher on a very hot day, fresh and cool, it was most pleasant. But it was light and slightly too acid, and I can quite understand why the wines of Châteaumeillant are hardly seen outside the region of production.

Coteaux du Giennois – not quite forgotten

Coteaux du Giennois (or alternatively Côtes de Gien) is another of those curious vineyards of the Loire that manage to survive – just – when logic would dictate that the few remaining *vignerons* would have upped their vines and started growing something else. Nor do they make a great but ignored wine. What they produce would be of less than passing interest elsewhere. Yet the fact that this relic of a much greater past is still with us is surely cause for quiet rejoicing.

Gien, the town from which the *appellation* gets its name, is on the right bank of the Loire about sixty kilometres upstream from Orléans in the *département* of Loiret. It is a fine riverside city with a comfortable rather than grand fifteenth-century château and a waterfront of elegant bourgeois houses. The river is crossed by a graceful, seven-arched stone bridge which, now the city is bypassed, no longer takes the heavy traffic.

In fact, though, Gien is not the centre of this small VDQS *appellation*, created in 1954. That is further south at Cosne, in the *département* of Nièvre and not far north of the edge of Pouilly Fumé. Here are the bulk of the 85 hectares that remain of an *appellation* that, even at the beginning of this century, covered 2,000 hectares, fuelled by the proximity of Paris. There are still sixteen *communes* – nine in Nièvre and seven in Loiret – which can have the *appellation*. But the bulk of vineyards are found at Cosne, which has the right to add its name to the description, as in Coteaux du Giennois Cosne-sur-Loire.

Given its proximity to Pouilly, it is hardly surprising that some of the production is in the hands of either the Pouilly co-operative or the few growers in either Pouilly or Sancerre who are interested – or curious – enough to make a wine from this neighbouring *appellation*; for example, Joseph Balland-Chapuis in Sancerre. However, there are growers whose cellars are in the area of the *appellation*

– the best that I discovered are Hubert Veneau of Domaine des Ormousseaux at Saint-Père, just east of Cosne, Alain Paulat at Cosne-sur-Loire, and Jean Poupat et Fils at Gien. They are the producers who are contributing to a slight revival of interest in the wines, along with the active research station of the Institut National de la Recherche Agricole (INRA) at Gien.

Like most vineyard areas, its origins are ecclesiastical. In this case, the two abbeys of Saint-Benoît-sur-Loire and La Charité-sur-Loire are believed to have been the main creators. Today, with both church and Parisian patronage removed, the vineyards rely on passing tourist trade and on local restaurants for the bulk of their sales.

The wines made here come in all three colours. Reds and rosés are made from Gamay and Pinot Noir, whites from Sauvignon Blanc and Chenin Blanc; the existence of the Pinot Blanc in the vineyard is no more than a distant memory, although still permitted. The vines are planted on light chalk or gravel soil. The reds and, to a lesser extent, rosés are growing more important at the expense of the whites. Inevitably in such a northerly *appellation*, the style of all the wines is light. The reds, generally a blend of the two grape varieties but also produced as separate varietal wines, are simple and fruity; the blends benefit from the vivacity of the Gamay, although some of the Pinot Noir wines can have a pleasant, delicate perfume. The whites are pale imitations of Pouilly Fumé.

Vin de l'Orléanais – in the shadow of the big city

The vineyards of Orléans are, like so many of the lesser *appellations* of the Loire, but a shadow of their former selves. Where once 700,000 hectolitres a year were produced, now the figure is down to just over 7,000 from 150 hectares of land. In 1816 Jullien could write in praise of the wines of Saint-Jean-de-Bray, in particular those from the *clos* of Sainte-Marie, and vines stretched along the Loire on both sides of Orléans. Now, Saint-Jean is a suburb of Orléans and vines are practically confined to the villages of Mareau-aux-Prés and Mézières-lez-Cléry downstream of the city.

But all is not lost. Compared with the vineyards of Gien, the wines of Orléans are comparatively thriving, thanks entirely to tourists, and there are a handful of producers who are producing wines that are of more than passing interest.

The wines of Orléans date back to Roman times, but the reconstruction of the vineyard after its disappearance in the Dark Ages is due to the monks of Saint-Mesmin and to the bishop of Orléans, Theodulf, who lived at the time of Charlemagne. The vineyards thrived because of their proximity to Paris – of all the Loire vineyards these are the closest to the metropolis – and to the royal nature of the city of Orléans itself. At the time, the wines produced were almost entirely red, from the Auvernat Gris (the Pinot Meunier), and in the early nineteenth century Jullien describes them as having had a 'good colour and a pleasant and honest taste'.

But the *vignerons* of Orléans, with their captive Parisian market, became greedy. In the seventeenth and eighteenth centuries they replanted with the high-yielding, coarse Teinturier. But with the arrival of railways, when bulk wine could more easily, and reliably, come from the Midi rather than the northerly vineyards of Orléans, sales collapsed and the vineyards all but disappeared.

Today there are five *communes* on the left bank of the Loire downstream from Orléans which are permitted to produce VDQS Vin de l'Orléanais: Olivet, Saint-Hilaire-Saint-Mesmin, Mareau-aux-Prés, Cléry-Saint-André and Mézières-lez-Cléry; and a further nineteen *communes* on the right bank where in practice there are few vines. The VDQS, created in 1951, permits the planting of Pinot Meunier (Auvernat Gris), Pinot Noir (Auvernat Rouge) and Cabernet Franc for reds; and Chardonnay (Auvernat Blanc) for whites. The vines, planted among the vegetables and fruit trees which are the predominant crop along the fertile banks of the river, are on patches of gravel soil.

The most interesting wines come from the Pinot Meunier, sometimes also called the Gris Meunier on account of the colour of the underside of its leaves. This produces a particularly light red wine which is splendid as a drink in the summer following the harvest. Whites, from Chardonnay (Auvernat Blanc), can be surprisingly full-bodied for such a northerly vineyard. The Cabernet Franc is the base for light, refreshing rosés, while wines from the Pinot Noir (Auvernat Rouge) emphasize perfume rather than fruit.

The best producer in the *appellation* is reckoned to be the Montigny family of Clos Saint-Fiacre, but the bulk of the wine from the fifty or so growers goes through the co-operative in Mareau-aux-Prés under the name of Les Vignerons de la Grand'Maison.

7

Touraine and the wines of the Loir

Touraine, land of the great châteaux of the Loire, land of green river valleys, of wide forests and vast plateaux, land of the gentle light. For many – both French and foreigner – this ancient province epitomizes France at her most welcoming, at her most beneficent. For the wine traveller, it is the melting-pot of the Loire, the land where every grape variety is planted, every wine style made. For the researcher, it also demands the greatest amount of driving between cellars, between districts that can be as much as twenty or thirty miles apart, so diffuse are the vineyards.

As of the 1993 harvests, there were fifteen *appellation contrôlée* wines and one VDQS wine produced in Touraine, some made in enormous quantities, some existing only in theory. In the seventy or more miles from Candes-Saint-Martin, on the border with Anjou in the west, to Blois in the east, and in the forty miles from Loches in the south to Château-Renault in the north, you can find the finest Loire reds at Chinon and Bourgueil, some of the greatest whites at Vouvray and Montlouis (all of which will be treated in separate chapters) and in between, some of the best-value drinking wines produced in the Loire Valley, under the generic Touraine *appellation*. On the fringes are the increasingly interesting wines of Cheverny and Cour-Cheverny – promoted to *appellation contrôlée* from VDQS in 1993 – and the small VDQS region of Valençay.

This multiplicity is a product of the long history of wines in Touraine. The remains of a stone press dating from the second century have been found near Azay-le-Rideau, while stories relating to Saint Martin of Tours in the fourth century tell of how he was the first to plant vines in the vineyards of Vouvray. In the eleventh century, Abbé Baudry of Bourgueil was accustomed to inviting friends to come and drink the wines from his abbey vineyard. Chinon is associated with Rabelais in the sixteenth century, while the vineyard of the château of Chenonceaux is as old as the building itself.

The influence of the great châteaux of the Loire, and of the kings of France, on the vineyard is regular and recorded. It was a certain Abbé Breton who, at the command of Cardinal Richelieu, in 1631 brought the Cabernet Franc grape from Bordeaux to plant in his vineyards in Touraine and Chinon. It is suggested that it was the good Abbé who is referred to in the local name for the Cabernet – Le Breton, although it is more likely that it was called after the people of Brittany to whom the wine was sent. The Chenin arrived even earlier, since Rabelais is quoted as praising it. The *ampélographes,* or experts on vines, believe that it is derived from the Pineau d'Aunis, itself a native wild vine described by the poet Ronsard.

Jullien, writing at the beginning of the nineteenth century, lists a gallery of vines that were then planted in Touraine. In the Touraine vineyards themselves, there was the Arnaison, the Grolleau, the Pinot Meunier, the Morillon, and the Mace-Doux, some of which have survived, others of which have completely disappeared. The red wines of Bléré on the Cher, now in the Touraine *appellation,* were, he believed, better than those of Chinon. Amboise, on the other hand, produced wines that were green and dry, lacking body or spirit, 'ageing less well than other wines from the same region'. Cyrus Redding, in the 1860 edition of *French Wines and Vineyards,* comments that the red wines of Joué (the Noble Joué produced near Esvres, south of Tours) 'are highly esteemed'.

Disease, in the form of oidium and phylloxera, dealt its usual deadly blows to the Touraine vineyard. But even in 1900 there were 65,000 hectares under vine, and production was three times what it is today.

The Touraine *appellations*

There are now four *appellations* under the Touraine name, all of which were created in 1939. By far the largest is Touraine generic, which started life as Coteaux de Touraine in 1939 and changed its name in 1953. There are now 4,500 hectares under vine. Wines for this *appellation* can come from all the viticultural corners of the *département* of Indre-et-Loire, and a small portion of Loir-et-Cher south-west of Blois – provided the vineyards are not already in one

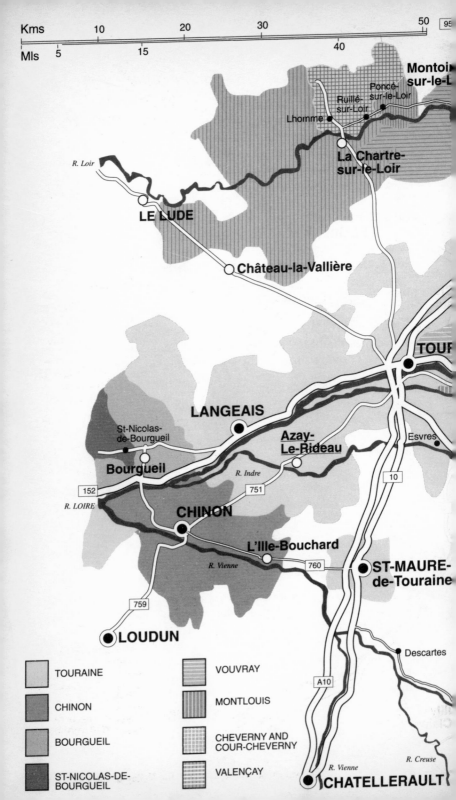

The vineyards of Touraine and the Valley of the Loir

of the other *appellations*. Thus, for example, in the small village of Lerné in western Touraine – celebrated by Rabelais in *Gargantua and Pantagruel* – a grower who has Cabernet Franc vines produces Touraine Rouge. Just a mile or so up the road towards Chinon, his neighbour will be making wines from his Cabernet Franc under the superior *appellation* of Chinon. In practice, the bulk of generic Touraine comes either from an area between the Loire and the Cher valleys east of Montrichard and Tours, or on the slopes north and south of the Cher valley between Bléré to the west and Selles-sur-Cher to the east.

There are also three more localized Touraine *appellations*, which bear the names of villages considered historically to be producing superior wine: Touraine Mesland with 250 hectares under vine, Touraine Amboise with 200 hectares, and Touraine Azay-le-Rideau with 100 hectares. And there are two sparkling wine *appellations* – Touraine Mousseux and Touraine Pétillant – which are covered in Chapter 11 under Loire sparkling wines.

Touraine generic

The list of grape varieties permitted in Touraine covers pretty well anything that can be planted in the central Loire vineyards. For whites, there is Sauvignon Blanc, Chenin Blanc, Menu Pineau (the Arbois grape which originates in the Orléanais) and Chardonnay. For reds, the list is even longer: Gamay and Cabernet Franc are the lead players, followed on stage by Cabernet Sauvignon (difficult to ripen except in great years), Cot (or Malbec), Pinot Noir, Pinot Meunier, Pinot Gris, Pineau d'Aunis (a grape variety believed to come from Saumur, but now only found in Touraine). For rosés, in addition to all the red varieties, it is also possible to use Grolleau (another local variety, also encountered in basic Anjou Rosé).

Some of these grape varieties frequently appear as single varietal wines – most notably Sauvignon Blanc in white and Cabernet Franc and Gamay in red. Others appear as blends. A new 'tradition' is Touraine Rouge Tradition, a blended red which was created in the 1980s as an antidote to the prevailing fashion for young Gamays of Touraine Primeur, which was aimed at the same market as Beaujolais Nouveau. Tradition wines are meant to be aged; they are blends of around 50 per cent Gamay, 30 per cent Cabernet Franc, and 20 per Cot. Whether the idea will take off is currently still in doubt. Some producers argue that creating yet another style of wine in Touraine, when there are already so many, will simply confuse consumers. Others believe that Touraine reds are moving away from the simple Gamay tastes towards more complex flavours, and that the creation of Tradition does just that.

Inevitably in the widespread Touraine vineyard area, soils vary enormously. Red wine grape varieties are found in well-drained, stony *silex* soil known locally as *les perruches*; white wines, especially Sauvignon Blanc, come from the more sandy soils found on the plateau land. But the exposure of the vineyards is as important. Red grapes, needing the extra heat, like the slopes facing south by the rivers, while white grapes are content with the flatter plateau land.

Oisly, Thésée and the mould-breaking vignerons

I started my researches in the heart of the Touraine *appellation*, in the vineyards of two small villages on the road to nowhere in particular, lying on the sandy plateau between Saint-Aignan on the Cher and Blois on the Loire. Oisly and Thésée – the former on the plateau, the latter on the Cher with its vineyards on the slopes running down the north bank of the river – have become famous through the inspired initiative of six growers who in 1962, fed up with sending their grapes to the local co-operative or to the *négociants*, decided to form their own co-operative which they named, logically enough, La Confrérie des Vignerons de Oisly et Thésée.

From small acorns oak-trees grow; from small grape-pips, huge vines spread their leaves. What was a small, quality-minded group back in 1962 now produces wine from 400 hectares and fifty-four growers. Even today, though, quality is the key factor, and not all the grapes from the growers are sold as bottled wine by the Confrérie; a selection is made and below-standard wine is sold to *négociants*. Even so, that leaves 2.5 million bottles made in an average year.

When I first visited the Confrérie in the mid-1980s, I was taken around by its inspirational director Jacques Choquet, who was in at the foundation. At that time, it was certainly the most modern *cuverie* in Touraine, full of stainless steel when other cellars were still putting wine in cement tanks. By 1993, when my guide was Philippe Angier, son of one of the original *vignerons* and now sales manager, the tank farm had expanded enormously, with a series of small tanks which allows them to vinify grapes from each *vigneron* separately. They have big pneumatic presses – the last word in modern, gentle pressing – which, ironically, arrived in the great frost year of 1991, the year when production at the Confrérie was down to a third of normal.

Their production is large, but it is also varied. In just over an hour I tasted twelve wines, all different *cuvées*, not just different years. They specialize in wines from Sauvignon Blanc and Gamay, with smaller amounts of Cot (or Malbec), Chenin Blanc and Pinot Noir thrown in for good measure. It was the Confrérie which pioneered the idea of varietal Sauvignon de Touraine and Gamay de Touraine, an idea now threatened by the insistence of INAO, the French body responsible for controlling *appellations contrôlées*, that the name of the *terroir*, the land, should appear on a label, not the grape variety. M. Angier argues – and I can only agree – that Sauvignon de Touraine on a label tells you not just the grape variety, but emphasizes the *terroir* from which it comes. Surely this must be the way forward. If only, we agree, the French wine bureaucracy was not ruled by the barons of Bordeaux and Burgundy!

From the basic range we tasted the Sauvignon Blanc that swept the British market back in the early 1980s, the 1992 version crisp, green, herbaceous, saying all the things Sauvignon Blanc should. The Gamay 1992 was light, fresh, strawberry-flavoured. Then there are wines which are individual *cuvées* from the estates of member *vignerons*: the elegant Sauvignon of Domaine du Grand Cerf at Oisly, the fuller style from Domaine de la Chatoire at Saint-Romain-sur-Cher. Then there is the top prestige range, under the name Baronnie d'Aignan: the white a blend of Sauvignon, Chardonnay and Chenin Blanc, with a hint of wood from the fermentation of the Chardonnay (which under Touraine AC rules can never be more than 20 per cent of a wine); a sparkling Crémant de Loire, soft, creamy; a 1990 red blend of Cabernet Franc, Gamay and Cot full of serious, chunky fruit and piles of colour. There is even a light, fresh Cheverny, as three members have vineyards in that *appellation*.

The next day I visited the neighbouring co-operative at Saint-Romain-sur-Cher. In one sense, this is the classic old-fashioned co-operative, taking grapes from 200 hectares of land in the Touraine *appellation* – with some in the Loire-wide Vin de Pays du Jardin de la France – owned by eighty growers, some of whom have less than one hectare of vines. But in another sense, the co-operative has followed the path set by the Confrérie of Oisly and Thésée. Only the top 15 per cent of their production is bottled for sale, while another 40 per cent is sold direct to locals who turn up with their cubitainers – a service as essential as the local petrol station. The rest – just as it does at Oisly et Thésée – goes off to the *négociants*, which, I'm afraid, says a lot about *négociants* and not much for the wine.

Vincent Mureau is the director of the Saint-Romain co-operative. He tells me they have installed temperature-controlled fermentation equipment. It is a clean cellar – an important factor in making decent wine – and there is obviously new equipment in use. As we taste, locals pop in with their plastic bottles and cubitainers which are filled up from pumps. They make the three main Touraine varietal wines – Sauvignon Blanc, Gamay and Cabernet Franc – and what they bottle is stored in newly-excavated tufa caves.

The wines themselves, while not exceptional, are all clean, well-made and good value – all attributes for which Touraine wines should be designed. The Sauvignon Blanc is fresh, light and fruity, with a drier *cuvée* having greater elegance and style. The Gamay is designed as a Primeur, to be drunk as young as possible. There are two Cabernets: a rosé, soft, round and slightly sweetened, but with good acidity, and a red from the 1990 vintage, with smooth, full fruit rounded out with a vanilla aftertaste.

Touraine south of the Cher

Straight down the road from Saint-Romain, across the Cher and on the southern slopes of the river is the other concentration of Touraine vineyards. They are slighter higher than the slopes on the northern side and, looking over the Cher, I could see for miles across the plateau of Oisly, and to the east the strange area of lakes and sandy forests known as the Sologne, glimmering in the heat-haze of the early afternoon.

Just down the slope, above the village of Meusnes, Jacky Preys has his cellars. When I arrived, the door of the corrugated-iron shed was firmly shut and the sounds from inside made it seem as though I had reached the Duchess's house in *Alice in Wonderland*. There was shouting and crashing going on above the row of one of the noisiest bottling lines I've ever encountered. M. Preys, when he appeared from his house next door to let me in, seemed quite unfazed by it all.

We tasted at one end of the shed, at a bench littered with old bottles, tall ones with immensely long necks sold as ornaments, piles of labels and a general air of satisfying clutter, while clanks continued to come from the bottling line where Sauvignon Blanc was being put into the handsome, recently-introduced Touraine bottles embossed with the Val de Loire coat of arms. Occasionally we made a diversion up some narrow stone steps to the stainless-steel tanks to taste wines from the 1992 vintage.

If all this seems chaotic, it does not detract from the quality of the wine or the importance of M. Preys's operation in Tourangelle terms. A small, energetic man with short-cropped, greying hair, very sure and confident, he is the owner of a sizeable vineyard of 70 hectares which is divided into three: one part is on the slope above the cellars, the second is at Saint-Aignan, a few kilometres downriver, and a third is in the VDQS of Valençay – of which more later in this chapter.

We tasted the Preys Sauvignon from Valençay first. After the crispness, almost leanness, of this wine, the Touraine Sauvignon Clos des Pillotières 1992 which came next was almost fat, but – a hallmark of all the Preys wines – was bursting with fruit and freshness. He seems to specialize in some of the more unusual grapes of Touraine. As we tasted a Fié Gris, M. Preys explained to me that he was, he reckoned, the only producer anywhere to grow this vine, also called Sauvignon Rosé, which produces grapes with a slightly pinky-grey skin. It goes, pressed gently, into his Touraine Blanc, a wine that tastes quite earthy when young, concentrated, and needs ageing.

Another curiosity of the Preys range is Pineau d'Aunis, from grapes with a light pinky-red tinge to them that can only be used to make rosé wines. It certainly is enjoyable: his 1992 was ripe, soft, with a light vanilla taste, very easy to drink. From this rosé we moved on to reds. Pinot Noir is obviously one of his strengths, to judge by the lightly-perfumed Touraine Pinot Noir 1992, whose flavour, M. Preys told me, comes from the flinty *silex* soil in which the vines are planted. His 1991, aged in wood, is more Burgundian, very fleshy and well-shaped.

His other strength in red wine is his Cot, which he kept back to the end of the tasting, offering it to me without explanation and pleased – and probably surprised – that I worked out what it was. It is a big tough wine, his 1992, but full of flavour and red fruit tastes, designed for ageing.

Experiments in Cot

M. Preys's enthusiasm for the Cot is spreading in Touraine, as producers discover that this vine – originally from the deep south of France – which reached the Loire via Cahors and Bordeaux (where it is the Malbec) can produce wines with great staying-power and strength even this far north. It has been one of the many strands of experimentation at the Domaine de la Gabillière, the experimental 16-hectare vineyard at Amboise, whose wines, made by the 150 students, are available in sufficient quantities for sale to the public and even export.

The Cot is part of a programme which includes work on the major Touraine grape varieties: Gamay, Sauvignon Blanc, Chenin Blanc and Grolleau. Sparkling wines – Crémant de Loire – are made as well as still wines. Microvinification in 600-litre tanks is a regular part of the work, as are clonal studies in the vineyard. Despite the experimental nature of the programme – perhaps because of the extra care that is taken in the vineyard and the *chai* – the wines that come out of the Domaine are of good quality: I tasted a really herbaceous, full-flavoured Sauvignon Blanc 1992; a pink Crémant de Loire 1990, blended from 50 per cent Pinot Noir, 40 per cent Cabernet Franc and 10 per cent Grolleau, which had a salmon-pink colour and well balanced fruit and acidity; and a Crémant Blanc Brut, made from Chenin Blanc, Pinot Noir and Chardonnay, light and very fresh with slight hints of creamy flavours.

California on Cher

I stopped at Domaine de la Gabillière on my way to what must surely be the most romantic wine estate in all France. Château de Chenonceaux is the only one of the great Touraine châteaux to make wine; but a visit to the cellars in the beautiful eighteenth-century farm buildings, set apart from the main château on its bridge over the Cher, reveals serious, top-quality wines being made not, as a casual visitor might expect, in an ancient *chai* but in the most modern winery I had seen on the Loire. It was a scene that could have come from California or Australia: the immaculate rows of stainless-steel tanks, the modern presses, the tiled floors and walls, the air-conditioning. Only an ancient press in the entrance reminded me that wine-making has been going on here since the château was built in the sixteenth century, when Thomas Bohier ordered the planting of the first vineyard. Subsequent owners, including Diane de Poitiers and Catherine de Medici, continued the tradition.

Chenonceaux is now a privately-owned estate, the property of the Menier family of chocolate-making fame. For thirty years, until he retired in 1993, the making of wine was in the hands of M. de la Morandière, a formal, correct, utterly dedicated man who was given a free hand to make the best wines possible. Money is no object – not surprising, perhaps, when the name of the château on the wine-label tends to push the price up. The new *chai*, first used for the 1992 harvest, is one sign of this. So is the use of helicopters for spraying, an expensive activity normally associated more with estates in Bordeaux than in Touraine. Another is the fact that you cannot do anything as vulgar as buy a bottle at the château. 'We want to be thought of as the Margaux of Touraine,' said M. de la Morandière, referring to the first-growth Bordeaux estate. 'You wouldn't be able to buy a bottle of their wine at the château, so we don't think it's in keeping with our image to sell our wine to visitors.'

There are 30 hectares of vines situated on the slopes behind the château, facing south. The area has been increased in the past few years, with the purchase of 14 hectares in 1991. From this land they make two ranges of wine. The top one is Château de Chenonceaux, which comes in a smart, wide-bellied bottle with elegant, minimalist labels and a neck capsule which incorporates a silhouette of the château. The other is called Les Dômes de Chenonceaux, after the elegant domes – the *dômes à l'impériale* – which grace the roofs of the château.

Curiously for a Touraine estate, they only made a Sauvignon Blanc for the first time in 1992, and the benefit of the new installation showed in the crisp, clean, herbaceous flavours which were international in style, midway between France and New Zealand. Their more traditional white has been made from Chenin Blanc: the 1992 is dry, well-balanced, with just a hint of honey and creamy apple. Reds come from a blend of Cabernet Franc, Gamay and Cot, or as a 100 per cent Cabernet Franc, or as 100 per cent Cot. The blended wine, with its strain of fresh Gamay, is designed for relatively early drinking, whereas the two reds – especially the hugely-coloured Cot – are designed for power and longevity. I tasted the 1990 Cot, which was deep enough in colour; with the new equipment for stirring the red grape must during fermentation, I can imagine that the colour of the wines after 1992 will be almost black.

A tradition revived

From the most modern winery in Touraine it is something of a leap to the small farmyard of Michel Mousseau, the Clos de la Dorée near the village of Esvres on the river Indre. This is the scene of the rebirth of a wine that had disappeared. Le Noble Joué is a wine whose history goes back at least to the fifteenth century, when it is recorded as being drunk by Louis XI at his nearby château of Plessis-le-Tours. Although it was still being produced at the turn of the twentieth century, the vineyards, centred on the Tours suburb of Joué-les-Tours, were fast being replaced by urban development.

Not until 1975 was it revived, by a group of *vignerons* from Joué-les-Tours, Chambray, Saint-Avertin, Larçay and principally Esvres – all villages with vineyards on the plateau between Tours and the Indre valley to the south of Tours, land within the Touraine *appellation*. What they were re-creating is perhaps not a great wine, but it is more than a passing curiosity. Noble Joué is a *vin gris*, a pale rosé, made of at least 50 per cent Gris Meunier, 30 to 40 per cent Pinot Gris (known locally as Malvoisie) and 10 to 20 per cent Pinot Noir. Gris Meunier, of course, is the curiosity, a rare appearance of the Champenois Pinot Meunier which lends the wine its crisp fruit, while Pinot Gris, a white grape with a mottled skin, gives the wine weight rather than colour, and Pinot Noir introduces an element of roundness and length.

M. Mousseau is the largest producer of Noble Joué, from his 12 hectares of land on which he also makes Touraine Rouge. His *chai* is across the yard from the farmhouse; to one side is the chicken-coop and the vegetable garden. It is simple wine-making, using stainless steel with separate, short macerations of the two red grapes and pressing of the Pinot Gris. The 1990 Noble Joué, which of course came from a particularly good year, had a light orange-pink colour – *oeil de perdrix* ('partridge's eye') as it is described in French – and delicious, refreshing acidity, with a firm, earthy after-taste removing it from being just another rosé. It is, as I discovered later, a wine that is best with food, especially with *rillons* and *rillettes*, the local *charcuterie* for which Tours is famous.

The place of the négociant

Small-scale such production may be, but it represents the myriad strands of tradition that are covered by the simple name of Touraine. At the other extreme are the wines of the *négociants*, which have the widest distribution simply because of their quantity. As so often, those *négociants* based in the region make the best examples of the wines. Paul Buisse, whose cellars at Montrichard on the banks of the Cher are some of the largest in the region, restrict their activities to wines from Chinon, Bourgueil, Vouvray and Touraine. They have 10 hectares of the Domaine Paul Buisse, buying grapes for their Touraine wines from the villages on the north bank of the Cher, particularly Oisly and Thésée. Essentially, they make *vins de cépages*, 100 per cent single grape-variety wines, using low-temperature fermentation for whites and occasional hints of wood for reds, especially those in their prestige range, which is found in restaurants all over Touraine and beyond. The reds in particular I found very good, full of firm, tannic structure and always very pure.

Above the town of Amboise, on the banks of the Loire, are the modern cellars of Pierre Chainier, run by Pierre Chainier and his son François. When I first went there in 1991, they were big – seven million bottles a year – and growing, acting both as *domaine* producer and *négociant* covering wines as far away as Muscadet. They had constructed smart offices and were experimenting with different styles of rosé, as well as making some really crisp, modern-style whites. But the frosts of that year put paid to development, almost indeed to the family firm itself; they have subsequently reorganized, and now concentrate exclusively on wines from Touraine. They have 20 hectares of their own land, in Vouvray and Chinon as well as Touraine. Their Selection Chainier is less interesting than their *domaine* wines; some of them, especially the reds from Chinon and a Gamay-based Touraine wine which is made from carbonic maceration, bringing out the strawberry fruit flavours, are particularly flavoursome. Their best whites, rather than the Chenins from Vouvray and Montlouis, are their Touraine Sauvignons, good fruity examples with plenty of herbaceous character.

Having tasted, back in 1991, their other *négociant* wines – a fairly bland Muscadet, for instance – I think that their decision to concentrate on the wines they know best, those of Touraine, makes good sense. It shows up the limitations that Loire *négociants* bring to wines from outside their area: an inevitable lack of local knowledge, of good growers, information which has to come through agents rather than direct.

Pierre Chainier – a friendly, if serious, man with self-made but discreet wealth – told me of his belief that the cheap Loire *négociant*, the one who buys wine from the whole river valley and bottles it, has given the Loire its poor image; and that this style of *négociant* will disappear as the Loire moves from being an area supplying cheap, bulk wine to one of higher quality. The successful *négociant*, according to M. Chainier, is the one who specializes.

Touraine Mesland

With 250 hectares under vine, Touraine Mesland is the largest of the three village *appellations* of Touraine. It has a long and distinguished history dating back probably to the Romans, certainly to the monks of the abbey of Marmoutier, who had vines in the eleventh century. In this century it received its separate *appellation* in 1955. Situated on the northern bank of the river around the villages of Onzain and Mesland, which face the château of Chaumont on the south bank, this is a vineyard dedicated to red wines, which thrive on the sandy soil.

Gamay, Cabernet Franc and Cot are the main grape varieties. Gamay is by far the most important and appears by itself, while the other two varieties only appear as blends with Gamay (in which Gamay must account for between 40 and 50 per cent). A pale rosé is made from Gamay alone. Small quantities of whites are also made, from Sauvignon and Chenin Blanc.

Château Gaillard is the largest *domaine* in the *appellation*. Run by Beatrice and Vincent Girault, it has 40 hectares of vines in the village of Mesland. Beatrice Girault is the dynamic, sales side of the business. Her accent immediately gives her away as not being a native: she is from Bordeaux, and trained – like her husband – at the viticultural school of Blanquefort. They bought the estate in 1984, and its mix of stony *silex* soil, sand soil and a small portion of granite soil allows them to make a mix of wines. The bulk of their production, however, is very much in line with Mesland: up to

70 per cent red, the rest split between small quantities of rosé and a larger amount of white.

The Giraults have made an interesting distinction in their styles of wine-making. They make what they call 'fruity wines' and 'wines of the soil' – what we might also call 'modern wines' and 'traditional wines'. In the first category, for example, are the early-drinking Gamays, strawberry fruit flavours to the fore. In the second are essentially much more exciting wines: their blend of Gamay, Cabernet Franc and Cot, a rich, full-bodied wine with considerable tannins when young. There is no wood, because the Giraults believe it is out of character with the wines of Touraine.

Touraine Amboise

The great château of Charles VIII dominates the Loire town of Amboise, a charming, comfortable little town marginally spoilt by tourists during high summer, but otherwise a bustling local centre for the land between the Loire and Cher east of Tours. On the plateau land behind the town and in the neighbouring *communes* of Limeray and Cangey are spread 200 hectares of vines. As with Mesland, it is reds, in particular those from Gamay, which are the most important. However, the *vignerons* of Amboise have decided to give themselves a little bit of self-importance by making *cuvées prestiges*, blends of Gamay, Cabernet Franc and Cot which go under the generic name of Cuvée François 1er, after the king who made Amboise his own. The idea is that each grower's Cuvée François 1er will have tannins, colour and the ability to age – as a contrast to their lighter Gamays, which are designed for rapid drinking.

Jacques Dutertre is one of the leading lights in Amboise, as well as one of the bigger landowners, with 32 hectares that he works with his son Gilles. It all started, he told me, with a gift of one hectare from his grandfather. Dutertre were the prime movers in the Cuvée François 1er, and he has now gone one step further down the road of making 'serious' Amboise wines with the launch of a blend of Cot and Cabernet Franc, which can also go under the François 1er name.

Not that he neglects Gamay. He makes this young wine using a type of carbonic maceration, with a fermentation of five to six days followed by early bottling. The blended wines have a classic long fermentation, with maceration on the skins and then some wood ageing before bottling eleven months after the harvest. I tasted M. Dutertre's Cuvée François 1er 1990, a blend of 60 per cent Gamay, 20 per cent Cabernet Franc and 20 per cent Cot: very perfumed, with firm, earthy tannins, a excellent deep colour, obviously a wine that will age for up to ten years. His blend of Cot and Cabernet Franc was more vegetal and seemed somewhat less harmonious, but had attractive flavours of hedgerow fruits, overlaid in its youth by heavy tannins.

Whites and rosés seem to be something of an afterthought in Amboise, although M. Dutertre makes good examples of both. His rosé, a blend of the three grape varieties – Gamay, Cabernet Franc and Cot – is a big, powerful wine, one to be drunk a couple of years after harvest. His delicious white Clos du Pavillon, made from Chenin Blanc, is again powerful, the 1990 deliciously creamy with a streak of grapefruit acidity and, equally, a wine for ageing.

Touraine Azay-le-Rideau: Château de l'Aulée

The smallest of the three Touraine village *appellations*, Azay-le-Rideau covers 60 hectares over eight *communes* on the banks of the Indre. The pretty village of Azay with its fairy-tale château is buried deep in the steep Indre valley, while the vineyards, scattered among orchards, are on both slopes above the river.

The two permitted styles are white and rosé. The white comes from Chenin Blanc, the rosé mainly from Grolleau (whose origin is sometimes traced to Cinq-Mars-le-Pilé a few kilometres further north on the Loire). Cot, Cabernet Franc, Cabernet Sauvignon and Gamay are also allowed for rosés.

There are no producers who devote themselves exclusively to Azay-le-Rideau. Some, such as Pibaleau Père et Fils, also make straight Touraine Rouge wines. Others, such as Château de l'Aulée, whose 36 hectares make it the largest producer in Azay-le-Rideau, also make sparkling Crémant de Loire. Château de l'Aulée – which does not make a rosé – also produces a white Azay-le-Rideau which is recognized as one of the best in the *appellation*, a classic slow-maturing Chenin Blanc.

Cheverny and Cour-Cheverny

The Loire's newest *appellation contrôlée* regions, elevated from VDQS with the 1993 harvest, are situated just to the west of the flat forest and lake region of the Sologne, south of Blois. There are 400 hectares under vine, worked by between fifty and sixty growers. To the west and south are vineyards within the Touraine *appellation*, and there are producers who cross both *appellations*.

It is flat, plateau countryside with only the hint of slopes, but sufficient for drainage for the vines. There are concentrations of vines around the twin towns of Cheverny and Cour-Cheverny, around the imposing château of Cheverny and west of the village of Fougères-sur-Bièvre which marks the western edge of Cheverny.

The arrival of the *appellation* will, it is hoped, act as a further stimulus to an area which is showing signs of achieving higher standards and making more interesting wines. The problem has been the low price these wines can command, which has inhibited investment. With the *appellation*, producers like to think that prices for their wines will rise and so will their chance to invest.

However, it has not all been plain sailing. Inevitably, this being France, the politics of *Clochemerle* have played a part in establishing the AC. Everything revolves around whether it should be permitted to make a 100 per cent varietal Cheverny or whether Cheverny should be a blended wine. There is, of course, no reason in wine terms why one should be more unsatisfactory than the other. It is much more a legalistic question of which is the more traditional – the sort of question which lies at the arcane heart of French wine law.

In the line-up, it seems as though it is the producers against the Paris bureaucrats. The producers know that a wine labelled Sauvignon, Chardonnay or Gamay sells, but the bureaucrats are not much interested in sales, more in preserving the rules. Then there is the question of the Romorantin grape, the variety that appears to be unique to Cheverny (although twenty years ago there were still plantations of it in Burgundy, from where it was brought in 1519 by François Ier to be planted at his château at Romorantin just to the south) and makes a very particular, high-acid wine, one which blends badly with other grape varieties.

What has emerged, and what will be enshrined in the new *appellation* rules, is a compromise which will appeal to neither side: the creation of two *appellations* out of the one former VDQS area. In the larger *appellation*, called Cheverny and covering twenty-two *communes*, producers will only be able to make blended wines – white from Sauvignon Blanc, Chardonnay (to a maximum of 15 per cent) and Pineau de la Loire, red from Gamay, Cabernet Franc, Pinot Noir and Cot. There will be a separate *appellation* for Romorantin called Cour-Cheverny, and covering the four *communes* close to the village of Cour-Cheverny where, it is thought, the best Romorantin grows.

The producers are not happy with this legalistic solution. They argue that promoting one unknown *appellation* will be hard enough; to promote two will be nigh-on impossible. It is a shame to make the job more difficult, especially since they have been promoting Cheverny at the big Loire Valley wine show held each year in Angers – where they have had a prominent stand – making the task of getting to know them and their wines so much easier.

It was there that I met both Philippe Tessier and the Romorantin grape for the first time. He is the great proponent of the grape, and has been prominent in beginning a replanting programme after a decline in the 1970s. The decline was precipitated by the greater popularity of other white grapes and the problems of growing the Romorantin – it needs to stay on the vines for a month after the rest of the harvest is finished, which means its thin skin risks being damaged by autumn rains.

In 1993 I visited M. Tessier, a shy, modest man, in his equally modest cellars near Cheverny, hard by the jewel-like Château de Toussay where, he told me, his father had worked and he had been born. Today he farms 13 hectares of vines, of which 1.5 hectares are currently Romorantin. Tasting his 1990, it is apparent that, with its high acidity, this is a wine that improves with ageing. After nearly three years, and from an exceptional year like 1990, it has developed a very special character, smelling a little like a herb tea and with a soft, nutty taste. In more normal years it becomes like old Chenin Blanc, balancing acidity and blackcurrants with soft, mature flavours.

The rest of M. Tessier's production is of more familiar grape varieties. Currently he makes a blended Sauvignon and Chardonnay white, the 1992 about as crisp as the palate can take – a good year for whites, he tells me, although not for reds. It does exhibit the limitations of Cheverny, where acidity is naturally high, even in good years, and where, as far as reds are concerned, getting colour and ripeness is always a problem.

Tasting the reds, it seems that the most successful are either the straight varietal Gamay or Pinot Noir wines (both now to be forbidden under the *appellation* rules) and the blends in which Gamay, Cot and Pinot Noir are predominant. This is not the land for Cabernet Franc, which ripens with difficulty.

The difficulty with reds is why the Delaille family have decided to concentrate on whites. Their Domaine de Salvard, in the hamlet of Le Salvar (they add the 'd' to their estate name because that is how it appeared in old documents) near Fougères-sur-Bièvre, has 25 hectares of vineyard, 20 of them in Cheverny, 5 in Touraine. Gilbert the father, mayor of the *commune*, and his trained oenologist son Emmanuel have just built a large modern *chai* within the ancient buildings of the farm courtyard, which used to be part of a château. They are happier about the *appellation* for Cheverny than M. Tessier, since they already make blended white wines and had their 1992 VDQS wines re-tasted so that they could be awarded the AC.

So it was at Domaine de Salvard that I first tasted AC Cheverny in the form of the 1992, a blend of Sauvignon and Chenin Blanc which gave a full, but always light and crisp, wine; and which compared well with the 1992 Touraine Sauvignon AC – much earthier and weightier – which they produced from the Touraine portion of their land.

The previous evening, while eating in Cour-Cheverny, I had drunk a less elevated Cheverny than either M. Tessier's or M. Delaille's. It was sharply acid, super-crisp and really only came into its own with the fish – the Loire *sandre* – I was eating. I found it difficult to see even the best Cheverny travelling much beyond the Loire. One can only hope that the arrival of the *appellation* does something for the commercial chances of this small region.

Valençay

The hilltop town of Valençay lies at the borders of two famous regions of France: Touraine and Berry. To the south and east stretch the cornfields of Berry, punctuated by the small vineyard areas of Reuilly and Quincy. To the north and west is Touraine.

The town is dominated by the huge Renaissance château, best approached down the long avenue of forest and trees on the road from Blois and Selles-sur-Cher. It is best known as the home of the politician Talleyrand, acquired in 1803 when he was one of Napoleon's ministers but retained as he managed to shift allegiance from Emperor to King.

In the small squares that lead away from the château's walls, a cluster of restaurants and a few pavement cafés give the place a pleasant air. A short walk across the market square and there is a view from the castle end of the town to the church at the other, across the narrow valley of the little river Nahon.

The main vineyard area of Valençay is to the north and west of the town, along the slopes above the Nahon valley and near the villages of Villentrois, Lye and Fontguenand. This is a continuation of the undulating land which stretches down from the Touraine vineyards on the south bank of the Cher. It has the same flinty *silex* soil, known in French as *pierre à fusil* ('gun-flint'), giving a slight mineral trace to the taste of the wine. In essence, the wines of Valençay are lighter, sometimes fresher and certainly crisper, cousins of those of Touraine.

There are currently 130 hectares in the VDQS zone of Valençay, which was recognized as recently as 1970. For an area so small, it is complicated: there are white, rosé and red Valençay wines, made from pretty well anything grown elsewhere in Touraine. There are Sauvignon Blanc, Chardonnay, Menu Pineau, Chenin Blanc and Romorantin for whites, although in practice Sauvignon and to a lesser extent Chardonnay predominate. For rosés and reds, it is possible to plant Gamay, Cot, Pinot Noir, Cabernet Franc, Cabernet Sauvignon (almost unknown because it does not ripen), Pineau d'Aunis and Grolleau, although only Gamay, Cabernet Franc, Cot and Pinot Noir can dominate, with other grape varieties never exceeding more than 25 per cent of a blend.

Many of the producers of Valençay wines also make Touraine wines. Typical of these are Hubert Sinson, Jacky Augis and Jacky Preys, all based at Meusnes, some fifteen kilometres north of Valençay, and for whom Valençay is a small part of their production. The main co-operative which handles Valençay grapes is Les Vignerons de Fontguenand, on the edge of the Touraine *appellation* area.

The style of wines is pleasant, the whites – which make up a quarter of production – offering much more than the reds or rosés. Whites, particularly from Sauvignon, offer a crisp counterpoint to Touraine Sauvignon. The reds and rosés are of much more local interest, although the most successful are either the young Gamays or the fuller-flavoured wines entirely from Cot or Pinot Noir.

The wines of the Loir Valley and Vendôme

Le Loir – to be distinguished from the great river La Loire – flows along a course twenty-five miles to the north and roughly parallel to the Loire until it joins the Sarthe just above Angers. The valley of the Loir is right at the division between Normandy and Touraine, where the landscape is green and enclosed rather than the more open land of great forests and plateaux found further south.

It is at the very limits of viticulture. Harvests in the three *appellations* of the Loir rarely start before November, and in many years the grapes hardly ripen at all. Yields are consequently kept low, down to 25 hectolitres per hectare. Given the tiny parcels of vineyard land and the difficulties of cultivation on the steep, south-facing slopes necessary for the grapes to have a chance to ripen, it is a wonder that the *vignerons* of the Loir continue.

This was certainly in my mind as I drove north from Tours to visit Joël Gigou at La Chartre-sur-le-Loir. I found him in his shop-cum-house on a Saturday morning, busy selling wine to a seeming convoy of passing tourists who had heard of his wines and wished to know more. He is a lithe, lean man with a narrow face that widens out as he discusses wines. We quickly repaired to his cellars along the river, dug into tufa cliffs, damp and freezing after the warmth of the day outside, but ideal, as he told me, for the storage of wine.

There we tasted, and from the start I was fascinated by the strange tastes from familiar grapes I was being offered. M. Gigou has 10.5 hectares of land – enormous for the area – in the main two of the Loir's three *appellations*. The larger of the two is Coteaux du Loir, an *appellation contrôlée* area which currently covers 70 hectares of land on the south bank of the Loir, mainly in the four *communes* of Chahaignes, Lhomme, Marçon and Ruillé-sur-Loir, although permission exists for up to 350 hectares in twenty-three *communes*. Jasnières, smaller and finer, is within the Coteaux du Loir *appellation* and has 48 hectares under vine in the *communes* of Lhomme and Ruillé-sur-Loir, both on the north bank of the river, on slopes facing due south.

While Coteaux du Loir wines come in all three colours – using Chenin Blanc for white, Pineau d'Aunis, Cabernet Franc, Cot and Gamay for reds, Grolleau for rosés – Jasnières can only be white, and only from Chenin Blanc.

The history of both *appellations* is long and distinguished. Ronsard praised the wines, and had Bacchus plant vines at La Chartre. Rabelais commented happily on the number of wine merchants and taverns – twenty-seven – in the town. When Henri IV hunted in the nearby forest of Bléré, he drank only Loir wines. In the nineteenth century both Guyot and Jullien praised the wines, and Guyot commented on the longevity of both the reds and rosés. Jullien reckoned the wines of Jasnières were 'even better than their reputation, good as it is'.

Viticulture, though, has fallen prey to the pressures of competition from easier, more heavily-subsidized crops and the unreliability of the harvests. Even in the 1950s Pierre Bréjoux could say that there were 600 to 700 hectares of vines.

Difficult to produce they may be, but my first taste of Jasnières that morning with M. Gigou made me very happy that there are still *vignerons* with the dedication to make such wines. Jasnières is, in many ways, the distillation of the virtues (and the vices) of the Chenin Blanc. It can suffer extremely in bad years such as 1991, when its leanness can be overwhelming. But in the greatest years, such as 1990 and 1989, it can be one of the finest wines in the whole Loire region.

I realized this as I tasted M. Gigou's Jasnières 1992 Cuvée de l'Aillerie, with its aromatic, floral freshness and fleeting lightness, which in its way had as many connections with a fine German wine as with France. His superior Saint-Jacques Jasnières 1992, made from old vines, had a character which was full of racy, vivacious fruit but also higher acidity – a wine to keep, according to M. Gigou.

Jasnières wines seem to act much as other Chenins do: in the first year or so after harvest, they have a fresh, sometimes creamy character that makes them easily drinkable. They then close up completely, leaving acidity to dominate, for five to six years. His 1987 Jasnières had developed the goat-cheese flavours of older Chenin, but had managed to retain lovely, crisp fruit; and the even older 1981 had elegance, finesse and a kerosene flavour that put it in a class with old Riesling.

If Jasnières is the star in the tiny firmament of Loir wines, there are other wines of interest in the Coteaux du Loir. M. Gigou, who keeps all his wines – including his whites – in wooden *pièces*, produced a Gamay Coteaux du Loir Rouge 1990 which had spent one and a half years in wood and tasted more like a lightweight Burgundy than a wine from the cool Loir.

Then there was a Pineau d'Aunis 1990 which M. Gigou described as a red, but which was almost rosé, very perfumed, soft, with hardly any tannin; the 1992, in wood and still on its lees in the June after the harvest, was even paler, high in acid, and obviously to be treated as a rosé. A Coteaux du Loir Blanc 1992 had light, peachy flavours, more direct than the same year's Jasnières – reflecting the same difference, suggested M. Gigou, looking towards Anjou, as that between basic Anjou Blanc and the great dry whites of Savennières.

If the wines of the Coteaux du Loir, and especially Jasnières, have a rightful if small place in the world of French wines, what of their eastern neighbour, the VDQS area of Coteaux du Vendômois? With its 90 hectares of vines stretching along the banks of the Loir from Vendôme westwards to Couture, where the Coteaux du Loir starts, here are vineyards which have lost out to the growing of cereals, where there are now a mere fifteen growers and a co-operative scattered among thirty-four *communes*, tiny patches of vines which mingle with maize and sugar beet.

The bulk of the vineyards are concentrated – if that is the word – between the city of Vendôme and the pretty, church-dominated town of Montoire-sur-Loir, a distance of about twenty kilometres. The growers' cellars are dug into tufa caves, where wine-making takes place in often traditional conditions – with the temperature control coming from the ambient temperature of the cave rather than any modern equipment.

The wines, too, are very much in the traditional Loire mould. Reds, whites and rosés can be made, from the usual gamut of Loire grape varieties: Gamay, Pinot Noir, the two Cabernets for reds, Gamay and Pineau d'Aunis for rosé, Chenin Blanc and Chardonnay for whites. The region's particular speciality is the rosé from Pineau d'Aunis, a crisply fruity wine which can have a pleasant edge of nuttiness and is at its best when made from the first pressing of the grapes.

I tasted the Pineau d'Aunis of Colin et Fils, who have 14 hectares of vines around Thoré-la-Rochette, midway between Vendôme and Montoire. They have been here since at least 1735, and are typical of the Vendômois growers in that they grow both cereals and vines: father is the cereal man, son Patrice runs the vineyard. Their rosé

was a delightfully fresh wine, pale pink and grey in colour, produced from sixty-year-old vines. The other wine which stood out in
their range was a Chenin Blanc, fermented slowly in wood for one
and a half months and then aged in wood until bottling at Easter.
Whites here can be either pure Chenin, or blended up to 20 per cent
with Chardonnay.

Reds are normally blends of Gamay and at least 30 per cent
Pineau d'Aunis, very fresh, young styles made for early drinking. I
tasted M. Colin's 1990, a blend of Gamay, Pineau d'Aunis and
Pinot Noir which, thanks to the good year, had excellent colour
and a fresh, low-tannin, strawberry taste, almost ready to drink a
few months after harvest.

8

The wines of Vouvray

═══════

The wines of Vouvray are a microcosm of the problems and the triumphs of Loire wines. They can be the most unreliable, the most infuriating, the most confusing, but also the most marvellous wines. In any tasting of Vouvray you can expect to encompass most of the wine-taster's vocabulary from 'stupendous' to 'dreadful', sometimes from one wine to the next. Small wonder, then, that for years the reputation of Vouvray was mediocre at worst, merely passable at best. It has taken the work of a small – but increasing – group of dedicated growers to restore to the wines of this Touraine village the position they deserve.

Vouvray's problems are historical and long-standing. The misuse of the name can be dated back to the Renaissance, when from the fifteenth century onwards Dutch traders bought wine from Vouvray and added it to Málaga wine brought from Spain to make something rich, sweet and to the taste of the Dutch burghers. It was a practice that continued until the end of the nineteenth century.

The Dutch influence was so pervasive that many of Vouvray's best vineyard sites, or *clos*, have been named after the branding-irons used by the Dutch merchants to stamp the casks of wine that they were buying. The branding-irons acted literally as brand names and were important to guarantee the quality – and hence the price paid for the wine.

But it was not just the Dutch who abused the name; the locals did it as well. For years, right up to the creation of the *appellation* in 1936, Vouvray was used as the name for any white wine from Touraine, whether sweet, dry or sparkling. It was only after a series of lawsuits which lasted fifteen years that Vouvray's *délimitation* and *appellation contrôlée* could be confirmed.

Somehow, it seems difficult for Vouvray to get away from these historical problems. Not that there are Dutch wine merchants busy adding Málaga to Vouvray today, or Touraine wine-growers relabelling their Touraine AC wine as Vouvray. What is happening, though – and has been for many years – is that an awful lot of grapes produced in Vouvray end up in rather cheap, sulphurous still white or sparkling wines, which bear the *appellation* name but certainly have no connection with the sort of wine it can more properly produce.

It all relates to the fact that, because Vouvray can be produced in such a wide variety of styles, grapes can be picked at a wide range of intervals, depending on what the grower or wine-producer wants to make out of them. If what is wanted is sparkling Vouvray, then the grapes will be picked green. If it is dry or *demi-sec*, then they will be picked normally ripe. If – in particular years – what is wanted are super-sweet *moelleux* wines, then the grapes will be left to gather botrytis. It's part of the charm and pleasure of Vouvray that this variety is available; but it does mean that an unscrupulous grower is tempted to pick his grapes green and sell them on to a *négociant* – generally one from outside the region – who may make sparkling wine from this somewhat indifferent base, but could perfectly well turn out a still, *demi-sec* Vouvray with some heavy addition of sugar and plenty of sulphur to keep it all hygienic.

The message, then, to any drinker of Vouvray is to watch the small print on the bottle. Good Vouvray is bottled by a *domaine* in Vouvray – or by the co-operatives of Vouvray – and any bottle which doesn't have an address in one of the *communes* of the Vouvray *appellation* on the label should be immediately suspect until tasted.

Why should it be that Vouvray is the *appellation* of Touraine whose name everybody else has wanted to misuse? It is certainly one of the most ancient, since wine was being made in Vouvray at the time of Saint Martin of Tours in the fourth century. The village's proximity to Tours also helped its notoriety; being, along with Montlouis, the nearest vineyard to a major cathedral city meant that its wines had pride of place at the tables of the monks and priests.

Vouvray was celebrated in literature as well. Balzac's description of the village is often quoted, but is still true today: 'The village of Vouvray nestles, so to speak, in the gorges and the valleys between the cliffs which start to describe a line in front of the bridge over the

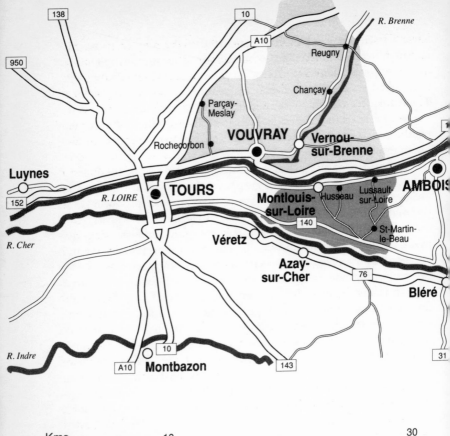

The vineyards of Vouvray and Montlouis

River Cisse. From Vouvray to Tours, the frightening crags of this jagged hill are inhabited by a population of *vignerons*. At more than one point, there are three storeys of houses dug into the rock and linked by dangerous flights of steps cut from the very stones. The smoke from a chimney rises between the shoots and the fruiting branches of the vineyard. The peasants are tilling almost perpendicular land. The vaults of the aerial cellars resound to the hammers of the coopers. The land is cultivated and fertile everywhere, though nature has here refused to provide soil for human industry.'

When I visit Vouvray I stay in rooms above a restaurant, Le Grand Vatel, in the centre of the small town itself. Each time I take the attic room, so that in the mornings I can look out over the roofs of the town, slate-grey, glistening in the morning sun, and towering above them the pale yellow tufa cliffs topped by vines. Even in the early morning you can hear tractors out there on the plateau that tops the cliffs, busy in the vineyards. In the other direction, not so far away – no more than ten kilometres – it is possible to see the dramatic spires of Tours cathedral.

The landscape of Vouvray is certainly one of the most charming, as well as the most idiosyncratic, along the Loire. While elsewhere there are many stretches of tufa cliffs bordering the river, with vineyards on top of the cliffs and human habitation below, there are few where the habitations are quite so intimately connected with the land on which they are built. There are still many inhabited houses where all that has been constructed is the façade, the rest having been dug into a cave quarried centuries ago for local stone. Most *vignerons* both work and store their wine in these caves which, with their constant temperature, provide ideal storage conditions. The tiny side valleys leading away from the broad expanse of the Loire have tight, steep sides on which perch small houses and cellar buildings, piled up one on top of another in a chaotic confusion where a roof of one house becomes the courtyard of another.

Along the front of the line of cliffs as they face south across the Loire are more imposing buildings: the grand hotel and restaurant Les Hautes Roches at Rochecorbon, the extended cellars of the *négociant* Marc Brédif, creators in the 1920s of Vouvray Pétillant and now owned by Patrick de Ladoucette of Pouilly, and on a platform halfway up the cliff the Renaissance Château de Moncontour, now the home and vineyard of the Brédut family, owners also of the sparkling wine firm of Monmousseau in Montrichard. Spaced between these are solid suburban villas built by the bourgeois of Tours as an escape from the city.

Up on the plateau, vines stretch in all directions. There are eight *communes* in the Vouvray *appellation*, which stretches from Sainte-Radegonde, now a northern riverside suburb of Tours, through Rochecorbon and Vouvray to Noizay, eight kilometres to the east of Vouvray. Away from the river, up the side valleys are the villages of Vernou-sur-Brenne, Chançay, Reugny, a good dozen kilometres north of Vouvray, and Parçay-Meslay, to the north of Rochecorbon.

The town of Vouvray itself, despite its proximity to one of the main tourist roads on the Loire between Tours and Blois, is pleasantly free from tourist clutter. It's hardly a showplace, more a comfortable, small shopping-centre with narrow streets, the best *charcuterie* in Touraine (Hardouin) and a splendid church which dominates the town, and whose ornate belfry can sometimes be seen poking up above the level of the tufa cliffs and appearing as a landmark to any *vigneron* returning home after a day's work in the vineyards.

In 1992 there were 1,742 hectares of land, all planted with Pineau de la Loire (Chenin Blanc), in the Vouvray *appellation*, on land which is either of limestone soil known as *aubuis* or of more flinty *silex* soil known locally as *perruches*. There are 356 growers, which means an average land-holding of a mere 4.8 hectares. The vineyard has remained relatively static in recent years – in 1982 the total was 1,697 hectares. The harvest, however, can fluctuate wildly. Total production in 1989, which as we shall see was a year of stupendous wines, was 108,111 hectolitres. In 1990, another great year, it was 110,666 hectolitres. But in the frost-devastated year of 1991, a mere 44,892 hectolitres were produced, while in the following year the harvest was an enormous 123,578 hectolitres.

The varieties of Vouvray

What makes life even more difficult is the way a harvest will split between still wines and sparkling wines. In hot years like 1989, much more still wine (63 per cent) than sparkling wine (37 per cent) was made. The reverse was true in 1992, with 67 per cent of wine being sparkling and only 33 per cent still. It makes reliability of supply for customers almost non-existent, especially if it is also borne in mind that still wine styles can range from dry to medium dry (the two styles normally made in average years) to occasional years, like 1989 and 1990, when there are comparatively large quantities of luscious sweet wines.

The three categories of still Vouvray are defined by grams of sugar. Thus a Sec Vouvray must have less than 15 grams of residual sugar, a Demi-Sec will have 15 grams or more, while a Moelleux must have more than 30 grams of residual sugar. A *moelleux* does not have to have grapes affected by the noble rot fungus, but in exceptional years such as 1989 or 1990 (and most recently before that, 1985), the wines which result will have high residual sugar levels of 40 to 50 grams or more.

Sparkling Vouvray also comes in different forms, depending on the pressure in the bottle. *Pétillant* will have 2.5 kg/cm^2 of pressure, while *mousseux* (the equivalent of a traditional champagne-style wine) will have a pressure of 5.5 kg/cm^2. The split in quantities between the two styles is roughly two-thirds *mousseux* and one third *pétillant*, but the low-pressure *pétillant* demands much greater skill to make and to ensure that the pressure remains even and permanent. While sparkling Vouvray is still an important part of the whole wine business in the *appellation*, it has lost some of the over-dominance it had in the 1950s and 1960s when up to 70 per cent of all Vouvray was sparkling. The more recent – and welcome – revival of the fortunes of still Vouvray is as much to do with the quality of the still wine-making as it is to do with the change in the market for sparkling wines.

The role of the *négociant* is still of crucial importance in Vouvray, although things have changed rapidly over the past decade. In 1983, 91 per cent of Vouvray was sold by *négociants*. By 1988 that figure had fallen to 64 per cent, while by 1992 the growers' wines were in a majority, with only 34 per cent of sales going through *négociants*.

The new generation of growers

While figures can give some picture of what is going on, the change in Vouvray from *négociant* beverage to growers' creations really came home to me one Saturday morning. I had asked to taste a range of growers' wines, and instead of having to travel between different cellars, I had been offered a specially-organized tasting in one of the huge tufa caves on the edge of Vouvray, the Cave de la

Bonne Dame. Normally it is used for parties, and when I arrived promptly at nine o'clock there was no sign of my tasting, but plenty of debris from the night before.

I waited in the already-blistering sunshine for the *vignerons* to arrive. I should have remembered that Touraine has a tendency to work on southern French hours, which to a northern European are charming and irritating in equal measure. No matter – within half an hour I was being greeted by Frédéric Bourillon, owner of Domaine Bourillon d'Orléans and chairman for that year of an organization that could not have existed even ten years ago in Vouvray, but which represents the most exciting sign of the future. The Vouvray Club Tradition has brought together the new generation of young growers who are now taking over from their parents, or are setting up their own new vineyards, and who aim to bring Vouvray to a level of quality which it may never have had in the past.

They are enthusiastic and innovative. They have also had the most superb head start with two of the greatest vintages they or their fathers will ever have seen, or are likely to see for a very long time. In both 1989 and 1990 the weather in Vouvray, as along the rest of the Loire, was perfect for producing that rarest and most sought-after style of wine, a *moelleux*. That morning I was to taste a succession of the most memorably sweet, sticky wines, all full of the taste of the noble rot which affects Chenin Blanc when the autumnal weather offers damp, misty mornings and clear, sunny, warm afternoons. Here and in Anjou, in the Layon valley, are the only two regions of the Loire where these sweet wines are possible.

I sat in the cool – almost cold – of the Cave de la Bonne Dame while one by one *vignerons* brought me bottles of these superb wines, along with some more normal offerings. I met Catherine Champalou who with her husband Didier owns 10 hectares of vines. They both studied at the viticultural school at Montreuil-Bellay near Saumur, and Didier made his first wines in 1985. She told me that Didier is a great believer in what is called *sec tendre*. Instead of making the full, traditional range of a Vouvray producer – dry, *demi-sec*, *moelleux* – he makes a wine that is slightly drier than a *demi-sec* and sweeter than a *sec*. In addition, he makes a sweet wine in years when the grapes are ripe enough. His vinification is traditional, with fermentation in *demi-muids* (small casks of 120 litres), although the base wine for his sparkling *pétillant* is made in stainless steel.

I tasted the 1990 Vouvray Tendre, with 17 grams of residual sugar, a lovely soft, creamy wine with long-lasting flavour, the result of long maceration of the grapes during fermentation. Then came the first of the sweet wines, a 1989 Moelleux, not overly sweet, more concentrated and rich. A second Moelleux 1989, the result of a second pass through the vineyards to pick the grapes affected by noble rot, was sweeter but – as any great sweet white wine needs to be – was perfectly balanced between sweetness and acidity, never too powerful, preserving delicacy.

The Champalous were followed by Bernard Fouquet of Domaine des Aubuisières, who has a young vineyard of 11 hectares on the *coteaux*, the slope of the hill as it reaches down into one of the side valleys on the edge of the town of Vouvray. Since his land has the two types of soil found in the Vouvray vineyards – the limestone and the *silex* – he likes to make two wines 'to express the nature of the soil', as he puts it. I tasted his two 1990 *secs*: the *silex* wine was mineral to taste, almost as flinty as the soil, but the limestone wine was much softer, easier to drink when young. Then I tasted a Moelleux 1990 with 40 per cent of botrytized grapes, not overtly sweet, while a second *moelleux* with nearer 100 per cent botrytized grapes and 160 grams of residual sugar was overpoweringly rich and sweet.

Next to visit me in my cave was the bearer of one of the great names of Touraine wine, Armand Monmousseau. Until recently his family owned and then managed the sparkling wine firm of Monmousseau in Montrichard. Now he is owner of Château Gaudrelle, a 14-hectare estate on the top of the plateau above Vouvray, dominated by a simple, tumble-down château which M. Monmousseau visits occasionally and a spacious courtyard around which the old cellars are built – unusually for Vouvray, Château Gaudrelle's wines are not kept in a tufa cave.

There are three different parcels of land, or *crus*, in the *domaine*: Clos le Vigneau, Les Gues d'Amants and La Gaudrelle itself. Grapes from each parcel are vinified separately, but are then blended into one wine which, in 1990, represented 60 per cent of production, although in some years Clos le Vigneau provides a single-vineyard wine. In addition, there is a reserve wine produced from grapes off vines up to 100 years old and with very low yields.

I talked to M. Monmousseau about the curious phenomenon of the disappearing Chenin. The wines from the Chenin all seem to exhibit a peculiar habit of being delicious within one to two years of the harvest and then closing up completely, losing fruit and emphasizing only acidity for anything between five and ten years, before reappearing as completely different wines, fully mature and often with the ability to last for twenty or thirty more years. It's one of the attractions of Chenin, but also its problem: today, few consumers are willing to wait to drink their wine, and so end up drinking Chenin-based wines when they are in their closed-up stage and invariably being disappointed.

The disappearing Chenin was very apparent in the 1989 Réserve Spéciale of Château Gaudrelle. Here was a wine which with its 90 per cent of botrytized grapes should have been lusciously sweet. Six months ago, said M. Monmousseau, this was delicious; tasting it in 1991, it was more acid than sweet, a layer of firmness covering it and hiding the fruit. 'Give it at least seven years,' I was told. 'Come back in 1998.'

Another producer who has decided to make just one wine, rather than the multiplicity of styles possible in Vouvray, is Christian Chaussard of Domaine la Sabotière. He has eight hectares in Rochecorbon, in a vineyard that was set up only in 1987. What a start to life: three fine vintages in a row – 1988, '89 and '90 – before the frosts of 1991. M. Chaussard's 1989 Sec, his main wine for that year, was surprisingly old-fashioned for a young man, very full, somewhat uncompromising. Only in 1989 has he so far made sweet wines, simply because the year demanded it, and his *moelleux* of that year, with its enormous sweetness and ample richness, explains why a wine could be blowsy were it not restrained by a balance of acidity.

M. Chaussard's neighbour in Rochecorbon, Benoît Gautier, was the last of my visitors that morning. Since I was beginning to feel the chill of the cave and could see the sunshine beating down outside, I'm afraid that at first I didn't give M. Gautier all the attention his wines deserved. But I did learn that in his Clos Château-Chevrier he has 10 hectares and that he makes two ranges of still wines, one from the Clos itself, one from other vineyards, as well as a *pétillant*. He started to pour out wines and suddenly I was all attention. For here was a mature Demi-Sec Vouvray from the classic 1985 vintage that revealed how the wines can develop after their closed-up period: a wine of great ripeness and richness, with a deliciously-perfumed, slightly dusty character and hints of minerals, superbly balanced, and promising years ahead of it.

Traditional Vouvray stars

The wine gave me all the encouragement I needed to come back to Vouvray and this time to make a tour of the cellars. I was already impressed by the younger, more recently-established *vignerons*. Now it was time to see how some of the traditional star *vignerons* of the *appellation* were getting on.

So it was that two years later, in the summer of 1993, I found myself turning into the tree-shaded courtyard of Gaston Huët. Although now officially retired, he was mayor of Vouvray for as long as anybody could remember and is still owner of one of the largest *domaines* in the *appellation*. M. Huët (the 't' at the end is pronounced) has always been the bench-mark against whom all other Vouvray producers are judged. He has three vineyard parcels: Clos de Bourg, Le Mont and, around his house, Le Haut Lieu. As we stepped out into the vineyard past the ornamental garden and shady trees, it was obvious that Le Haut Lieu, 'the high place', was a good description for the land, with its views in all directions, to the north over the sweep of vineyards, to the south over the church spire of Vouvray, to the west towards Tours. Recognized as one of the best vineyard sites as early as the fifteenth century, Le Haut Lieu even drew words of praise from Sir Walter Scott, who visited it in 1827.

Now working alongside his son-in-law Noël Pinguet, M. Huët seems to have taken on a new lease of life, as well as a new philosophy. His vineyards are now operated on biodynamic principles, which aim to restore to the land what the chemicals used in conventional viticulture have taken out, encouraging natural predators to attack the pests of the vineyard and using strictly organic techniques of cultivation (for more on this, see Chapter 13 on Savennières and Roche-aux-Moines). The effect on the wildlife of the vineyards has been dramatic, M. Huët told me; since the change to *biodynamie* seven years ago, the wild tulips which once covered the slopes, but had disappeared as a result of chemicals, have returned, along with the grass between the vines which now provides food for the rabbits who had previously attacked the vines.

Instead of visiting the impressive Huët cellars, M. Huët took me into his lovely house of pale stone, where we tasted in the cool, a pleasant contrast to the heat of the day outside. He told me that the wine-making is kept as simple as possible. Low-temperature fermentation in stainless-steel tanks takes place over three months, using natural yeasts. The wines are then racked to remove the lees, and left in tank until bottling in April.

We started by tasting two dry wines: one from 1992 was very dry indeed, with hints of almonds and greengages; a second, from 1987, had the kerosene character that sometimes links Chenin wines with Riesling wines of Alsace or Germany, and was very high in acids, still developing. It seemed that the Huët style is to make wines which have initial austerity and develop slowly. That was reinforced by the *demi-secs* that followed: a soft 1992 from Clos du Bourg, not as floral as might have been expected; a 1988 which was developing a blackcurrant flavour, perfumed, with plenty of fruit, just beginning to show its paces.

Then it was into a succession of sweet wines, each more delicious than the last. There was an elegant 1990 made from grapes gathered in the first pass through the vineyard, sweet rather than botrytized. There were more apparent honeyed botrytis flavours in a 1990 Clos de Bourg Moelleux, gorgeously rich and unctuous, and a rather firmer Le Haut Lieu – the wines from this vineyard always develop more slowly, I was told, and this is a wine 'that will go on for ever and ever'.

It seemed that the wines of the Grand Old Man of Vouvray had not lost their pre-eminent quality, and when M. Huët finally poured out a refreshing glass of Vouvray Brut 1991, I found myself drinking probably the best sparkling Vouvray I was to encounter. A blend of grapes from the three different vineyards, it has piles of character, more *terroir* than technology, with slightly sweet, very fresh fruit, and definite Chenin piercing acidity. It is not a style that would appeal to all drinkers of sparkling wine, I reflected, but certainly one that would make a lover of great Chenin wines go weak at the knees.

M. Foreau's English garden

My next visit was just down the hill from M. Huët. There, in another lovely stone house – surrounded by a garden, ornamented with a magnolia tree, that would not look out of place around an English vicarage – lives Philippe Foreau. His cellar is in a cave just across the narrow road that climbs the valley of La Croix Buisée from the centre of Vouvray and which also passes the Huët cellars. It was obviously a busy morning for M. Foreau, who kept darting back to the house to check on some work builders were doing and running back into the cellar to open another bottle for me.

Philippe's father, André, was for many years another of the Grand Old Men of Vouvray. Philippe, who took over in 1983, told me he is now the third generation to cultivate the family estate of Clos Naudin, which has 12 hectares on limestone soil. He is first and foremost a viticulturalist, believing that the quality of the vineyard is of the greatest importance; he has virtually abandoned chemicals and at harvest time, aiming for low yields of 35 hl/ha, he picks his vineyard over several times to get grapes at the optimum maturity for the wine he thinks they will make. In the cellar his methods are as traditional as possible: few chemicals, fermentation in 300-litre barrels (although there are also stainless-steel tanks to be seen in his cellar), no chaptalization (because he believes it changes the nature of the alcohol in the wine) and long, natural fermentations at cellar temperature.

We tasted in the most marvellously fusty, wood-panelled office with fitted cupboards full of old labels and corks. It was, said M. Foreau, more comfortable than the circular room in the cellar, with its round stone table and old wooden press, which suffers from the high humidity of 95 per cent – good for wine but not for tasters. We started by tasting a Sec 1992. In 1992 M. Foreau made one-third of his wine still and dry, and the other two-thirds as the base for sparkling wine. Like many producers in Vouvray, he does not like the idea of malolactic fermentation (which reduces the high acids); he feels that, when the acids are reduced, the wine becomes too ripe and also needs to be heavily filtered, something he does not approve of.

The straight *sec*, although acid, was also rich enough to sustain the dryness of the fruit, and had a delightful, slightly smoky character and fresh, floral flavours. It made an interesting contrast to an experimental 1992 fermented in new wood which, we both agreed, did not work, as it had lost its fruit and tasted flat – not something he will try again.

We then went back seven years to a 1986 dry. Here the smokiness I had noticed in the 1992 was still attractively present, but was now part of a really complex set of flavours, mineral and kerosene and honey all balancing – although, according to M. Foreau, the wine was by no means ready. 'Give it another fifteen years,' he said. Even older was a 1980 *demi-sec* tasting of honey and truffles, smoky and hinting at lemon curd. Despite its age it had enormously high acidity, something I found quite difficult to come to terms with, but M. Foreau suggested that this meant it would also develop for many more years.

Then we moved on to wines from the great 1990 vintage. A *moelleux* with 110 grams of residual sugar had a taste of jelly or *confit*, with balanced sweetness and acidity, while a *moelleux réserve* with an amazing 220 grams of residual sugar was almost too rich and sweet, only becoming balanced after a moment in my mouth, when a hint of the dryness always present with a heavily-botrytized wine came through.

The methods of Clos Naudin were echoed in the cellars of Philippe Brissebarre, who lives in the next little valley to M. Foreau, La Vallée Chantier. To get there I had to pass under the new TGV railway line whose path from Paris to Tours cuts right under the Vouvray vineyards. There was enormous outcry when the line was proposed: '*La nouvelle voie TGV va massacrer le site de Vouvray*' (the new TGV line will destroy Vouvray), shouted the placards – but today it is as if nothing has changed. Fears that vibrations from the trains, as they passed underneath in their tunnel, would damage the roots of the vines have not materialized. All the locals now resent is the fact that they have to go to Tours and cross the river to the station of Saint-Pierre-des-Corps to catch the TGV to Paris.

The cellar of the President

M. Brissebarre seems to exist in a delightful muddle. Maybe it was because he had had a party in his cellar the day before, but his tiny tasting area at the front was littered with old glasses and bits of cheese. His small son played in the sandpit outside, while his wife was dispatched every so often to find clean glasses from the house, or to search out a bottle from the cellars. His house, a modern two-storey affair, was set right against the cliff, while in a shed to one side granny was organizing bottling and packing. Two large dogs stayed firmly inside their pen.

Despite the rustic scene, M. Brissebarre was an important man in Touraine viticulture at the moment I met him: president of the Comité Interprofessionel des Vins de Touraine, the grouping that represents the producers and growers, he was taking the turn of a grower to be president after a *négociant* had had his turn. The French wine industry is decidedly democratic and egalitarian: a small grower has just as much chance of being president of the powerful Comité as a wealthy, big-business *négociant*.

The Brissebarre *domaine* now consists of 13 hectares, with 2 more just planted but not yet producing. As it has expanded, M. Brissebarre has needed to excavate more cellar space, working with his father to dig further back. When the work was finished, in time for the 1992 harvest, he erected a finely-carved stone plaque at the entrance to record the moment for posterity.

I was walked quickly round the cellar to admire the new work – which struck me as an amazing feat for just two men to perform, and which would certainly be banned under any health and safety regulations – before moving to the kitchen-cum-tasting room at the front of the cellar. I first tasted his sparkling Méthode Traditionelle, a full-pressure *mousseux* which forms, depending on the year, an important part of his sales – 80 to 90 per cent in France, he told me. He believes that a sparkling wine should taste of its origins just as much as a still wine should; so a sparkling Vouvray should taste of Vouvray. His 1989 certainly did, full of firm fruit, with a hint of dusty Chenin flavours and rich, peppery alcohol.

Then followed a succession of still wines. First came a soft, per-fumed and floral Sec 1992, almost *demi-sec* in its sweetness and delicious to drink now. 'When a Chenin wine is young,' he said, 'it explodes with flavour and then gradually closes up. This wine is still in the explosive stage.' Two *demi-sec* wines from the 1989 and 1990 vintage showed how there is a hint of botrytis even with this level of sweetness, so ripe were the grapes that year. I found myself preferring the slightly less overpowering flavours of the 1989; M. Brissebarre agreed that he found this vintage to be more elegant, the 1990 being more opulent. The year 1990 was strange, he said, with no rain at all in September, which actually stopped the development of the grapes until right at the end, when some rain had the effect of raising the sweetness of the grapes by a degree of sugar every day for a week and setting off the noble rot.

We then tasted two *moelleux* wines from those years: the 1989 Grande Réserve, hugely botrytized, magnificent, just waiting to develop slowly. 'C'est pas mal,' said M. Brissebarre, understating madly, and then, looking at his small son: 'I hope when he drinks this in fifty years' time he will think of me.' The 1990, by contrast, was more sugary, less botrytized, altogther less complex.

Leaving M. Brissebarre, I travelled through Vouvray to Rochecorbon to visit the cellars of the man who had so admirably organized the tasting in the Cave de la Bonne Dame two years before. Frédéric Bourillon is a big, heavily-set man who has obviously had some successful years, because he has built himself a very smart new cellar with expensive wooden ceilings and lots of stainless steel. However, his problem, he told me, is that he now makes more wine from his 18 hectares than he can sell. He had been selling his wine to one of the British supermarkets, he said, but it was just too expensive: 'The problem with the price of Vouvray in 1990 and 1991 was that it was too expensive, first because the wines were so good (the 1990 vintage) and then because there was not enough (1991).' With the 1992 harvest prices could fall, but by that time the damage will have been done – Vouvray is now seen as expensive, and consumers are seeking alternatives. This has happened right along the Loire, from Sancerre to Muscadet, and it has created an image of high prices which will take some years to eradicate.

The ageing ability of Vouvray

It was with M. Bourillon that I tasted a range of venerable Vouvrays made by his grandfather from some of the great post-war vintages. First there was a 1955 which, when young, was a *moelleux* but is now almost dry; it is, however, still impressively rich and certainly not just a museum piece. This was followed by a 1949 which tasted amazingly young, very fresh with the sweetness of the botrytis still in evidence. Here was a wine that would slip down as easily as one from a much more recent vintage. Equally remarkable was a 1945, very deep gold in colour, tasting rich and old, but still with sweetness and freshness. We finished with a 1947 which was the only disappointment; with a taste of old mushrooms, this bottle at least was now too old – although, said M. Bourillon, other bottles he had tasted recently were much more alive.

It was a marvellous exercise, showing the ageing ability of Chenin wines in Vouvray and also putting into context the great wines of recent vintages such as 1985, 1989 and 1990. With the enormous strides in wine-making techniques since those wines of the 1940s and 1950s, it will be a wonder, for those of us still drinking, to discover whether the more modern wines can keep their freshness and greatness for as long.

The Domaine Bourillon d'Orléans has a high proportion of old vines – 35 per cent are over seventy years old – and M. Bourillon vinifies the juice from these vines in wood, a mix of old and new barrels. Although he does not want the taste of the barrels to affect the wine, he does want the oxidative quality of barrels and the fact that vinifying in barrels cuts down the acidity. He showed me the proof of this in a 1992 *sec* made from old vines, where the wood maturing has the effect of making the wine rich and soft rather than giving it a wood taste. He uses his brand-new stainless-steel tanks – first used in 1992 – for his sparkling wines and for his lesser wines.

For a view of stainless steel in its full glory, I had to visit the largest *domaine* in Vouvray, at Château de Moncontour. With 140 hectares of vines, this estate, which centres on an enormous Renaissance château standing on a wide platform overlooking the Loire, has been owned by the Brédut family from Bordeaux since 1989. Although they also own Monmousseau sparkling wines in Montrichard, their home will be at Moncontour, and I was given a quick chance to see the extensive renovation going on at the château – all in the best possible taste – before Mme Brédut, who runs Moncontour while her husband attends to Monmousseau, took me proudly into what she called her 'cathedral'.

The new underground cellar of Moncontour – which is right next to, but below, the château – is certainly big, impressive, full of stainless-steel tanks, with high ceilings and vast open spaces, a complete contrast to the narrow tunnels and chambers more often found in Vouvray. I was taken up steel steps, past the huge round columns which support the edifice, to the highest point, where the grapes arrive, to view the huge space set out before me, with its rows of big tanks and high-tech machinery.

Part of the reason for all this modernity is the sheer size of the estate. Another is their involvement in sparkling wines, which they believe are best made in the most up-to-date conditions to give reliability and quality. To prove the point, I was given a series of still base wines for *vins mousseux* to taste. They do not just make sparkling Vouvray here, but also Crémant de Loire, which – as will be explained more fully in Chapter 11 – can be made from a blend of grapes in which the classic Champagne grapes, Pinot Noir and

Chardonnay, can play a part. With its lightness and utter freshness, it made a revealing contrast to the more earthy taste of a base wine for Vouvray Mousseux which I tasted next, and which spoke just as much of that *terroir* I had first discovered with M. Huët.

When we moved on to tasting still Vouvrays, Mme Brédut told me that in her view the wine should never be too alcoholic. It is very easy, she felt, to make wines that are high in alcohol if the grapes are ripe enough. What she wanted, though, was delicacy. This she had certainly achieved in a deliciously light and delicate 1991 *sec,* and a 1992 *demi-sec* which was more freshness than sweetness, easy to drink, absolutely clean and fragrant. If character was perhaps lacking here, there were the compensations of easy enjoyability and none of the harsh acids of the Chenin.

There is more large-scale wine-making at the two co-operatives in Vouvray. Quite why there should be two co-ops within a few hundred yards of each other is, I was told, more to do with local politics than any practical purpose. Both the Cave des Producteurs de Vouvray, whose cellar is in La Vallée Coquette, and the Cave des Viticulteurs de Vouvray, based at the Château de Vaudenuits not far from M. Huët's cellars, have roughly the same number of grower members: fifty for the Producteurs, forty-five for the Viticulteurs. But there, I am afraid, the resemblance ends, for while the Producteurs are making some extremely good wines – especially in the sparkling categories – the Viticulteurs still seem to be back in the days when quantity rather than quality was the rule of co-operatives throughout France. Both co-ops also make Touraine *appellation* sparkling wines and, indeed, concentrate much more on sparkling than still wines.

It must be obvious that a Vouvray producer has the chance to make a huge variety – up to ten different styles – of wine each vintage. It is equally obvious to me, and to many others, as consumers that this means Vouvray's variety is also Vouvray's confusion and, therefore, its enemy out in the wide commercial world. This situation has obviously been recognized by many of the younger generation of growers; look at Didier Champalou, who makes a *vin tendre* rather than producing both a *sec* and a *demi-sec*.

It is the same with sparkling wines: under the *appellation* of Vouvray it is possible to make both a *pétillant* and a *mousseux* but, for many growers, to make and then try to sell both is only adding to their problems. So, like Philippe Brissebarre, they prefer to make either one or the other and then, with his full-pressure *mousseux*, to call it simply Vouvray Brut – a nice, neat description that is understood by wine-drinkers everywhere, but which leaves *pétillant*, a style particularly appropriate to Vouvray because of its capacity for richness and depth, somewhat out on a limb.

That Vouvray is capable of producing both great still wines and fine sparkling wines should be a fact it can take advantage of not only viticulturally – in poor years leaning heavily on sparkling wines, in better years turning to still wines – but also commercially. What the growers need to do, though, is to agree on some way of restricting their choice so that the consumers are not too confused, and then of persuading the bureaucrats who govern French wine to change the complex and over-constricting rules.

Once the problems imposed by the restrictive and complicated rules of the *appellation* are sorted out, Vouvray looks set for a good period in its long history. Nowhere else on the Loire is there such an enthusiastic and dedicated generation of younger growers. And nowhere else is there the sense of unity of purpose which allows them to work together on the future of their great wine.

9

The wines of Montlouis

Montlouis faces Vouvray across the Loire. But to drive from Vouvray to Montlouis is not just to cross the Loire from the north bank
to the south – a journey made difficult enough by the fact that
you have to go via Tours or Amboise, which are the nearest river
crossings. It is also to move from an *appellation* with a big name
and a long, illustrious history to one which has really only existed
with a separate identity since 1937, and whose name is still almost
unknown in the wider world.

That Montlouis should suffer the fate of being poor cousin to
Vouvray is unfair. It is a result of history, which came down on the
side of the big guys against the little guys. For years Montlouis
wines were sold under the name of Vouvray; they were, after all, in
the same style, made from the same grape variety – the Chenin
Blanc or Pineau de la Loire – and came from the same type of
land. You bought a Vouvray de Montlouis instead of a Vouvray de
Vouvray and found that you had a wine which tasted much the
same and was slightly cheaper.

History suggests that the vineyards of Montlouis were created in
the fifth century under the auspices of the cathedral of Tours. The
Chenin Blanc has long been the most renowned variety; in the
sixteenth century François Ier, whose château of Bourdisière was
close by, is recorded as having drunk and praised the wines, as did
Henri IV later. The trade to the Low Countries, vital for Vouvray,
was equally beneficial to Montlouis.

In 1919 the *vignerons* of Montlouis awoke with a shock to the
realization that their name was about to be taken away from them.
From now on they would have to stand on their own, selling their
wines as Montlouis pure and simple. At least that is what the
growers of Vouvray wanted. A court case ensued as the Montlouis

producers argued for their historical rights, a case which they finally lost only in 1937 and which led to the creation of the Montlouis *appellation* in 1938.

This may be history, but it is still important to Montlouis, whose wines have never subsequently achieved the renown of Vouvray and which are always seen as slighter, lesser alternatives. Perhaps the question to ask today is whether that reputation is deserved.

The answer lies, as with so much to do with wine, in the soil. While the Loire itself flows between the two vineyard areas, the soil on both banks is roughly similar. There are the same tufa cliffs with the vineyards planted on the flat plateau land on the top. The soil is chalky at base, mixed with *silex* and gravel on top. In Montlouis, however, there is also a proportion of sand in the soil, something not encountered in Vouvray, and this has the effect of making the wines lighter than those of Vouvray. The result is, stylistically, that Montlouis wines tend to mature more quickly, to fade earlier and to be of a lighter, less heady disposition than those of Vouvray.

It is probably this characteristic which leads to suggestions that the wines of Montlouis are inferior to those of Vouvray. Certainly you will rarely find the blockbusters to be found in Vouvray. You will find many more easy-going dry and *demi-sec* still wines and sparkling wines, with few of the sweet *moelleux* wines. But that is as much to do with economics as viticulture: Montlouis wines sell for less than those of Vouvray, and therefore the return on the risk involved in leaving grapes to hang on the vine to attract noble rot – and so to make *moelleux* wines – is commensurately smaller.

Montlouis's vineyards are compact, not large – currently around 360 hectares divided between 95 growers – and lie in a narrowing spit of land between the Loire and the Cher east of Tours. If you drive through the eastern suburbs of Tours, past the main railway station of Saint-Pierre-des-Corps and on along the south bank of the Loire, the tufa cliffs, so familiar in Vouvray and other parts of Touraine, begin to rise above the road. At times the road runs on reclaimed land, so close do the cliffs come to the river. On the north bank, Vouvray and Rochecorbon can be seen, and the vineyards of Vouvray commence. A couple of kilometres later, just after you pass under the two railway bridges that form the only direct link between Vouvray and Montlouis, the small town appears perched on top of the cliff.

The town of Montlouis-sur-Loire is a little like its vineyards: it is small, slightly run-down, with hints of a tourism that has almost passed it by, a few indifferent restaurants and an awkwardly-shaped square. To reach the top of the cliff from the river-bank, small lanes, often blocked by cars or lorries, twist precipitously upwards. The vineyards lie behind the town and to the east, stretching along the banks of the Loire to Lussault and sloping gently down to the Cher at Saint-Martin-le-Beau. These two *communes*, along with Montlouis itself, are the only villages within the *appellation*. To cross from one side of the *appellation* to the other takes maybe a quarter of an hour.

Statistics confirm that this is not a large *appellation*. Production is generally between 13 and 16 per cent of that of Vouvray: the size of the harvest ranges from the tiny 3,292 hectolitres recorded in 1991, the year of the frost, to 18,688 in 1989, the first of the two great years in which, as a rare exception, a quantity of sweet wines was produced. Montlouis can make the same styles of wine as Vouvray: dry, *demi-sec* and *moelleux* still wines, and sparkling wines which are fermented in the bottle.

The split between sparkling and still wines – and the proportion of *demi-sec* to dry still wines – varies according to the weather conditions. In 1989 and 1990 a much greater proportion of still wines was made: 72 per cent in 1989, 62 per cent in 1990. In the cooler year of 1992 the proportions were almost reversed: 43 per cent of production was still wines. In the mind of the consumer, therefore, there is always a certain confusion about what Montlouis really is, what sort of wine it really makes; a situation exacerbated by the fact that, while it is easy to spot a sparkling wine by the bottle, to tell the difference between a dry and medium still wine is not always possible – especially when, as is often the case, the label is of no help.

On a hot summer morning I made the journey along the road from Tours to Montlouis. Passing in front of the town along the road on the river-bank, I continued for a few kilometres, passing the co-operative on the left – which I was to visit later – and continuing on to the small village of Husseau. There I was to meet Yves Chidaine.

He turned out to be a vigorous sixty-year-old, bursting with enthusiasm, keen to get me to taste as many wines as possible, extolling the qualities of the 1989 and 1990 vintages (this was in

1991) and full of the virtues of the Montlouis *appellation*. Like so many *vignerons* in Touraine, his cellars are carved out of the tufa rock, with an entrance that, until you look hard, appears forgotten, closed-up and neglected. Inside, out of the sunshine, all is cool and damp. He told me he has 12 hectares of land on the plateau above where we were standing. He also told me – and this was apparent from looking round at the old casks – that he is a traditionalist, preferring to ferment in old wood, only using stainless steel for his sparkling wines. By using wood, he believes, he can get extra aromas and a greater variety of wines, which lend more character to the final *assemblage*.

His vineyards are on typical Montlouis soil: high in *silex* and with a good mixture of sand. From this land he likes to make around 40 per cent of his production as sparkling wine, although in 1989 and 1990 he found this impossible because of the ripeness of the grapes and their lack of acidity.

We tasted rapidly, not through lack of time, but because of the speed with which M. Chidaine produced wines and enthused about them. We started with a 1990 *sec*, at this stage harder than I would have expected, probably because, M. Chidaine said, of the weight of the fruit, a wine that is going to take years to develop. Then came a dry wine from his best vineyard, Clos du Breuil, a 1989 with delicious crisp fruit and ripe quince flavours, and with a hint of mineral taste that comes from the higher proportion of *silex* in the soil.

We followed with increasingly sweeter wines. M. Chidaine told me that a dry Montlouis can have no more than 5 grams of residual sugar and a *demi-sec* 27 grams, levels which are lower than those of Vouvray. Clos du Breuil wines again showed well, always with an extra oomph of fruit from the older vines. Then there was a sweet wine which M. Chidaine produced almost with glee, so rare is this style of wine in Montlouis. His 1989 *moelleux* with 50 per cent botrytis was full of floral fruit, not too heavy, acidity almost floating on a layer of sweetness. Cuvée Les Lys 1989, an *assemblage* of wines from older vines, was obviously a wine that will need many years' ageing – in itself not as common in Montlouis as in Vouvray.

After the succession of sweet wines, a taste of a *pétillant* (low-pressure) sparkling wine and a glass of the full-pressure *mousseux* Montlouis came almost like a shower of crisp, clean water, and its creamy, floral fruit certainly left my mouth clean, and ready for the next tasting.

That was in the cellars of Berger Frères in Saint-Martin-le-Beau. I thought I would be late for this visit, since M. Chidaine had been so enthusiastic with his wines. But I arrived dead on time, such is the short distance between the banks of the Loire at Husseau and Saint-Martin-le-Beau on the Cher. Berger Frères's cellars are situated on the outskirts of the village, a tight warren of narrow streets centred round a church that appears much larger than the place warrants.

The cellar that grew like Topsy

Laurent Berger, son of Michel Berger, was waiting for me, although obviously not expecting such a prompt arrival since he had just started a long telephone call. It gave me time to peer into the functional cellars which house the stainless-steel fermentation tanks and to realize that, since my previous visit some five years earlier, this firm had growed like Topsy. It has been run as a family business since the last century, now by two fathers, Michel and Jean, and two sons, Laurent and Philippe. They have 20 hectares of land, a lot by local standards, mainly on the slope behind the village facing south towards the Cher. The company is sometimes known by the name of its best vineyard, Domaine des Liards.

Unlike many producers in Montlouis, Berger deliberately makes half of its production as sparkling wine each year, picking under-ripe grapes if the weather conditions demand it. They say this is due to popular demand – and it also helps that sparkling wines have a higher unit price than still wines. In addition to these sparkling wines and to still Montlouis, they also make red Touraine wines. Fermentation of the still Montlouis is in wood, sparkling and red wines are made in stainless steel.

All this came out as Laurent, fresh from his phone call, produced bottles which were stood on an upturned wine cask in the middle of an almost-empty cellar. The sun was warm and inviting for a visiting Brit, but to the locals, used to the heat of the summer, tasting in the cold is absolutely normal.

Laurent is responsible for the vineyards and the cellar. He uses some of the latest techniques with the vines, trimming them to increase exposure of the grapes. For the reds and for sparkling wines, they harvest mechanically. In the cellar, a modern pneumatic press is in evidence, while whole-bunch maceration has been practised for the past fifteen years. But behind all this modernity is still strong tradition, especially for the still wines, which are fermented in wood and which rest in typical tufa cellars dug out of the hillside behind the modern *chai*.

So there is this mix of modern wines – with clean, fresh, slightly anonymous Montlouis Mousseux and Crémant de Loire, and light, fresh reds of Touraine Rouge – and the traditional, with some classic, richly-flavoured Montlouis *tranquille*. I tasted a range of these, from a very fresh, open, lightly acid Montlouis Sec 1990 and a much firmer, tighter 1989 (a better vintage, M. Berger told me). These were followed by a *demi-sec* 1990 from old vines, using grapes selected at pressing, densely-textured, with firm acid and fruit, a little early to be properly balanced. As a final *pièce de résistance* M. Berger produced his Moelleux 1990, from late-harvest grapes picked at the end of October, with 100 per cent botrytis. It was fermented in wood for three months, the sweetness of the grapes slowing down the work of the yeasts. The result was certainly remarkable, with delicately-poised acidity and sweetness, a definite dry honey taste of botrytis. It was obvious, as M. Berger said, that this was a wine that would go against the normal tradition in Montlouis, that of making wines which matured quickly.

My next visit was over lunch. Not that I needed to miss out on the cellars of the Cave Co-operative de Montlouis, since they were right next door to the restaurant in which I ate, and I lunched with the manager of the co-operative. It was a strange restaurant; because it was in a cave it felt highly humid, despite massive fans, and it was full of coach-parties of German tourists and ornamental fish-tanks, with a string orchestra playing ancient French pop songs in one corner. Despite these unpromising surroundings, the food was surprisingly more than adequate, and the regular arrival of new bottles of the co-operative's wines more than satisfying.

The co-operative, I learned, was established in 1960 and has twenty-two members with 100 hectares of vines between them, meaning that it produced just under a third of all Montlouis wines. By far the largest proportion of their production, as much as 75 per cent, is of sparkling wine, since that is what their customers want, and what they can sell most easily both at the cellar door – a vital part of their business – and through their extensive mail-order sales.

We drank an aperitif of the Montlouis Mousseux Cuvée Prestige in question, and while I found it smelt of very little, it did have an attractive fresh flavour, some attractive acidity and a creamy mousse. It was, however, much less interesting than some of the still wines we tasted during lunch: *sec* from 1989 and 1990 – the 1989 a finer wine, the 1990 easier to drink now – followed by *demi-sec* 1990 with 18 grams of residual sugar, soft, crisp, easy to drink, and then by two *moelleux*, a disappointingly tart 1990 and a hard, closed-up 1989 with underlying promise of a slow maturity.

After lunch, it was a short drive back to Husseau and a visit to Dominique Moyer. For once, as a real treat, I was received not in a tufa cellar but in a proper house, and was seated at a table in a drawing-room. Dominique Moyer is a charming, cultured man, and his family have been making wine for, as he put it, 'several generations', now owning 12 hectares of vines in Montlouis and Saint-Martin-le-Beau. We tasted wines from 1989 and 1990; he was one of the few growers in either Vouvray or Montlouis who felt that 1990 was better than 1989. It is not a view I share, preferring to agree with the majority, but certainly for M. Moyer, it did appear that there was more depth and flavour in his 1990 wines.

He told me that he picks grapes for his *sec* wines from young vines, reserving older vines for the *demi-sec* and the oldest of all for the *moelleux*. I then tasted a *demi-sec* 1989, which was just entering that harsh, closed-up stage which all Chenin wines pass through, and when, sadly, so many are drunk. I noted: 'You would really have to like Chenin to drink this wine at this stage,' but it was obviously a wine that, given ten years, will be superb. The same was true of the 1990 *moelleux*, except that it was also delicious when I tasted it, being still in the earliest stages of development: full of raisiny fruit, piles of botrytis, low acids, sweet after-taste combined with a nutty edge. The last time a wine like this was made, said M. Moyer, was in 1959, and before that in 1947. I wonder when the next time will be.

Cellars of old wines

My last visit in Montlouis was back in Saint-Martin-le-Beau, to the vast catacombs of Deletang et Fils. I was shown round at high speed by Olivier Deletang, who is obviously used to dealing with visitors by wowing them with the huge quantities of old wines maturing in neat piles in the spotless, spacious cellar. Right in their heart is a small tasting counter where we stood. It was during this visit that I made my first underground telephone call, via M. Deletang's portable phone – something I had imagined technically impossible, but which proved much easier than visiting a nearby call-box.

The Domaine Deletang is the largest family vineyard in Montlouis, with 20 hectares – 14 hectares are planted with Chenin, the rest with Touraine Sauvignon Blanc and Cabernet Franc Rouge. Techniques are modern: the fermentation cellars are smart and brand-new, and the underground cellars are only used for bottle storage. Still dry wines are left on their lees before bottling, after a slow, three-month fermentation, and certainly I found the *sec* 1990 Les Batisses deliciously concentrated and creamy, modern in style but not without good Chenin character.

After this dry wine we launched immediately into *moelleux* wines, of which Deletang made a number of different *cuvées* in 1989 and 1990. Their two best vineyard sites, Les Bâtisses and Petits-Boulay, both produced very sweet wines: the Petits-Boulay, from sandier soil, rounder; the Bâtisses more complex, obviously with a longer future ahead of it.

In those two years Deletang also made what they call *super-trie* wines from 100 per cent botrytized grapes, specially selected at the end of the harvest. These were even sweeter, overpowering with their botrytis flavours, but here again it was the Bâtisses 1990 which proved the more complex, with its firmness and balance of dryness to offset the sweetness.

As a sign of how Montlouis wines can develop, I was given a chance to taste a *demi-sec* 1959, carefully poured by M. Deletang from a dusty bottle produced from deep in one of the darker corners of the cellars. It was, he said, '*souple*' – an understatement, I felt, for a wine that sang of honey and ripeness and exotic fruits, which was still remarkably sweet, but which had softened and rounded and lost any trace of Chenin acidity and harshness. If only we would all wait that long to drink such wines.

When I visited Montlouis in 1991, the newest star in the *appellation* had hardly been born. So it was not until 1993, at the annual Angers wine fair, that I discovered the Domaine de la Taille aux Loups, whose name seems to refer to pruning and to wolves, a connection I find difficult to make. It is run by Jacky Blot, a dynamic, ever-smiling, moustachioed technical genius, whose enthusiasm and forceful personality have both fascinated Montlouis and upset plenty of apple-carts. His main theme is organic farming: all artificial fertilization on the eight-hectare vineyard has been stopped, chemical treatments have been drastically reduced, and he is the first in Montlouis to have a 'green' harvest of excess grapes during August to reduce the crop. In the cellar, they encourage natural wild yeasts, have almost cut out sulphur by keeping everything as hygienic as possible, and keep temperatures low to allow slow fermentations, for sweeter wines sometimes as long as twelve months.

The first vintage on this estate was 1989, but the vines are not young – the average age is fifty years. They pass through the vineyard two or three times at harvest, selecting grapes according to ripeness, only making still wines. Fermentation is in small, four-year-old *barriques*, mainly purchased from Château d'Yquem in Sauternes.

In the space of a quarter of an hour on their stand at the Angers wine fair I tasted seven of their wines. These were certainly something new for Montlouis, simply because of their concentration. The sweet *moelleux* wines are superb, particularly the top *cuvée*, Cuvée des Loups 1990, with its 100 grams of residual sugar, its almost syrupy texture. But equally impressive are the *sec* and *demi-sec* because of their huge concentration: the 1992, which I tasted as a cask sample, was full of enormously rich, if dry, fruit flavours; the 1989 *sec* was serious, complex, rich, balanced with acidity, just waiting to settle down for a long maturation.

Maybe, I thought as I walked away from this tasting, Montlouis is coming out of the shadow of Vouvray if such serious, exciting wine-making and investment can be coming to the *appellation*. It certainly needs this sort of kick-start to enable it to develop its own personality and confidence as a separate entity, and to prevent it from quietly stagnating. In the future, perhaps, we will go to Montlouis just as naturally as we will visit Vouvray, rather than passing it by on the other side of the river.

10

The great red wines of Touraine: Chinon, Bourgueil and Saint-Nicolas

——

One name dominates the history of the red wines of Touraine: Rabelais. You find him in Chinon, in the form of a statue on the waterfront. He was supposedly born a few miles away, just south of the Chinon vineyards, at Le Logis de la Devinière, now a heavily-signposted place of pilgrimage. In Bourgueil, his family owned a house in the vineyard of Gravot. His often-quoted eulogy to Chinon – '*Chinon, trois fois Chinon, petite ville, grand renom, assise sur pierre ancienne, au haut le bois, au pied le Vienne*' – while not poetry of the first order, neatly sums up the town's position straggling down the slope between the forest on the top of the hill and the river Vienne at the base. In other words, Rabelais is to the reds of Chinon and Bourgueil what Robert Burns is to Scotch whisky.

Rabelais's principal interest in the wine was not as grower but as consumer, which as any producer will tell you is a much easier and safer position to be in. Not so long ago the affairs of red wine producers in the Loire region were in a state of benign neglect, from a combination of ignorance on the part of the public and of wines which tended to fail in any quality comparison with Bordeaux or Burgundy.

I think that situation has been righted today, even if – as also in the case of Sancerre Rouge or Saumur-Champigny – it has not always been for the right reasons. When their wine suddenly takes off in fashionable Paris, any typical group of French producers will take the money and ask questions afterwards. In Touraine, this has been the fate of Saint-Nicolas-de-Bourgueil, which has joined Saumur-Champigny (and followed on from Sancerre Rouge) as the red wine to drink chilled and young.

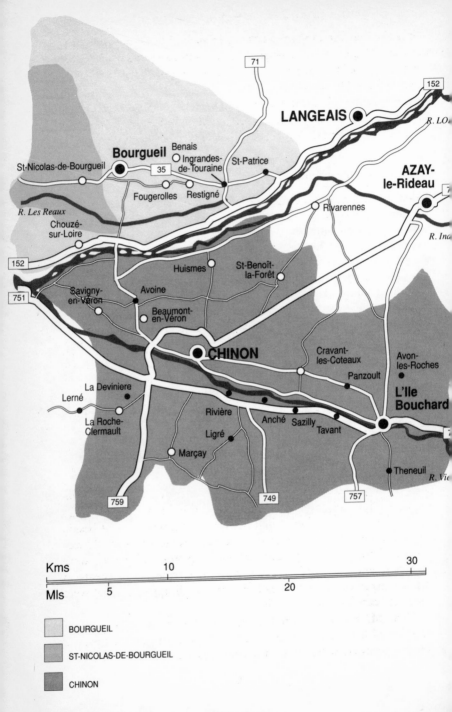

The red wine vineyards of western Touraine

It is the sad fate of many of the red wines of the Loire that they are seen as flighty little numbers to be consumed in this way. And it is especially sad for the great *crus* of Touraine – for Chinon, Bourgueil and Saint-Nicolas-de-Bourgueil.

The next stage in putting these wines in their rightful place, well up the quality league of French reds, will be the realization – and the common acceptance – that they age, and age well.

Cathedrals in the ground

I first appreciated this in the cellars of Jean-Maurice Raffault in Chinon; for cellars, in fact, read caves, carved out of the tufa rock which forms the subsoil of much of this part of Touraine. These caves are ubiquitous: every producer has one, or shares one, or is excavating one. To keep your wine in a *chai* – as they do in Bordeaux – would be considered deeply eccentric when the countryside is littered with these perfectly ambient natural cathedrals in the ground.

M. Raffault's cave is a good one. You reach it by way of a semi-subterranean passage covered over with hanging bushes and trees. Once inside, M. Raffault, a man of great enthusiasm for his wines and the wines of Chinon, invites you to admire the mould which covers most of the available surfaces. It is on the ceilings, on the walls, and it covers small mounds on the floor which, as you look more closely, turn out to be bottles of wine. The mould – a form of penicillin – is a good sign, because it shows that the humidity is right, the temperature is constant, and that the wines are being kept in the best conditions for ageing.

As M. Raffault and I reached the heart of the cave a large trestle table, suitably encrusted with mould, could be seen. The two large food-boxes, one of which I had been carrying, were placed beside the table and their contents unpacked. A large white cloth was produced to cover the mouldy table-top, plates and glasses were laid out, and the food was unwrapped: terrines, cold meats, a serious array of cheeses, bread and butter all appeared and were arranged carefully on the cloth.

Then M. Raffault started a series of forays into the dimmer recesses of his cave, coming back each time with bottles, the next more encrusted with mould than the last. An ancient corkscrew with a vinewood handle was produced, and the meal could commence.

At first all was silence, as the French ritual of the breaking of the bread and the slapping-on of the terrine took place. Several bottles followed swiftly upon each other, M. Raffault merely indicating the vintage and leaving me to write notes: 'from wines of the 80s to the 1969, the 1968' etc. It was when we reached the 1953 – mature, yes, but certainly not dried-out – that I began to realize there was a purpose behind what had seemed an attempt to prove the spirit of Rabelais lived on. Here was proof that these wines developed outstanding characteristics with age.

They moved in a logical progression, allowing for differences in vintages, from wines with a deep purple colour, considerable green tannin but also raspberry fruit, through a closed-up period when dryness took over, into a golden age of tobacco and truffles, interwoven with violets, and then into comfortable old age, when truffles and vegetal tastes predominated and the fruit faded into obscurity.

Le Breton and the vineyards

The Cabernet Franc is the grape that produces the wines in all three *appellations* – Chinon, Bourgueil and Saint-Nicolas-de-Bourgueil. And, apart from in the vineyards of Saint-Émilion in Bordeaux, this corner of the Loire is where it comes most into its own. The local name for the vine is the Breton, and gentle controversy bubbles along about its origins.

Putting aside the attractively romantic theory that it was first planted in the seventeenth century by an Abbé Breton on behalf of his master Cardinal Richelieu, the most likely origin of the name is simply that the wine was bought by the inhabitants of Brittany, because it was the nearest convenient source of red wine. It was the wine *for* the Bretons rather than *of* the Bretons.

The arrival of the Cabernet Franc can be dated reasonably precisely. It was certainly mentioned by Rabelais, and records suggest that it actually arrived in the second half of the twelfth century from Saint-Émilion. Both Anjou (the region into which Chinon and Bourgueil fell at the time) and Aquitaine were then in the possession of the English crown, so politically it would have been the best time in several centuries for vineyard development to be co-ordinated between the two regions.

Quite why the choice fell on the Cabernet Franc is easier to answer. The fact that the grape is fairly resistant to mildew, that it manages to produce wines with a good colour even in cool years, and that it ripens earlier than its close relative the Cabernet Sauvignon, all go a good way to explaining why it should have prospered in the most northerly fine red wine vineyards in Europe.

There is a little Cabernet Sauvignon planted, but its presence is very limited (around 2 per cent in Chinon, even less in Bourgueil) and the reason for it being there – to give structure to the all-too-soft Cabernet Franc wines – has now become less important because of its poor performance in cool years (it hardly ripens) and because changes in technology have given more colour and shape to Cabernet Franc wines.

Chinon and Bourgueil are the easternmost vineyards along the Loire where the Cabernet Franc reigns supreme. Beyond that, in the vineyards east of Tours, it shares place with the Pinot Noir and Gamay, as well as the lesser Pineau d'Aunis.

Although the two regions of Chinon and Bourgueil can be, and are, conveniently bracketed together, that is only just possible with the wines. And the style of the two towns is quite different. Chinon is the aristocrat, with its castle, its narrow streets lined with half-timbered houses, its elegant river-front and ancient bridge. Bourgueil is the bourgeois, a working town with little to remark on architecturally (apart from the ruins of the sixteenth-century abbey) and fewer points of gastronomic interest.

There are definite differences between the wines, though most consumers would find them hard to spot. Generalizing, it seems that the wines of Chinon have a greater softness and roundness, while those of Bourgueil have a more rustic quality, greater tannins and perhaps less finesse. The smaller *appellation* of Saint-Nicolas-de-Bourgueil (which only managed to get recognition separate from Bourgueil because the local *commune* got in quickly back in 1936) makes wines which have the rusticity of Bourgueil without the longevity – hence their current attraction as young wines in Paris.

The vineyards, too, are contrasted in appearance. Bourgueil's look south over the broad Loire flood-plain towards the nuclear power station, which is itself just north of Chinon. Saint-Nicolas-de-Bourgueil's vineyards are a western extension of those of Bourgueil itself. Chinon's vineyards are mainly in the narrower, more attractively-wooded valley of the Vienne further south and east, although there is a sizeable outcrop near the power station itself at Savigny-en-Véron, a narrowing spit of land between the Vienne and the Loire.

The bulk of Chinon's vineyards lie in eleven *communes* on the north bank of the Vienne, from Savigny-en-Véron in the west – a *commune* that lies both on the Vienne and the Loire – to Crouzilles in the east, east of the town of L'Île Bouchard. On the south bank of the Vienne there are nine *communes*, from Theneuil, just east of L'Ile Bouchard, to Marçay, which lies due south of Chinon just off the road to Loudun. While the vineyards on the south bank are scattered, those on the north bank are found in considerable concentrations, although always interspersed with other crops. The biggest wine villages in the *appellation* are Cravant-les-Coteaux, just to the east of Chinon (with 600 hectares of vines), followed by its neighbour Panzoult (with 265 hectares) and by Beaumont-en-Véron (with 284 hectares) and Savigny-en-Véron (with 252).

Bourgueil's vineyards are in seven *communes*, from Saint-Patrice in the east, not far from the Loire town of Langeais with its fearsome castle, down to Chouzé-sur-Loire, which is on the banks of the river. It is a more concentrated *appellation* than Chinon, with long stretches totally devoted to viticulture. Here the largest wine *communes* are Bourgueil itself (with 970 hectares) and neighbouring Restigné (with 764 hectares). A small enclave cut out of the north-western corner of Bourgueil is the *appellation* of Saint-Nicolas.

The basic structure of the vineyards in both valleys is, however, similar. They are divided into three sections: the vineyards on the valley floor, producing light wines from gravel and sand soil; the vineyards of the slope, where gravel and stones predominate, and whose wines are more elegant and long-lasting; and the wines from the chalk soil of the plateau, which are the most long-lived. Saint-Nicolas is the only one of the three *appellations* without much vineyard on a plateau; this, and the sandier soil found there, are normally cited as reasons for the lighter, faster-maturing wines.

The production differs considerably between the *appellations*. In 1992, Chinon produced 124,661 hectolitres of red and rosé wines – by far the greater proportion was of red – and 838 hectolitres of white (from the Chenin Blanc grape), Bourgueil produced 78,463 hectolitres entirely of red, and Saint-Nicolas-de-Bourgueil 53,872 hectolitres. Those proportions remain fairly constant despite variations in the total harvest: in 1989, for example, the figures for Chinon were 103,290 hectolitres of red and rosé and 599 hectolitres of white, for Bourgueil 70,533 hectolitres of red and a minute amount of rosé, and for Saint-Nicolas 47,276 hectolitres of red and a yet smaller quantity of rosé.

That difference is echoed in the vineyard areas. In 1990, Chinon had 1,765 hectares of vines, while Bourgueil had a relatively comparable 1,136 hectares and Saint-Nicolas 794 hectares. However, it is not echoed in the number of growers: Chinon has 329 growers, Bourgueil 335 growers and Saint-Nicolas 165. What I suppose those figures suggest is that Chinon has greater yields per hectare from fewer, more efficient growers, while Bourgueil has low yields and growers with smaller plots of land. Certainly, there is a greater air of prosperity among the growers of Chinon, who have smarter cellars and flashier cars than their more modest neighbours north of the Loire.

The place of wood

The best way to find out the differences between the wines of the three types of vineyard is to taste them, something best done when the wines are still in tank or wood. I arrived at the cellars of Bernard Baudry in Cravant-les-Coteaux, east of Chinon, at about five one evening, as M. Baudry was wrapping a huge sheet of plastic around a pallet-load of wine destined for Belgium. My mouth was dry from a day spent tasting young red wines in Saint-Nicolas-de-Bourgueil and Chinon, and when I smiled I probably showed teeth that were black with colour and tannin.

A sally into the Baudry cellars was enough to dispel any palate fatigue. His 25 hectares of vineyards are divided between the comparatively flat gravel and sand land along the Vienne and a smaller proportion which are on the plateau above his house. This is the heart of the Chinon area – the *commune* of Cravant-les-Coteaux has one-third of the vineyards in the *appellation*.

M. Baudry's enthusiasm is wood. The small cellar which leads out of his office is lined with barrels. They are not new; like many of his colleagues, he is very wary of using new wood on wines which can lack weight in lesser years. So you do not get the rows of glowing fresh wood that you would find in Bordeaux. What he wants instead is a gentle rounding-out of the fruit.

We started tasting. In this cellar was wine from the 1990 vintage of one of his *lieux-dits*, his vineyard of Grezeaux on the plateau. There was richness to the wines, coupled with considerable tannin, and a hint of wood taste. Every barrel tasted slightly different – there was more firmness here, more roundness there, greater fruit from that barrel in the corner. 'They're all barrels from Bordeaux, you know,' said M. Baudry casually. 'That one came from Château la Lagune, and that was from Domaine de Chevalier. I want my barrels to have had a good start in life.' Indeed he does.

Then we moved out of the cellar and stood around an upturned barrel which doubled up as a tasting table. A newly-bottled wine was produced and poured out: the Haies Martels 1990, from Baudry land near the river. By contrast with the plateau wines in the barrels, this was light, fresh. It had fifteen days' fermentation on the skins in stainless steel, I was told. If any of these red wines can be drunk young and chilled, this was it – although the temperature of this bottle, straight from the cellar, was, we both agreed, much the best.

How old is an old vine?

Apart from the soil, there are other factors which decide whether a wine is to be made for ageing or for comparatively early consumption. Many producers have patches of what they term *vieilles vignes*, old vines. It is a pretty loose term: one producer's *vieilles vignes* at fifteen years old would be another's babies, just coming into full production. But it does seem to imply two things: first, a selection of grapes, and second, lower yields. Both are recognized as helping the quality of the wine.

I tasted the Vieilles Vignes of Jean-Yves Billet at Domaine des Forges in Bourgueil. Jean-Yves is an important man: when I met him he was president of the local growers' syndicate, and busy with it. I had to arrive at two o'clock, and he could spare me an hour. So I got down to questions quickly. He has 17 hectares of land at the eastern end of the Bourgeuil vineyards in Restigné. Of these, 6.5 hectares are *vieilles vignes*; and by that he means vines which are over forty years old. He is one of those producers who prefers stainless steel for all his wines, believing that fruit quality is the most important characteristic of Bourgueil wines.

We descended to the small cellar underneath his courtyard, by way of a little hut which covered the top of some stairs. The tasting followed no particular order: old vintages mingled with young wines randomly. Some of M. Billet's friends appeared half-way through and were invited to join in as willing participants. We tasted his young wine, Cuvée Printemps, which comes from low-lying sand and gravel soil and young vines. Fruit was certainly the dominant quality here, along with an earthy *goût de terroir* which is a characteristic sometimes found in young Cabernet Franc wines.

His range includes a blended Bourgueil from different areas of his vineyard, a special *cuvée*, Les Bezards, which seems to mature after five or six years – and the Vieilles Vignes. Both the 1986 and 1988 relied on tannin and structure as well as fruit; the 1988 in particular was concentrated, with big chewy fruit and acidity coupled with tannin. Neither was remotely mature. It was perhaps no coincidence that M. Billet bottles his wines in Bordeaux-shaped bottles (with high shoulders) rather than the more usual Burgundy shape (with sloping shoulders). Here again the reference was to Saint-Émilion, although in fact M. Billet was simply returning to an older sort of bottle which had been replaced after the Second World War by the Burgundy-shaped bottle.

The allotted hour had long passed before we emerged from the cellar, and whatever M. Billet had to do after seeing me was now completely forgotten, since he demanded that I go with him to see his new cave. As I was still new to tufa caves at this stage of my tour, I agreed, and we drove at speed across country and through fields made red by poppies, into the sides of the slope that marks the boundary between the vineyards of the plain and those of the plateau in Bourgueil. The cave was enormous, high-ceilinged and seriously under construction; the sound of pneumatic drills was quite adequate to drown out any chance of conversation. It made a perfect excuse to leave for my next appointment, already an hour late.

While M. Billet's cave was obviously going to be big enough to hold a reception for the whole of Bourgueil when construction work was finished, the same could hardly be said of the tube in the rock that currently constitutes the cave of Pierre-Jacques Druet in the Bourgueil *commune* of Benais.

The advent of fruit

M. Druet is a newcomer to Bourgueil. He studied in Bordeaux and came to the Loire in the mid-1980s, full of ideas which must have seemed shocking to the old-timers, and still impress by the care with which they have been thought through. He is, he says, making wine which can age well, but which tastes good when young. It is in contrast, he believes, to the older producers, who either make wine which is undrinkable when young and needs an age to mature, or wine which is to be drunk young but does not age.

He is a serious young man who expects serious interest from his visitors. Perhaps he is a little intolerant – especially when a party of senior citizens, out for a good time, turns up in the middle of our tasting. His wife Martine was deputed to pour out the wine, and they were left to mingle outside while the cellar door was firmly shut, and we continued to move from barrel to barrel in the cellar.

The Druet style calls for wood. It also calls for considerable colour and extract. They are all elements in making wine to last. To give the Cabernet Franc every chance, M. Druet brings technology into play. Like many of the younger generation of producers in Chinon and Bourgueil, he uses stainless-steel tanks for fermentation. And, again like the more up-to-date producers, he uses a system called *pigeage* which breaks up the 'cap' of grape skins which forms on top of the fermenting must. Huge paddles churn up the skins and ensure that they do their job of giving colour to the wine. But M. Druet has gone one better. He has devised a fermenting tank that narrows towards the top. This shape – one I have never seen before, but which is so obvious when it is all explained – is designed to force the grape skins down as they are churned about and therefore assist the system of *pigeage*.

There is no question but that Druet wines are highly-coloured and have what the wine trade calls 'extract' but which I would simply call plenty of flavour and taste. His style is also helped by the fact that most of his vineyards are in the chalky soil of the plateau of Bourgueil. So his three *lieux-dits* (single-vineyard) wines are all from land that naturally makes powerful wines.

The lightest of the three seems to be Beaunais, although the 1989 had excellent colour and concentration due to the warmth of the vintage. Somewhere in the middle is Le Grand Mont vineyard, certainly more concentrated, which in its intensity moves you further south to Bordeaux. Biggest of the three in wine terms is Vaumoreau; the 1989 was aged partly in new wood, a radical departure for Bourgueil – although to hear how M. Druet prepared the barrels by rinsing with water and cheap red wine, it seems even he was cautious about the effect of new wood tastes. But it works: the wood certainly is strong, but there is so much fruit its future seems assured. And, like the other two wines, it could even be drunk soon, though that might be infanticide.

Another young producer has cellars in another small cave in the *commune* of Saint-Patrice, at the eastern end of the *appellation*. Christophe Chasle, a slight, shy man with a somewhat ragged beard, claims to be the only *vigneron* who bottles his wine in the *commune*, although there are obviously other growers, since there are 80 hectares and he only has seven of them. A former nursery-man, he started up his vineyard in 1982, replanting land that had not seen vines since phylloxera.

His cave is an old one, housing in one corner a remarkable collection of Gallo-Roman pieces which he has dug up, and a wall painting of a *gabarre*, the flat-bottomed boat that was used in the eighteenth century to ferry travellers across the Loire at this point. His wines, however, are very much in the modern style of Bourgueil, designed as much for ageing as for drinking young. His earliest-maturing wine he calls Les Gravois, coming from gravel soil close to the river, which he bottles in the spring after the harvest: the 1990 was, he said, much chewier than his normal style because of the harvest, and the 1989 had developed a delicious cassis flavour. Rochecot is a much bigger, richer style of wine from land on the slope of Bourgueil. The vines were planted in 1986, so even in 1990, when the wine was well-structured and perfumed, they were still young.

Poet and trend-setter

Many of the trends in red wine-making in Bourgueil and Chinon come together in the person of Charles Joguet. His vineyards at Sazilly on the southern bank of the Vienne are among the few in Chinon to face north. It seems to cause him few worries; the slope, he argues, is so gentle here that the sun manages to stay on his land for much the same amount of time as it does on the south-facing vineyards across the river. Having said this, he then admitted that he harvests later than most Chinon producers, which suggests a definite difference.

M. Joguet is a poet and artist as well as a wine-producer – some would say, of course, that making wine is an art-form anyway. But his artistic nature does seem to allow him to wander in from lunch a good hour or so late, and to be immediately forgiven because he has piles of charm. He walks elegantly, pullover draped over his shoulders

Like so many Frenchmen, once behind the steering wheel of his small, very dusty Renault, he assumes that all roads are straight and that every other car is a mirage. We drove, at breakneck speed, from his office at Sazilly to his tufa cave where he keeps his wine in bottle. We had already tasted his younger wines in wood. He is of the school that is happy to put wine in wood, but, he says, because of the high natural acidity of his wines, he prefers to use barrels that are two years old, which cuts down the wood taste and allows the fruit to survive.

The Joguet range, like that of many of the new wave of producers in both Chinon and Bourgueil, consists of a Jeunes Vignes alongside separate *cuvées* from each of his parcels of land, his *lieux-dits*. He has four of these. The lightest in character is Clos de la Curé, from a patch of land next to the church in Sazilly, down towards the river. The next in weight is the Clos Varennes de Grand Clos, slightly higher up the slope. The two richest, biggest wines are Clos de Chêne Vert and Clos de la Dioterie, both planted with older vines.

Charles Joguet is also one of the few producers in Chinon to make much of a rosé. It is a *vin gris*, slightly grey-pink in colour, and has only à short maceration on the skins for five to six hours to give its attractive touch of colour. Considering how much acid there is in the red wines, this is surprisingly low in acidity, and would need to be drunk young before it fades into softness.

We hurtled up to the cave entrance, only to find it blocked by builders' materials. Charles is another producer who has felt impelled to enlarge his already enormous cave; it certainly made a spectacular sight – but I still cannot work out why they have to be so big.

We walked around the piles of sand and cement and found a small packing-case, a couple of rickety chairs and two glasses, both of which had lost their stems and so could only be put down on their sides. Nothing daunted, M. Joguet produced wines which entailed disappearing off into what seemed like side-chapels and coming out with the inevitable dusty bottles.

The contrast between the 1990 wines in wood and the 1989 in bottle told more about the effect of wood on the wine than the vintages. Both were superlative years, and both sets of wine exhibited rich fruit that is very rare in the region. The 1989 wines had already lost the dominant wood tastes that were just too strong in the 1990 wines. It was the tannins that now dominated, and there was no question, we both agreed, that these would be wines that would last for many years.

From the elegant M. Joguet's cellars I went to see yet more elegance, this time in the form of Château de la Grille. An ancient but heavily-restored château on the flat plateau land above Chinon, it is at the centre of an 18-hectare estate which most closely resembles an estate in Bordeaux, with its avenue of trees and *chai* to one side. No tufa caves here; this is a proper underground cellar, high and square, jam-packed with fermentation tanks and barrels between which it is sometimes difficult to pick your way.

The château has belonged to Champagne Gosset since 1950, and they are keen to promote their Chinon with much the same image as in Champagne. There is the smart packaging, the tasting room, the fine château; it is all a world away from the small growers down in the Vienne valley below. Great care is taken in the production, with hand-harvesting and special eighteenth-century bottles (not dissimilar in shape to an old Champagne bottle) for the single wine they make from the estate

After fermentation in stainless steel, with automatic *pigeage*, the wine is aged in wood for twelve to eighteen months. It is quite a mixture of wood, with 25 per cent new and the rest up to four years old. It was fascinating to taste the same vintage still in different woods – the 1990, which I had tasted in 1992 just before bottling. The older the wood, the more the obvious juicy fruit, so that fourth-year wood revealed lovely redcurrant fruits. Third-year wood again showed more fruit than wood. But by the time I reached second-year and new wood, it was the wood and the structured tannins which dominated. Put together, as I tasted later, the 1990 is initially dominated by that wood, but there is also weighty fruit and richness which make Château de la Grille the style of Chinon that needs to be aged.

Saint-Nicolas and the Mabileaus

Having already seen the effect of ageing on Jean-Maurice Raffault's wines, I should not have been surprised at how well wines from Chinon age. I was much more surprised when, the next day, I visited Jacques Mabileau (one of eight producers with the same surname) in Saint-Nicolas-de-Bourgueil. This is the *appellation* that is supposed to produce wines for early drinking. So what were we doing, down in M. Mabileau's tufa cave, tasting his 1981 and finding that there were enormous ripe-fruit flavours that showed no sign whatever of fading?

Much is to do with the fact that M. Mabileau's 13 hectares are on the small part of the extension of the Bourgueil *coteau* that is in the Saint-Nicolas *appellation*. The fact that we were also tasting a wine made from *vieilles vignes* also helped to give it extra weight.

This 1981 came at the end of a tasting which had started badly. We were on time – a surprise in itself after a day's tasting – but M. Mabileau was somewhere in the vineyard, no doubt expecting us to be keeping Tourangelle hours. His son was packed off to fetch him. A few minutes later he roared in, perched high on one of those tractors designed to straddle the vines, looking rather sheepish and shy.

It was not until after we had tasted his 1990 wines in tank – first a *jeunes vignes* and then his Domaine Jacques Mabileau, followed by a *vieilles vignes* – that he became relaxed enough to issue the standard invitation to come along to his *cave*. This was a somewhat more exciting event than usual, because it meant following him in my car into the pitch darkness, negotiating past pillars and along narrow passages, desperately trying to keep his car's rear lights in view and to avoid turning off into the maze of side-passages.

Once there, we launched into a series of vintages of *vieilles vignes*: the 1988 in a light style after the 1989s, the 1987 with tannin and firmness, the 1986 well-structured with deliciously ripe fruit, the 1985 with a fine smoky, gamey bouquet and an almost caramel richness, the 1982 with perfumed, dusty fruit with an edge of dryness (it was the only wine in the series to be aged in wood). And so finally to that 1981, remarkably youthful, a tribute to high quality wine-making as well as to the perfect conditions in which the bottle had been stored.

The place of the *négociant*

Considering their dominance in other parts of the Loire valley, Chinon and Bourgueil are remarkably free of *négociants*. Each *appellation* has a locally-based *négociant* (Couly-Dutheil in Chinon, Audebert et Fils in Bourgueil), both of whom own top-quality vineyards and produce a range of wines which do credit to the *appellation* – and neither of whom is much involved with wines from outside. A few outside *négociants* do produce *appellation* wines (and the few really unpleasant bottles of Chinon and Bourgueil that I have tasted seem to come from these firms), but they are in comparatively small quantities and show nothing like the dominance *négociants* do in Muscadet.

Couly-Dutheil have their own vineyards, 65 hectares of them, including the showpiece, Clos de l'Écho, which is on top of the steep cliff beside the castle at Chinon. Their cellars in the heart of Chinon, with storage for 6,600 hectolitres of wine, are a remarkable feat of engineering. Out of yet more tufa caves have been carved the offices and warehouses of a late twentieth-century wine producer, replete with large-scale bottling lines, lifts and huge stainless-steel storage tanks.

Their history is easily told. The Dutheil part of the name comes from the Corrèze, the poorest part of France. Many Corréziens drifted from the region into wine – the Moueix family of Pomerol being perhaps the most famous. The Dutheils came north, and in Chinon Madeleine Dutheil married into the Couly family. Today, it is the sons of this marriage who run the business.

There is plenty of romance in the cellars, something which is regarded as a vital part of the visit. A tour will not just show you modern equipment, but will bring out the old barrels, the stock of ancient vintages of wine, as well as the relationship between *terroir*, vine and finished wine. Bertrand Couly, in charge of vinification, spends time over tasting the wines to show how each style of soil gives different styles of wine. He delights in producing samples of the clay and limestone soil of the Clos de l'Écho for you to hold in your hand and examine, urging you to taste the wine as you do so – to feel the product from its start to its finish. Maybe my French was rusty that day, but I am still not quite sure what benefit I was supposed to obtain from this exercise.

Clos de l'Écho is the wine you inevitably taste in the cellars of

Couly-Dutheil. They are situated right by the main entrance to the Château de Chinon, and the name is supposed to come from the echo that bounces off the castle walls if you shout from the top. It was purchased by the Coulys in 1952 and now produces their finest estate wine, one of the best-reputed in Chinon. During my time in the Couly-Dutheil cellars, which are high in humidity and designed to give you cold feet from the damp earth floor, I was given seven vintages of the wine to taste, dating back to 1964 – a stunning wine, still full of delicious smoky fruit, still with tannin, and with acidity which certainly suggests it has a long way to go yet. At the other end of the scale the 1988, the youngest wine I tasted, had very sweet fruit balancing tannin and acidity – signs, said M. Couly, of considerable potential.

Lighter, less long-lived wines are produced on their other *domaines*: Domaine René Couly, with 22 hectares, is in the hamlet of Saint-Louand just to the west of Chinon; Clos de l'Olive is on the main road to Cravant-les-Coteaux; and Les Gravières d'Amador is on the lower, sandy soil by the Vienne. For their lesser *cuvées*, they purchase grapes which are vinified at their cellars in Chinon. All told, they have about 9 to 10 per cent of total Chinon production.

I think it is quite instructive for other areas of the Loire to speculate about this relative lack of *négociants*. One of the fundamental reasons is that neither area is a bulk wine-producer; none of the three *appellations* is in the business of supplying large quantities of inexpensive wines. A high percentage of producers bottle their own wines. In addition, it does seem that supply and demand have run parallel rather than veering wildly apart.

Rabelais's caves

But that does not mean that growers in the region do not feel threatened by big firms moving in. A recent consequence of this is the formation in 1990 of a group rejoicing in the evocative name of Les Caves des Vins de Rabelais. This is not a co-operative in the traditional sense because much of the vinification is still done at the cellars of the 107 members, and they are still able to sell their wines independently.

What this group does is to produce a Special Cuvée in amounts large enough to compete with the *négociants*. Under the name of the house in which the group has its offices, Les Aubois, they make a rosé and a red, as well as tiny amounts of a white from Chenin Blanc. There is also the superior *cuvée*, Cuvée Jeanne d'Arc (it was in Chinon that Joan of Arc first arrived at the court of Charles VII), which boasts a garish black, gold and red label. They also sell the individual *domaine* wines from their members.

Which brings me full circle, because one of those *domaine* wines that I tasted at Les Caves de Rabelais came from the Domaine de la Croix of my old luncheon partner, Jean-Maurice Raffault. I have to say that his 1989 will age just as well as those other vintages I tasted back in his tufa cave.

Sparkling wines of the Loire

Saumur lies at the boundary between Anjou and Touraine, in the heart of the Loire vineyards. But its central position is not just one of geography. It is, in many ways, the wine capital of the Loire, and is certainly the focal point of one of the largest concentrations of vineyards and the home of the region's sparkling wine industry.

The affinities with Champagne are numerous. The chalk soil of the plateaux and slopes that surround Saumur and where the vines are planted, exactly parallels the soil of Champagne. The white wine that comes from these vineyards is light, rather green and has the same tendency to re-ferment as does the white, still Coteaux Champenois. It is not surprising that Saumur became home to a sparkling wine industry that has brought style and elegance to the town - just as it does to Epernay or Rheims - and along with that, employment and prosperity.

Saumur, 'the pearl of Anjou', is certainly one of the most attractive towns along the Loire valley. Dominated by its imposing, many-turreted castle, which stands four-square on a ridge high above the town, it is one of the relatively few towns on the banks of the Loire that actually takes advantage of its situation, with a splendid row of riverside buildings: the theatre, the Hôtel de Ville, the domed, fifteenth-century church of Notre-Dame des Ardilliers. Behind this imposing façade lies a delightful warren of tall, half-timbered buildings with pitched slate roofs, leaning towards each other above ancient streets – now, mercifully, mainly pedestrianized and a pleasure to walk in. Pavement cafés and boutiques show that this is not just another quiet French town, but an important tourist centre.

For a town whose name is associated with one of the most famous wines of the Loire, the existence of a thriving wine industry is not immediately obvious. There are no cellars, no tasting rooms in the centre of the town, despite the attractions of a captive tourist market. True, it is very easy to get a glass of sparkling Saumur in one of the many bars, and all the restaurants have a wide selection on offer. But to find where the wines are made you have to travel away from the town.

To reach the main Saumur cellars, you first have to pass Saumur's other claim to fame. That is the École Nationale d'Equitation, the national riding school with its famous troupe, the Cadre Noir. In imposing eighteenth-century buildings built around huge squares, the Cavalry School is full of mementoes to the glory of marshals and generals of the Cavalry that was still the pride of the French army at the beginning of the First World War.

And so you arrive at Saint-Hilaire-Saint-Florent, along the Rue Ackerman. The name of the road commemorates Jean Ackerman, who created Saumur sparkling wines at the beginning of the nineteenth century. He was a Belgian by birth but had worked for many years in Champagne, where he learnt the method of giving wine a secondary fermentation in the bottle. He arrived in Saumur, aware that the local wines were just as suitable for the same method. There he discovered that not only were the wines available, but also the cellars needed to store them. As in Touraine, the yellow tufa cliffs which line the river-bank at Saumur are riddled with caves from which building materials have been taken over the centuries. Here was the Loire equivalent of the *crayères* of Champagne.

The firm of Ackerman-Laurance was formed in 1811, in cellars in Saint-Hilaire-Saint-Florent. The company's name recognized the fact that Jean Ackerman had met and married Emilie Laurance, the daughter of a wealthy local banker: a marriage not only of love, but also of great convenience to Ackerman's plans.

Strangely, Ackerman-Laurance was for nearly forty years the only firm in Saumur to make sparkling wine. In those days, even in Champagne, the breakages resulting from unsuitable bottles were a costly business, and discouraging to other local wine-producers. But from the mid-nineteenth century onwards, other firms – Bouvet-Ladubay, Gratien et Meyer and a little later Veuve Amiot and Langlois-Chateau – were created. They too were mainly situated in Saint-Hilaire-Saint-Florent (although Gratien et Meyer decided to be different by setting up on the other side of Saumur), which quickly became a mini-Epernay and Rheims on the Loire.

For a long time – indeed, right up to 1919 – the producers in Saumur regarded their product as Champagne, and sold it quite openly as such. Ackerman-Laurance marketed 'Dry Royal Champagne, Finest Imported from Saumur' on the British market – an advertising slogan that would now send the Champenois, seething and frothing, straight round to their lawyers. At the same time, the Champenois saw nothing wrong in investing in Saumur; the house of Gratien et Meyer was always part of the same company as Alfred Gratien Champagne. It's a practice that has continued right up until today, with Langlois-Chateau being part of Bollinger and Bouvet-Ladubay part of Taittinger.

The companies still have their offices along the narrow Rue Ackerman. Courtyards open off this street, in which huge TIR lorries have to manoeuvre with their loads of bottles, and to which, after harvest-time, finished wine is brought from press houses in the vineyards for bottling and for the secondary fermentation. Many of the buildings, in pale yellow stone, are elegant, with big offices at the front where official business is done, and where tastings for the public or for visitors can be organized. The elegant style is not dissimilar to that of Champagne, since any sparkling wine seems to lend itself to public display.

The grapes and vineyards of Saumur

Behind this public façade lie cellars, bottling halls and computerized equipment. And behind them again lie the vineyards and the multiplicity of small growers who supply the Saumur houses with their grapes. For the producers own few vineyards, relying on a network of growers to supply either wine or, increasingly, grapes. These grapes can come from any of 93 *communes* spread across a wide area in the *départements* of Maine-et-Loire, Vienne and Deux-Sèvres. It is an area that stretches south from the Loire to Thouars and Montreuil-Bellay, west to Doué-la-Fontaine and east to Fontevraud-l'Abbaye, an area covering, in 1991, 1,457 hectares of vines.

The range of grapes that the growers can offer to the Saumur houses is wide: for white wine, there are the white varieties of Chenin Blanc, Chardonnay and Sauvignon Blanc (the last two up to a maximum of 20 per cent), plus (up to a maximum of 60 per cent) a range of red varieties, which are all permitted for rosé: Cabernet Franc, Cabernet Sauvignon, Cot, Gamay, Pinot Noir,

Grolleau and Pineau d'Aunis. In effect, most sparkling white Saumur is now a blend of Chenin and Chardonnay with some Cabernet Franc.

Production of Saumur Mousseux, sparkling Saumur – or, as it is now called in all the publicity, Saumur d'Origine – averages 91,000 hectolitres a year. In 1992 it was 120,000 hectolitres, but in 1991 it was well below average at 64,000 hectolitres. Of this production, by far the greater part – up to 80 per cent – is made by the houses, the big brand owners, the equivalent of the Champagne houses. Much of the remainder is produced by the co-operative of Saint-Cyr-en-Bourg, and mostly sold under labels of convenience to supermarkets around France and Europe. Only a tiny proportion – one or two per cent – is made and sold by growers.

The houses have long-term contracts with roughly 550 growers who send grapes to the press houses that have been established in the vineyards. There, as in Champagne, there are different pressings: Cuvée, Premier Taille, Deuxième Taille and a final pressing called locally Rebêche. Limits for the quantities produced by each pressing are one hectolitre of must per 150 kilos of grapes. Yields for Saumur d'Origine wines are restricted to 60 hectolitres per hectare, giving an average alcohol of 10.5 per cent and a maximum of 13 per cent before the addition of any dosage at final bottling. Prices for grapes, though, are still ridiculously cheap: in 1990 the price was 5 francs per kilo (compared with 30 francs a kilo in Champagne), and 6.30 francs per litre for *vin clair*, the finished wine.

Saumur d'Origine is made using exactly the same method as for Champagne. It is no longer permitted to describe this as the 'Champagne method' – which is why the phrase Saumur d'Origine was invented – but that is precisely what it is. Today, the first fermentation normally takes place in stainless-steel tanks, although one house – Bouvet-Ladubay – is using barrels for fermenting part of its top *cuvée*. The wine is then bottled with the addition of yeast, and a secondary fermentation takes place in the bottle.

To remove the dead yeast cells from the bottle after the second fermentation, the practice – as in Champagne – was to carry out a riddling process, gradually turning the bottles until their necks point directly downwards and the yeast cells form a small lump in the neck. Traditionally this was done on wooden racks called *pupitres*, or desks, with holes into which the bottle was placed. Today, however, the bottles are normally put into big metal cages called *gyrasols* which can twist and turn semi-automatically by adjusting the angle of the base, which is on something that looks like a huge hinge. This process of *remuage automatique* was developed at the firm of Bouvet-Ladubay by the director Patrice Monmousseau and is now widely found throughout the Saumur houses. The *pupitres* are still kept for show, though, because they are more romantic than metal cages.

After the *remuage* is complete, the dried yeast is removed by freezing the neck of the bottle and opening it to allow the lump of ice to pop out under pressure. Then there is the addition of what is called *liqueur d'expedition*, which consists of wine and sugar to sweeten the often too-dry wine. The bottles are then recorked with the typical sparkling wine cork, shaped rather like a toadstool. Under the rules of the *appellation*, the bottles then have to be stored *sur lattes*, on their sides, for nine months before they can be sold.

This classic method is the one practised by all the houses, and is the only one permitted for wines labelled Saumur. There used to be a business in sparkling wine made by injecting carbon dioxide into tanks of wine – the *cuve close* method – but although before the Second World War this accounted for 40 per cent of Saumur's business, and even as recently as the 1950s a million bottles a year were produced in this way, today it is no longer made.

Jean Ackerman's company still exists in its premises in Saint-Hilaire-Saint-Florent. Now Ackerman-Laurance is associated with the *négociant* Rémy-Pannier and with the brand of De Neuville, whose premises are next door; the largest wine firm in the Loire valley, it has interests stretching right through Touraine, Anjou and the Pays Nantais.

The Ackerman-Laurance cellars are typical of the wine cellars of Saumur: seven kilometres of tunnels and caves lined with maturing bottles. Every so often, clanks and crashes indicate bottles being moved, while in the distance there is the hum of modern cooling equipment maintaining the temperature of wine still in store in stainless-steel tanks. By contrast, the firm's modern cellars at Chacé, to the south of Saumur, are where the wines are disgorged, at the rate of 8,500 an hour and where bottling takes place on highly-automated lines.

The wines produced in these cellars are mainly of the 1811 Brut, or dry – a term used in Saumur as in Champagne. A new superior *cuvée*, Jean Baptiste, has 20 per cent Chardonnay. The *brut* accounts for about 80 per cent of production, the remainder being *demi-sec*. Sadly, the quality of what is produced by the oldest and still the largest – six million bottles a year – of Saumur houses has not kept pace with the changes in other firms.

Gratien et Meyer is the exception among Saumur wine producers, since its cellars and offices are not in Saint-Hilaire-Saint-Florent. If you approach Saumur from the direction of Chinon and Montsoreau, driving along the banks of the Loire, just before you arrive in the town you will see a huge, white 1920s building apparently stuck to the side of the cliff-face. This is Gratien et Meyer. It is the only firm in Saumur to have had a permanent link with a Champagne house, since it was founded in 1864 by Alfred Gratien, who also set up the Champagne firm which today bears his name. The Meyer part of the name was the result of a partnership with Jean Meyer, and today the firm is run by the Seydoux family, descendants of M. Meyer on his daughter's side.

Gratien et Meyer is the only major Saumur house to own a substantial quantity of vineyards – 25 hectares, representing 10 per cent of its requirements – for its sparkling wines. They also need to buy in grapes, which go to the Centre Pressurage du Val de Loire, the pressing station at Le Puy-Notre-Dame which is jointly owned with Ackerman-Laurance and Veuve Amiot. In total, they make 1.8 million bottles a year, which are stored in six miles of caves and kept there for between eighteen months and two years (compared with the legal minimum of nine months).

The top Gratien et Meyer wine is Cuvée Flame, a blend of Chenin Blanc and Cabernet Franc with a little Chardonnay, a rich, full wine that has only a slight hint of hardness from the Chenin when it is young. The standard *cuvées* are Brut and Demi-Sec. The Brut is light and easy to drink, and the Demi-Sec takes advantage of the honeyed flavours of Chenin Blanc to balance these with a little acidity. A more acquired taste is the red sparkling Cardinal, made from Cabernet Franc, slightly sweet, whose big advantage is that it makes a splendid accompaniment to chocolate.

Saumur pace-setter

The company that has really set the pace in Saumur is Bouvet-Ladubay. Since the arrival of Patrice Monmousseau, scion of a

Tourangelle family long dedicated to wine, Bouvet has acted as the pioneer as well as the stylistic leader among the wine houses of the Rue Ackerman. In addition to making exemplary wines, they have created a museum of modern art and have renovated a miniature theatre which occupies the first floor of one of the houses in Rue Ackerman. They also sponsor racing cars in the Le Mans 24-hour race. And they have fine blue and silver horse-drawn carriages which journey around the streets of Saumur. They believe that, for sparkling wines, promotion and public relations are an essential part of selling. As a result they have the highest profile of all the Saumur houses.

Patrice Monmousseau's office in Saint-Hilaire-Saint-Florent is large, with panelled walls and a wide, tidy desk dominated by calculators. Panelled doors open on to a conference room, and the windows look out on a courtyard. Across the courtyard is a large public reception room, laid out rather like a winter garden with plants and white furniture; here, tourists and groups come to taste the range of wines. Upstairs, if they are lucky, they will be shown the collection of old Bouvet labels – 8,000 different designs – housed in a collection of huge wooden filing cabinets that swing out on runners.

The production of Bouvet-Ladubay, since 1974 part of the Taittinger Champagne group, is around two million bottles a year. They only buy grapes from growers, but instead of taking the grapes to pressing houses, they press the grapes at the growers' cellars. This, according to M. Monmousseau, is to ensure the complete freshness of the wine. It also means they have a myriad of different *cuvées*, which allows for great flexibility in blending.

The wines produced under the Bouvet name do seem to live up to the promotional hype that goes with them. The basic Bouvet Brut is crisper and fresher than many other Saumur wines, while its companion Rosé has a slight hint of weight and tannin. More interesting, of course, are the prestige *cuvées*: Saphir, a vintage wine made almost entirely from Chenin Blanc, whose just honeyed flavours turn it from being quite aggressive when young into something much richer, balancing honey and apples, when mature.

The top *cuvée* is Trésor, which is packaged in an antique-shaped bottle with a stylish label and plenty of understated gold foil. This wine is unique in Saumur: it is a blend of Chardonnay and Chenin Blanc, and part of its fermentation and a short maturation before bottling take place in Tronçais oak casks. When I first tasted it in 1991, the wood and the Chardonnay dominated the wine initially – and it was too early to say whether the Chenin flavours would emerge. Later tastings have suggested that the Chenin appears to lift and lighten the wine, giving it great freshness but with more weight than other Saumur wines. Aged for three years in bottle – compared with the minimum legal requirement of nine months – and with a limited production of 30,000 bottles a year, Trésor is obviously intended to remain seriously exclusive.

Patrice Monmousseau is a great enthusiast for the wines of Saumur. He is delighted that the phrase *méthode champenoise* has been banned for all sparkling wines outside Champagne: 'Bouvet is older than 80 per cent of Champagne houses – we've just as much tradition here. I would much prefer to call my wines *méthode traditionelle*.' He is also somewhat cynical about the success of Champagne: 'The Champenois live in such a desolate place that all they can do is work to sell their wine.' And he is optimistic for the future of Saumur: 'We are waking up. We forgot about techniques and relied on tradition. Tradition brought the price down and it needed a new approach.' If M. Monmousseau represents that new approach – and despite local consternation at some of his methods, there is also grudging respect for the wines he is making – then Saumur sparkling wines do have a future.

Saumur's wine widow

Tradition still appears to reign supreme at one of M. Monmousseau's near neighbours, Veuve Amiot. With their pale wood panelling and fusty, linoleumed corridors, and the apparently complete absence of computers, the offices exist in a time-warp. This is somewhat surprising, since Veuve Amiot and its associated company Compagnie Française des Grands Vins are actually part of the Italian vermouth and sparkling wine producer Martini e Rossi.

As its name suggests, the company was for a long time dominated by one of wine's famous widows. As with La Veuve Clicquot in Champagne, La Veuve Amiot's husband died young, and in 1884, two years after his death, she set up cellars in Saint-Hilaire-Saint-Florent ready to sell her wines to the world. The family continued in ownership until the sale to Martini in 1971.

Despite appearances, though, technical innovation is in the wind here. Technical director Teddy Savary – his first name is not a diminutive, he assured me, but the whole thing – told me how they are able to cut down on the quantities of sulphur dioxide by using a yeast which encourages an automatic malolactic fermentation before the blending of the wine. They have also improved the filtration so as to cut down on the amount needed. The quality of the wines has certainly improved in the ten years since I first tasted them.

Veuve Amiot makes three million bottles a year. They do not have vineyards, buying grapes which are taken to their pressing houses at Mesure and Chacé. Two-thirds of their production is of a Brut, mainly Chenin Blanc with 15 per cent Cabernet Franc, a wine which undergoes the statutory nine months in bottle before sale. Any longer, M. Savary believes, and the wine would lose the freshness which is its most important characteristic.

Cuvée Réserve, their superior non-vintage *cuvée*, has some Chardonnay and Sauvignon Blanc as well as Cabernet Franc in the blend, and is a much fuller wine, very fruity and ready for some bottle ageing. The top of the range is Haute Tradition, a Blanc de Blancs with 10 per cent Chardonnay and 90 per cent Chenin Blanc. The 1986, with plenty of years under its belt, was delightfully perfumed and had developed an attractive honeyed character.

The Veuve Amiot belief, as set out for me by M. Savary, is that the name Saumur is an important asset. He likes the idea of making a sparkling wine which, like Champagne, comes from a tight geographical area. Which brings him into direct conflict with the view of one of his neighbours in Rue Ackerman, the firm of Langlois-Chateau.

The big success and small failure of Crémant de Loire

It was over lunch in the cellars of Langlois-Chateau that M. de Montgolfier, the director, explained to me why his company had abandoned production of Saumur d'Origine. It was because of the controls, he said. The *appellation* of Crémant de Loire was created in 1975, to control not just sparkling wines that could be made in Saumur but also those from other parts of Touraine and Anjou. They are therefore blended wines from across a wide region of the Loire Valley, meaning that any geographical links are diminished.

What is not diminished, though, is the quality of the *crémants* that have been made. For a start, they have a much higher percentage of classic Champagne grapes, Chardonnay and Pinot Noir. Then the yields have to be much lower than with Saumur: 50 hectolitres per hectare compared with 60 for Saumur. Harvesting must be by hand, allowing whole berries to be sent to the presses. The minimum bottle ageing period is also longer, one year compared with the nine months for Saumur.

All this should be encouraging quality-conscious producers to make Crémant de Loire instead of Saumur. But it has been slow to take off: compared with the 120,000 hectolitres of Saumur made in 1992, only 22,000 hectolitres of Crémant de Loire were made. And compared with 1,457 hectares under vine for Saumur, only 381 hectares were under vine for Crémant de Loire.

There is much argument in the offices along the Rue Ackerman about the relative merits of Saumur and Crémant de Loire. While M. Savary of Veuve Amiot and M. Monmousseau of Bouvet-Ladubay both believe in the name of Saumur, there is M. Montgolfier of Langlois-Chateau arguing for Crémant de Loire. Outside Saumur, of course, there is less argument: in Vouvray, Montlouis and Touraine – all of which could produce Crémant de Loire instead of sparkling wines bearing the local *appellation* – there is scant interest, but in Anjou, where there is no reputable *appellation* for sparkling wine, *crémants* have been a considerable success. At Les Caves de la Loire in the heart of Anjou (a co-operative we will visit in greater detail in Chapter 14), Crémant de Loire is an important part of the range, as it is for a smaller grower such as Domaine Richou, also in Anjou. For them, it is a chance they never had before to make a quality sparkling wine under an *appellation*.

To return to the Rue Ackerman and to Langlois-Chateau. This is a much smaller firm than Ackerman-Laurance, Bouvet-Ladubay, or Veuve Amiot; about 500,000 bottles of Crémant de Loire now represents their entire production of sparkling wine. They also produce still wines, acting as both *négociant* and vineyard owner (with 30 hectares), from all regions of the Loire from Muscadet to Sancerre, as well as making still Saumur wines from their own vineyards. Their still wine estates include the eight-hectare Château de Fontaine-Audon in Sancerre, the 11-hectare Domaine de Grand' Maison in Muscadet and the Domaine de Langlois-Chateau in Saumur.

The sparkling Crémant de Loire is a blend of 60 per cent Chenin

Blanc, 25 per cent Cabernet Franc and 15 per cent Chardonnay and Groslot. After disgorgement, it spends two years in bottle (twice the legal minimum), and although each *cuvée* of Crémant de Loire produced by Langlois-Chateau does not bear a vintage date, most is from three years before release. I found the wine full, rich and much creamier than some of the Saumur wines I had tasted from other houses. As the wine ages – witness a vintage 1985 Langlois Crémant tasted in 1991 – the taste of Chenin tends to become more pronounced.

Touraine, Vouvray and other sparklers

While Saumur is the major Loire centre for sparkling wines, the natural acidity and lightness of many other Loire wines lend themselves to bubbles. In Touraine, for example, at the town of Montrichard on the river Cher, there are the cellars of J. M. Monmousseau, formerly linked with Bouvet-Ladubay of Saumur and now owned by the Brédut family of Château Moncontour in Vouvray; they produce a range of sparkling wines by the classic method, of which the top *cuvée* is Brut Mosny, a blend of Chenin Blanc, Pinot Meunier, Sauvignon Blanc and Chardonnay, the permitted varieties for sparkling Touraine wines.

Production is comparatively small within the context of the whole *appellation*: in 1992, 10,000 hectolitres of white Touraine sparkling wine were made, representing 2.5 per cent of total Touraine production, along with 3,000 hectolitres of rosé. But the creation of a separate *appellation* for sparkling Touraine in 1974 offered a lifeline to growers who were unable to sell their Chenin Blanc for still wines.

Other Loire sparkling wines come from Vouvray and Montlouis, from producers we have already met in the chapters on those *appellations*. The brand of Blanc Foussy is made in cellars on the banks of the Loire at Rochecorbon just outside Vouvray, which are certainly the most visible for visitors arriving from Tours.

The still wines of Saumur and Saumur-Champigny

Drive east or south of Saumur and the land quickly rises to a level plateau, punctuated by occasional streams. It is not exciting countryside, but the sense of wide open spaces is typical of the surrounds of the Loire. Roads are straight, hedges are few, trees are in scattered copses or stand alone at random. In winter, it is bare and barren; in summer, it is dotted with vines and vegetables, often in small plots, sometimes in large fields.

This is the region of the vineyards of Saumur. It is a large area, covering up to fifty-five *communes*, which can supply grapes for the sparkling Saumur d'Origine (see Chapter 11). But the same region, in more restricted form, also supplies grapes for still Saumur white and red, and for the rarer rosé Cabernet de Saumur and sweet white Coteaux de Saumur. And in one privileged corner to the east of Saumur, in vineyards on cliffs bordering the Loire, where the terrain undulates into sharp, secret valleys, is the *appellation* of Saumur-Champigny.

This is one of the most concentrated and one of the largest viticultural areas of the Loire. Between them, the *appellations* of still Saumur (that is, excluding sparkling wine) in 1992 produced 153,274 hectolitres of wine, divided into 41,323 hectolitres of Saumur Rouge, 32,501 hectolitres of Saumur Blanc, 75,446 hectolitres of Saumur-Champigny, 3,945 hectolitres of Cabernet de Saumur, and a mere 59 hectolitres of Coteaux de Saumur. The averages for the decade from 1980 to 1990 were as follows: Saumur Rouge 26,215 hectolitres, Saumur Blanc 27,424 hectolitres, Saumur-Champigny 49,078 hectolitres, Cabernet de Saumur 2,329 hectolitres, and Coteaux de Saumur 308 hectolitres. These figures show that 1992 was a bumper year for red and dry white

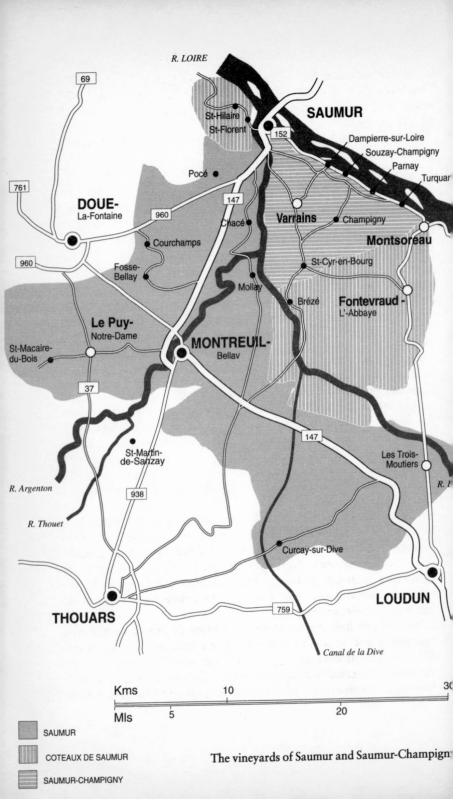

R. LOIRE

69

761

DOUE-
La-Fontaine

960

960

St-Macaire-
du-Bois

37

Le Puy-
Notre-Dame

938

R. Argenton

R. Thouet

St-Martin-
de-Sanzay

THOUARS

St-Hilaire
St-Florent

Pocé

147

Chacé

Courchamps

Fosse-
Bellay

Mollay

MONTREUIL-
Bellav

SAUMUR

152

Dampierre-sur-Loire
Souzay-Champigny
Parnay
Turquar

Varrains   Champigny

Montsoreau

St-Cyr-en-Bourg

Brézé

Fontevraud -
L'-Abbaye

147

Les Trois-
Moutiers

R. I

Curcay-sur-Dive

759

LOUDUN

Canal de la Dive

Kms   10   30

Mls   5   20

SAUMUR

COTEAUX DE SAUMUR

SAUMUR-CHAMPIGNY

The vineyards of Saumur and Saumur-Champign

wines, but a disaster for the sweeter wines like Coteaux de Saumur. They also show that the volume of Saumur-Champigny produced has greatly increased during the decade, from 42,904 in 1983 to 75,446 in 1992.

Those statistics reflect the proportion of the vineyard devoted to each *appellation*. The average in the years from 1983 to 1992 was: 525 hectares for Saumur Rouge, 478 hectares for Saumur Blanc, 864 hectares for Saumur-Champigny, 47 hectares for Cabernet de Saumur and 20 hectares for Coteaux de Saumur. In 1991–2 the figures were: Saumur Rouge 757 hectares, Saumur Blanc 518 hectares, Saumur-Champigny 1,057 hectares, Cabernet de Saumur 24 hectares, and Coteaux de Saumur one hectare.

Saumur-Champigny: co-operative success

To reach Saumur-Champigny, you take the road out of Saumur along the south bank of the river, past the church of Nôtre-Dame des Ardilliers and the cellars of the sparkling Saumur producer Gratien et Meyer. The tufa cliffs get closer and closer to the river, leaving space for little more than the road, the occasional riverside caravan park and a single line of buildings which often abuts right up against the cliffs. It's sometimes difficult to tell where buildings end and cliffs begin, since both are made of the same gleaming, off-white stone; some houses, known as *maisons troglodytes*, actually have rooms within the cliff itself.

Saumur-Champigny begins as the road enters the village of Dampierre-sur-Loire. For me, this village is memorable because of its restaurant – more a bar with a lean-to which houses a few tables where you can eat the cheapest, and one of the best, *steack frites* in this part of France. You can also drink an equally memorable red house wine, fruity, hinting at vanilla and truffles, bursting with colour. This is Saumur-Champigny, from the Cave des Vignerons de Saumur at Saint-Cyr-en-Bourg. This was not my first introduction to Saumur-Champigny, but it was the first time I had tasted the wines of the co-operative.

It is rare to base a tour of an *appellation* in France on the co-operative. But Saint-Cyr-en-Bourg is no ordinary co-operative. Since its inception in 1957 it has led the way in Saumur; it has virtually re-created the *appellation* of Saumur-Champigny and has supplied countless bottles of sparkling Saumur to supermarkets and wine merchants around Europe. From a mere fifty members at its start it now has 300, who between them control more than 1,000 hectares in twenty-eight *communes*.

The installation on the edge of the village of Saint-Cyr-en-Bourg is as impressive as the statistics. Two enormous craters in the ground, 25 metres deep, give on to seven kilometres of galleries dug into the tufa. They were used by US servicemen during the Second World War, and from then until 1991 they were used to house the wine-making and storage facilities. Everything was run on gravity: grapes were received at the top, de-stalked at the next level, pressed at the next, fermented at the next. A few months later, the resulting wine reached the bottom level, where it was bottled.

Gravity is still used in the new installation: a gentle slope goes down to a huge pressing hall, and is followed by an equally large chamber full of Vinimatic fermenters, Australian machines designed to extract maximum colour from red wines while avoiding too much tannin. A forest of 1,000-hectolitre stainless-steel tanks is used for storage and fermentation of white wines. And, just as before, the bottom level is the bottling hall, where 12,000 bottles an hour can be filled.

It is all enormous – and impressive. The fact that it also turns out some excellent wine is a bonus which does not invariably follow from having the most modern installations. A sign of its success is that the co-operative exports more than 40 per cent of its production, generally under private labels rather than its own name. Wines cover the whole spectrum of Saumur *appellations*, from sparkling wine to two prestige *cuvées* of red: Cuvée du Conseil, a Saumur Rouge, and Cuvée du Président, a Saumur-Champigny.

The co-operative, under its inspirational director Marcel Neau (whose brother Régis runs Domaine de Nerleux, a 40-hectare Saumur-Champigny property also in Saint-Cyr-en-Bourg), has been instrumental in creating the modern fortunes of Saumur-Champigny. From being a minor *appellation* making lightweight red wines, it has shot into prominence as a source of fresh, early-maturing red wines that have for a period been all the rage in Paris restaurants, often drunk with fish and generally served slightly chilled.

As an *appellation* Saumur-Champigny is only twenty years old. But the wine is, of course, much older than that. The name Champigny comes from the Latin *campus ignis*, 'field of fire', a reference to the particularly warm microclimate of this small area. It was recorded by Cyrus Redding in 1860 as a mere local curiosity ('a quantity of red is made at Champigny but does not go out of the *département*'), and Jullien in 1816 was even more dismissive ('red wines from Saumur are small in quality, the best coming from Champigne-le-sec [*sic*] near Saumur'). Curiously enough, its current reputation as a *vin de Pâques*, one that can be drunk in the Easter following the vintage, is relatively new. Writing in the 1950s, Pierre Bréjoux says that 'after a year or two in wood, the wines have to be kept in bottles for two to three years, and they keep very well'. It is obvious from this remark that the change to modern vinification methods, the use of stainless-steel tanks rather than wooden barrels, has wrought a change of character in the wines, allowing them to be drunk quickly – although it is also true that they can still age well.

Nine *communes* can produce Saumur-Champigny, all of them lying on the plateau bordering the Loire to the east of the town of Saumur. Parts of Saumur itself are within the *appellation*, and then the line of villages along the Loire: Dampierre-sur-Loire (and the hamlet of Chaintres), Souzay-Champigny, Parnay, Turquant – clusters of houses tumbling down the steep sides of the little side valleys that break up the cliff-face. On the borders of Maine-et-Loire and Indre-et-Loire is the château town of Montsoreau which marks the eastern end of the *appellation*. On the plateau south-east of Saumur are the villages of Varrains, Chacé and the home of the co-operative, Saint-Cyr-en-Bourg.

A narrow road runs the length of the plateau from near Fontevraud-l'Abbaye, home to the magnificent royal abbey, back to Saumur, passing through the main vineyards of the *appellation*, which are planted with Cabernet Franc and a small amount of Cabernet Sauvignon. The road undulates down into the little side valleys and up again. The spires of the village churches stick up above the tops of the cliffs. Looking back to the east, the lower land of Touraine stretches off into the distance.

Apart from the co-operative, many Saumur-Champigny producers have their cellars in the cliffs facing the Loire. Most prominent of these are the four turrets of the Château de Targé, which stands on a platform in front of the cliff, looking out over the Loire at Parnay. It has been the home of the Pisani-Ferry family since

1655, when it was used as a hunting lodge by one of Louis XIV's secretaries.

The current owner, Edouard Pisani-Ferry, has been in charge for the past fifteen years. He and his large dog welcomed me in the courtyard of the château, whose four sides consist of a cliff face, a sheer drop down to the road beside the Loire, and two pavilions. He told me how little-known Saumur-Champigny was when he took over: 'There was just us and Château de Chaintres which were known, and suddenly it's shot up.' We talked about the vineyard: there are two types of soil in Saumur-Champigny, the soil of the slopes of the cliff – the *côte* – which is chalky, and the soil of the plateau, which is more sandy. The chalk gives wines with elegance, the plateau wines which are more rounded. Château de Targé's 20 hectares of vineyard are mainly on the slope, giving a shape and structure to the wines. Structure is also provided by the 10 per cent of Cabernet Sauvignon which is blended with the Cabernet Franc.

We scrambled along a steep path that leads up behind the château. Without warning, our heads popped up over the edge of the cliff and there was a smart new vinification plant, gleaming with stainless steel and modern presses. M. Pisani-Ferry was eager to show me his new – I won't use the word toy, but it is obviously something he is very enthusiastic about. As we stood in the middle of the new building, M. Pisani-Ferry told me about his production methods. He uses both manual and mechanical harvesting on his land, keeping the manual work for young and very old vines. He believes that it is possible – if the driver of the harvesting machine is experienced – to go through the vineyard a number of times getting grapes at their ripest. To protect them he uses small wicker baskets. To keep the grapes whole while destalking, he uses a slow-moving screw.

During vinification, which lasts between twelve and fifteen days, the fermenting juice is regularly pumped over the cap of skins that forms on top of the must. Initially, the temperature is kept low by a cooling system on the outside of the stainless-steel tanks, but for the last few days of fermentation the temperature is taken up to 30° C in order to extract tannin and colour: 'I like a little tannin in my wine. I don't want it to fall down when I eat cheese.'

'Some of my wines can be hard when young. So to soften them I put a proportion into wood, which gives richness and roundness.

But I don't want too much – after all, Saumur-Champigny is all about charm, chic and esprit.'

Then we tasted. He only makes one wine, carefully defining why: 'I think there is a tendency for people to make too many different wines. I now prefer to follow the practice in Bordeaux, of making one *grand vin* and then declassifying, rather than making a basic wine and small quantities of a *vieilles vignes*.'

From tank – this was 1991 – I tasted the 1990 with its intense, almost purple colour, enormous fruit and young, earthy flavours. There was not much tannin and what there was was sweet, a product of what has proved to be a marvellous year in Saumur-Champigny. The 1989 too, which we tasted next, back in the cellars beside the château, had oodles of ripe fruit. There was more perfume on this wine, the dusty, slightly nutty sort of perfume. At two years old it was ready to drink, but there was tannin there to keep it going 'for at least three or four years', said M. Pisani-Ferry.

That these wines can mature was proved as we moved down the line. There was a 1987, from a leaner year, quite dry to taste, lighter in colour, but still with good balance. And there was a 1986 – nearly six years old at this point – which had mushrooms and strawberries combining with a heady perfume to make a wine that, while mature, is certainly not old.

I tasted still older Saumur-Champigny when I visited Philippe Vatan the next day. The Vatan family cellars of the Domaine du Hureau are cut into the rock face just above my favourite restaurant in Dampierre-sur-Loire. They were humming with activity when I arrived: it was the day the bottling lorry arrived. These huge pantechnicons are regular visitors to estates too small to purchase the sort of high-tech bottling line required today; the lorries, whose sides open out to reveal a bottling line inside, can be hired on a daily basis.

Today, Saumur Blanc was being bottled. Since there is no white Saumur-Champigny, any white a producer may make is treated as Saumur Blanc. There are, of course, Saumur Blancs and Saumur Blancs: some can reveal the worst characteristics of Chenin Blanc. This one, from the 1990 vintage, showed in its richness more the characteristics of Chardonnay. Because of the quality of the year, Philippe Vatan had put the wine into a tank still full of the lees of the sweet *moelleux* he was also making: a somewhat unorthodox move, it was also a very successful one, bringing out a delicious honeyed element and making a splendidly ripe wine.

That was a *bonne bouche* because, of course, the serious business was Saumur-Champigny. The family has 13 hectares of Cabernet Franc plus 3 hectares of Chenin Blanc, and Philippe is now in charge of the wine-making. That he is so successful is a remarkable tribute, since when he took over in 1987 he claims to have known nothing about wine (a claim I find hard to believe from one who grew up in a *vigneron*'s family, but one which is typically modest). He was only shoved into the wine-making role because of the tragic death of his brother in a car accident.

We walked into the huge, cavern-like cellar in the cliff. A big central chamber leads to little side chambers, some with stores of bottles, others with stainless-steel tanks purpose built to fit the variously-shaped spaces. We first tasted wines from tank, and it was quickly obvious that the Vatan style is chunky, concentrated, unlike the more elegant, restrained style at Château de Targé. A 1990 from old vines was powerful, rich in colour, intense with piles of fruit and tannins. After twenty-one days' maceration on the skins, so it should be.

From the tanks, we moved to bottles. They make two styles of Saumur-Champigny at Domaine du Hureau: one a standard *cuvée*, one from old vines. I tasted the 1989 of both *cuvées*: the standard wine was ripe, with a pleasant earthy perfume; the *vieilles vignes* more tannic, firmer, hinting at a perfume of vanilla rather than truffles. Then we moved back in time as, with a flourish, M. Vatan produced a dusty bottle. It was time for guessing games as the wine was poured. Colour very bright, still young. Palate with some fruit tannin, delicious ripe perfumes, concentrated in the house style. I hazard a guess: mid-1980s? There was a twinkle; no, this was 1981, a wine made by Vatan *père*, showing that with concentration a Saumur-Champigny can survive remarkably well.

There was a final wine to taste before we left. A Coteaux de Saumur was produced, that rare sweet wine of Saumur made from Chenin Blanc and really only produced, even in small quantities, in years when the weather conditions are propitious: warm with long, sunny autumns. As any student of Loire wines will know by now, 1990 was such a year, and this *moelleux* with its sweetness, taste of quince and its hints of botrytis proved the point. Even here, the house style of concentration was in evidence: part of the grapes were macerated as whole bunches to give extra flavour, something that shone out of this delicious wine – one which, as M. Vatan admitted, is unlikely to be repeated for many years.

From the Vatan cellars, it was but a short drive up to the top of the plateau and the hamlet of Chaintres. Here are situated two of the most famous names in Saumur-Champigny: Château de Chaintres and Domaine Filliatreau. I had but a brief moment at both because my visit, organized in advance but subsequently forgotten, coincided with the absence of both owners.

I went to Château de Chaintres first. In his book *The Loire Valley and its Wines*, James Seely paints a glowing picture of the château with its 'sun-warmed stone façade'. It certainly is a charming building, whose history goes back to the sixteenth century. It has had a mixed existence, having been the property of royal counsellors and religious fathers before coming to the present owners, the de Tigny family, in the late 1930s.

The vineyard of 15 hectares is enclosed within a wall, a rare and beautiful sight. Methods of vinification are still relatively traditional, and the resulting wine is satisfyingly concentrated and firm, obviously destined for an extended life. I had a chance to taste the 1990 in tank and it was huge, hard as nails and dominated by big tannins and serious fruit. Nothing could have been further from the role-model of Saumur-Champigny as a light restaurant wine.

If Domaine Filliatreau is more in that role, that is no criticism. The *domaine*, the largest in Saumur-Champigny with 39 hectares of vines – supplemented by the purchase of further grapes – is situated in a disjointed courtyard, one side a pleasant stone building housing offices, the other a modern metal shed where the wine is made. I was shown round by Mme Filliatreau senior, who made much of the fact that her grandchildren are now in the business.

They make, she told me, three *cuvées* of Saumur-Champigny as well as a little white Saumur Blanc. The first Saumur-Champigny is a normal *cuvée* from young vines which spends no time in wood, and is just right for those Paris restaurants since it can easily – and pleasantly – be drunk young. The Vieilles Vignes – the vines are at least fifty years old – is another proposition: still made only in tanks, it nevertheless has full fruit, perfume and concentration, along with tannins. And then there is the Cuvée Lena Filliatreau, named after Paul Filliatreau's wife (I was talking to her mother-in-law), a wine that comes from the chalk soil of the *côte* rather than the sandy soil of the plateau, and which spends eight months in wood, developing serious tannins and elegant fruit. It is a wine that shows the ageing side of Saumur-Champigny.

Saumur Blanc and Rouge

Considering how much Saumur Blanc and Rouge are produced, it is surprising how little of it is of more than average quality. It is also understandable, from tasting much of the still white from poor years, why sparkling Saumur is such a useful way of disposing of unripe grapes.

The reason is, of course, that away from the microclimate of Saumur-Champigny the climate of the Saumur hinterland is a difficult one in which to ripen grapes on a regular basis. The largest part of the vineyard is laid out along the slopes of two river valleys: the Thouet, which flows into the Loire just west of Saumur, and its tributary the Dive. Between the Thouet and the Loire is the most concentrated and best area – part of it is Saumur-Champigny, the rest is the source of what little Coteaux de Saumur is made. The valley of the Dive forms a separate area, flowing to the east of Montreuil-Bellay and on into the *département* of Vienne. A third section of vineyard is found on the west bank of the Thouet, centred on the village of Le Puy-Notre-Dame. In all, there are thirty-eight *communes* in three *départements*, Maine-et-Loire, Deux-Sèvres and Vienne.

Soils in the region are flint and sand by turns, quite shallow, rather exposed. On the whole the white wines, made from Chenin Blanc with a little Chardonnay and Sauvignon Blanc, come from the flinty, chalky soils and the reds, made from Cabernet Franc and a little Cabernet Sauvignon and Pineau d'Aunis, come from the limestone.

It is near Le Puy-Notre-Dame, the largest wine *commune* in Saumur, that I found one of the more interesting producers of the region, Domaine de la Renière. Owned by René Hugues-Gay, it is an old family estate that has been handed down from father to son since 1536. All the first sons have been called René – hence the punning name Renière. The current René has installed modern presses, stainless steel and mechanical harvesting, but has accompanied these innovations with a great attention to detail and low yields in the vineyard.

I found his reds more interesting than his whites, although both are good. Whites are made without chaptalization if possible, and in a year like 1990, where sugar levels were naturally so high, his approach has produced a deliciously fresh, ripe wine, full of nutty, creamy fruit and a hint of super-ripe grapes. M. Hugues-Gay makes two red *cuvées*, a Vieilles Vignes – the 1990 light, fresh, lightly-perfumed but not very exciting – and a much more interesting Cuvée Prestige which is aged in wood for up to eighteen months. A 1986, tasted in 1991, showed good style and fruit, plus firm tannins and little sign of maturity – a close relation to a good Saumur-Champigny.

On the other side of the *appellation*, in the village of Brézé on the eastern bank of the Dive, is the Renaissance Château de Brézé, family home of the Colbert family. They have 24 hectares – 13 of Chenin Blanc, 2 of Chardonnay and 9 of Cabernet Franc – on limestone and sand soils. Modernity is the watchword here: controlled fermentation at low temperatures for the whites, the use of Vinimatics to give colour to the reds, followed by ten months' ageing in wood.

Again, it is the reds which stand out more. The whites are in a modern style but no more, while the reds have a designed elegance, a restraint, and good fruit and wood balance. I tasted a 1990 which had all this plus good weight. It was, in its way, almost like a lightweight Bordeaux – perhaps hardly surprising, since the Colberts also own Château Saint-Ahon in the Médoc.

Apart from these two estates – and the excellent example of the co-operative at Saint-Cyr-en-Bourg – there are only flashes of excitement in this vast area of vineyard. There are the reds of Clos de l'Abbaye in Le Puy-Notre-Dame, the property of François Aupy, proud possessor of eleven kilometres of caves. There is a delicious Saumur Blanc from Château de Montreuil-Bellay, whose wines are worth tasting anyway just for the chance of getting the view of the château on its cliff from across the bridge over the river Thouet.

And there are the still wines of the Saumur-based sparkling wine producer Langlois-Chateau. A white 1989, tasted in 1991, showed good concentration from the maceration of the whole bunches in the fermenting juice; a red, made from old vines planted in the village of Bron on the west bank of the Thouet, is aged in large wooden barrels and develops a good perfumed taste with two or three years of ageing.

13

The wines of Anjou

Name a wine style, and you will find it in Anjou. From the driest white wine, through pale rosés which can be dry or sweet, and reds which are generally lightweight but can occasionally have some power, to the sublimest sweet whites – they are all there, grown in confusion and profusion. If much of what is made is of no more than average quality, the surprise is that in the middle of this chaos of *appellations* and vineyards, there are to be found so many nuggets of greatness.

Anjou is the name of the province centred on the city of Angers. Covering the whole of the *département* of Maine-et-Loire, stretching from the borders of Touraine in the east to the Pays Nantais in the west, it is a large region, much of it devoted to cereal and other crops. Apart from places like Saumur – which is technically Anjou, although in wine terms treated separately – most of Anjou's few major towns lie away from the Loire. To the south, there is Cholet, a large agricultural centre whose main purpose seems to be to hold up passing travellers in interminable traffic jams. Angers itself lies not on the Loire but on the Maine, a river of a dozen kilometres or so which forms a confluence of two other rivers, the Sarthe and the Mayenne, before the combined waters flow into the Loire.

Angers has none of the obvious tourist attractions of cities like Tours. Its castle is formidable rather than beautiful, its streets are ordinary if well-kept and wide, and the shops are much what you would expect in any medium-sized city in France. Yet it has its own charm, with the half-timbered houses in the centre and the hilltop situation of its cathedral, and it certainly is a good centre from which to explore the main vineyard areas of Anjou. Each year, at the beginning of February, it is the Mecca for wine producers and buyers from all the regions of the Loire, who come to the Salon des

Vins de Loire to taste wines from the previous vintage as well as to enjoy some serious banquets. Since its inception in 1987, the Salon has ensured that the Loire keeps a regular place in the wine calendar.

While there are vines stretching in a broken line south of the Loire from the borders of Maine-et-Loire and the Pays Nantais in the west right up to Saumur, the main centre for viticulture in Anjou is to the west and south of Angers. Vineyards lie in a concentration from the eastern slopes of the valley of the Layon, which flows into the Loire at Rochefort-sur-Loire, through such villages as Beaulieu-sur-Layon towards Brissac-Quincé and so to the edge of Saumur, a distance of perhaps twenty kilometres. A small outcrop of vineyards is on the north bank of the Loire at Savennières.

Within this area are to be found the *appellations* of Anjou, all twenty of them. There are the tiny, single-vineyard *appellations* in Savennières, the almost equally small super-*appellations* in the sweet wine areas of the Layon valley, the larger *appellations* covering a number of villages in the Layon or around Brissac-Quincé – and there is the main regional *appellation* of Anjou itself. Inevitably, the smaller the *appellation*, the greater the wine.

The *appellations* of Anjou: dry whites

The Chenin Blanc dominates white wine production in Anjou, whether the wines are dry, medium or sweet. Although it can suffer from the spring frosts common in Anjou, this grape can also produce, with comparative ease, any wine from the driest to the sweetest. The basic dry white is Anjou Blanc, which comes from an average of 1,289 hectares in 170 *communes* in Maine-et-Loire, seventeen in Deux-Sèvres and eight in Vienne, but which can also be medium sweet or sweet, depending on the vintage and the decision of the producer. The preferred soil is schist and granite, a complete contrast to the chalky soil found in both Touraine and Saumur; there are no tufa caves for storing wine in Anjou.

Production of Anjou Blanc averages 73,000 hectolitres a year. But it can vary wildly, from the huge 1982 production of 108,000 hectolitres to the minuscule 31,000 hectolitres in 1991 (due to the frosts of that year), followed by the comfortable quantity of 82,000 hectolitres in 1992. Producers in the smaller, higher-quality *appel-*

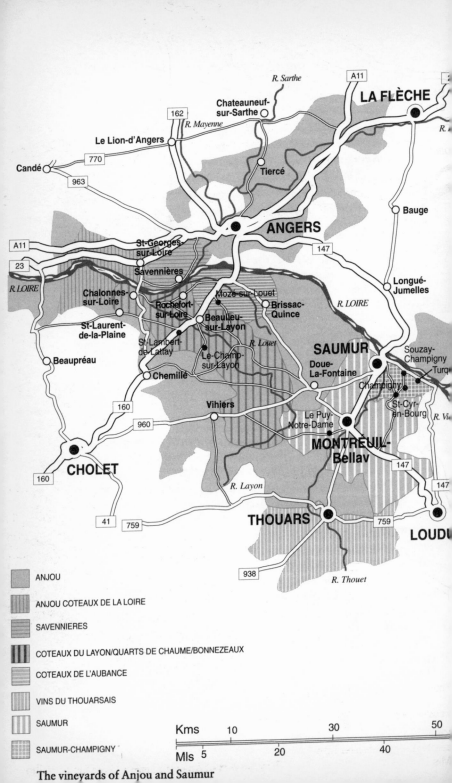

The vineyards of Anjou and Saumur

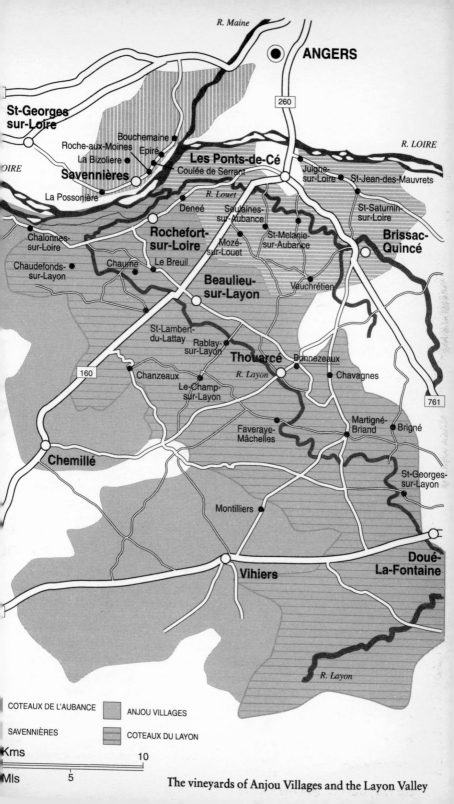

The vineyards of Anjou Villages and the Layon Valley

lations can also declassify their wine down to Anjou Blanc if the quality is not good enough; they cannot classify upwards.

Much Anjou Blanc is pretty ordinary. Those producers who take trouble with their wines are rarely recompensed with good prices, meaning that there is little incentive to do more than go for high yields – which can be as high as 72 hectolitres per hectare – and sell their grapes on to a local co-operative. In addition, there has been a move, especially since the arrival of the superior *appellation* of Anjou Villages for red wines, to convert vineyards from producing indifferent whites, often vaguely sweet, to reds which command higher prices.

However, there is one dry white wine *appellation* in Anjou which, apart from the fact that it also uses Chenin Blanc grapes, occupies a completely different world from Anjou Blanc. That is Savennières. The vineyards around the little village and in the neighbouring *communes* of Bouchemaine and La Possonière, situated on the north bank of the Loire twelve kilometres west of Angers, are on steep, south-facing slopes of volcanic schist, brilliantly able to retain heat from the sun. Yields are ridiculously low – no more than 30 hectolitres per hectare – a relic from the time when sweet wines were produced here. The vineyard area is small and concentrated, averaging 69 hectares over the past ten years. In addition to that small output, there are two even smaller *appellations*: Savennières-Coulée de Serrant of 7 hectares, a mono-*cru* owned by one producer, and Savennières-Roche-aux-Moines of 17 hectares, divided between three producers.

For many, the wines of Savennières and its two *crus* are the finest dry white wines of the Loire Valley, easily outclassing Sancerre or Pouilly Fumé, although I would argue strongly for the merits of the latter. They are certainly long-lived. Dry they may be, but they reveal all the traits of Chenin Blanc: the early attraction, the period of retreat and harshness, and the long maturity which fades gracefully over periods of twenty years and more.

The prestige of Savennières has overshadowed another white *appellation* whose vineyards, theoretically at least, include the area of Savennières. But if you can make Savennières, why bother to make Anjou Coteaux de la Loire, a wine which can be either dry or medium dry (of the same sort of sweetness as basic Coteaux du Layon)? It comes from eleven *communes* facing each other across the Loire between Ingrandes-sur-Loire and Brain-sur-l'Authion on the north bank – an area neatly divided by Savennières and the conurbation of Angers – along with a shorter stretch on the south bank. The vineyards currently cover a mere 60 hectares, and production is 2,000 hectolitres a year – and falling.

The *appellations* of Anjou: rosés

Rosé d'Anjou has been the success and the downfall of Anjou. This medium-sweet pink wine, sugared with anything from 10 grams of residual sugar, has kept Angevin wine-producers afloat in a period when other products simply did not sell. But it has also soured the image of Anjou as a serious wine-producing region. Along with its stable-mate Cabernet d'Anjou, generally even sweeter, it has flooded supermarket shelves, sustaining in its heyday the drinkers of Liebfraumilch – the ones who today have turned to wines which are drier and more sophisticated.

Even though these two rosés continue to dominate wine production in many of the lesser areas of Anjou, the figures tell a tale of decline throughout the 1980s and into the 1990s. In 1983 there were 3,024 hectares producing Rosé d'Anjou and 2,629 producing Cabernet d'Anjou. By 1992 those figures had shrunk to 2,214 and 2,296 respectively, and they continue to decline. Rosé d'Anjou comes mainly from sandy and gravel soils, while Cabernet d'Anjou comes from the schist soils of Martigné-Briand and Tigné.

Production has not fallen, however, as the yields have been pushed up: 196,000 hectolitres of Rosé d'Anjou were made in 1983 – and 170,000 hectolitres in 1992. The 138,000 hectolitres of Cabernet d'Anjou made in 1983 were actually surpassed in the bumper year of 1992, with 144,000 hectolitres. Quite where all this wine is going is not clear, since the market is stagnant and rosé is hardly a wine which can be stored until things pick up. The only explanation – given to me by a grower in Anjou who makes a little rosé – is that it is being sold at cut-throat prices, thereby further diminishing the image of Anjou.

That these sweet rosés are unfashionable should not hide the fact that Anjou is ideal country for pink wines – as demonstrated by the quality of the rosé from the third *appellation* in Anjou. Rosé de Loire is an *appellation* created in 1974 and, like the sparkling Crémant de Loire, was intended to cover Anjou, Saumur and Touraine. In practice, though, just as most Crémant de Loire comes from Saumur, so most Rosé de Loire comes from Anjou, from the vines that would previously have made Rosé d'Anjou.

The difference is that Rosé de Loire is dry, with a maximum residual sugar of three grams per litre. Fruity, fresh and fragrant, it can make a delicious summer aperitif wine. Sadly, although it is gaining in popularity, it is still not sufficiently recognized, and in 1992 production stood at 48,000 hectolitres a year from 669 hectares. This did at least represent an increase over the decade: in 1983 the figures were 21,000 hectolitres and 316 hectares.

The grape varieties for these rosés cover the usual gamut for red and pink wine. Cabernet d'Anjou is more restricted: Cabernet Franc and Cabernet Sauvignon only. Anjou Rosé offers the widest choice: Cabernet Franc, Cabernet Sauvignon, Pineau d'Aunis, Grolleau, Gamay and Cot, although Grolleau is normally the dominant variety. Rosé de Loire replaces Cot with Pinot Noir.

The *appellations* of Anjou: reds

While the rosés decline in prestige, the reds of Anjou move in the opposite direction. The creation of the superior *appellation* of Anjou Villages in 1987 gave a shot in the arm to producers who saw a future in red wine in the region, encouraging them, through higher prices, to go for quality rather than quantity, as stipulated in the low yield of 50 hectolitres per hectare. The other two red *appellations*, Anjou Rouge (properly known since 1992 as just Anjou – you have to guess that the wine is red) and Anjou Gamay, both have higher yields (55 hectolitres per hectare) and lower quality.

Between them, these three *appellations* cover an average of 2,342 hectares producing 126,000 hectolitres, less than half the production of rosé. But the figures are increasing: 1983 saw 104,000 hectolitres from 1,828 hectares (there was no Anjou Villages, and producers in what is now Villages simply produced Anjou Rouge), whereas in 1992, when all three *appellations* were up and running, production of red was 136,000 hectolitres from 2,595 hectares.

Anjou Rouge is still by far the largest of the three *appellations*; in 1992 it covered 1,995 hectares and produced 96,000 hectolitres. It can be made from Cabernet Franc, Cabernet Sauvignon and Pineau d'Aunis in any of the same 170 *communes* that can also make Anjou Blanc. The second red *appellation* of Anjou, Anjou Gamay, is obviously made entirely from Gamay. It comes from schist soils and is treated not unlike a Touraine or Beaujolais Primeur, with carbonic maceration to give freshness and fruit, and an early release before the Christmas following the harvest. In 1992, 338 hectares produced 19,000 hectolitres.

The third red *appellation*, Anjou Villages, is the most interesting of the three because of its potential for quality. It is centred on forty-six *communes*, of which the heartland is the area around Brissac-Quincé, south-east of Angers across the Loire. Other areas are in the valley of the Aubance to the west of Brissac, and around Thouarcé and Martigné-Briand in the valley of Layon.

It was pressure from the *vignerons* of Brissac which brought about the creation of this *appellation* in 1987. From 224 hectares in that year there are now 273, producing an annual average of 12,000 hectolitres over the six years up to 1992. Apart from the restriction on the growing area, the rules of production are more rigorous than for either Anjou Rouge or Anjou Gamay. Yields are lower: as we have seen, 50 hectolitres per hectare. Maturation is longer: the wine has to remain in tank, or increasingly wood (even new wood), for a year (technically until 15 September in the year following the harvest), compared with the spring or early summer sale of the other reds. There is a high proportion – up to 30 per cent – of Cabernet Sauvignon, in a blend which also includes Cabernet Franc. In keeping with this higher quality, Anjou Villages wines are normally put in special bottles embossed with the *fleur-de-lys* and crowns of the Dukes of Anjou.

The *appellations* of Anjou: sweet whites

Despite the fame of Savennières and the improving quality of the red wines, it is the sweet white wines which remain the glory of Anjou. Apart from Sauternes in Bordeaux and the *moelleux* wines of Vouvray, there is no other area of France which can make sweet wines of such quality and longevity. From vineyards in the valleys of the Layon, and to a lesser extent the Aubance, are produced botrytized wines which benefit from the benign mould which grows on the Chenin Blanc in the autumns when the weather is misty in the mornings and hot in the afternoons – glorious wines which combine intense sweetness and the natural acidity of the Chenin in perfect harmony.

The Layon valley is the heart of this sweet wine production: along the eastern bank of the river, slopes facing south-west follow its course from Rochefort-sur-Loire up to Martigné-Briand. Within the general *appellation* of Coteaux du Layon, there are three superior areas: the Coteaux du Layon Villages, which also includes the specific *appellation* of Coteaux du Layon Chaume; and the two top *crus* of Quarts de Chaume and Bonnezeaux.

Coteaux du Layon itself covers 1,400 hectares and produces an annual average of 44,000 hectolitres, rising to 54,000 hectolitres in a great year such as 1989 and falling to 25,000 hectolitres in a disastrous year such as 1991. Of this, 265 hectares and 8,000 hectolitres are entitled to the *appellation* Coteaux du Layon Villages from one of six named villages: Beaulieu-sur-Layon, Faye d'Anjou, Rablay-sur-Layon, Rochefort-sur-Loire, Saint-Aubin-de-Luigné and Saint-Lambert-du-Lattay. The hamlet of Chaume in the *commune* of Rochefort is entitled to its own *appellation* of Coteaux du Layon Chaume: 80 hectares here produce an average of 2,200 hectolitres. Yields here are lower than in the Coteaux du Layon: 28 hectolitres per hectare compared with 40 hectolitres per hectare.

Of the two super-*appellations*, Quarts de Chaume is the smaller. Whereas Chaume is on the top of the slope facing the Layon, the Quarts de Chaume consists of three ridges sticking out into the Layon valley away from the main plateau. Legend has it that a quarter (*quart* in French) of the crop from these ridges was always reserved for the lord of the manor, who knew good wine when he tasted it and knew that here was the finest wine of all. Ownership of the 34 hectares is divided between three major producers and seven other growers who have around one hectare each. Annual production averages 676 hectolitres of the finest nectar, with tiny yields of 25 hectolitres per hectare.

Bonnezeaux is another hamlet, further south-east near the larger village of Thouarcé. Again it is land on the slopes facing south-west over the Layon valley that has the right climatic conditions for botrytized wines. As at Quarts de Chaume, two small side valleys, or rather clefts, delimit three ridges named Beauregard, La Montagne and Fesles. Production, averaging 1,754 hectolitres from 68 hectares, is larger than Quarts de Chaume, but yields are kept to the same low level of 25 hectolitres per hectare.

The second sweet wine valley in Anjou is the Aubance. Conditions there are never as favourable as in the Layon, so although the wines can be delicious, they never have the intensity of the Layon wines. Since Aubance wines never command the same price as Layon wines either, the growers there prefer to stick to more reliable styles such as Anjou Villages or Anjou Blanc and Anjou Rouge. Nevertheless, the 73 hectares defined in the *appellation* do produce a respectable average of 2,380 hectolitres from relatively high yields of 40 hectolitres per hectare.

Savennières: the practice of *biodynamie*

Nicolas Joly has a reputation that is larger even than his wines. Whether he is an eccentric or a man ahead of his time depends on your point of view. What is certain is that, in applying his theory of biodynamic viticulture to his vineyards of Coulée de Serrant and Roche-aux-Moines in Savennières, he creates fabulous wines to go with his larger-than-life personality.

The drive to the Château de la Roche-aux-Moines takes you past a vision of medieval beauty – in the form of a jewel-like Cistercian monastery at the bottom of a narrow defile in the hills – out into the vineyard, down an avenue of mature trees and up to the elegant eighteenth-century house, which has some of the finest views over the Loire.

That is the theory at least. The fact that it was pouring solidly and steadily that June day, with a cloud of mist where the view should have been, did not cancel out the beauty of the situation – it was just that I had to imagine much of it. Once inside the house, however, no imagination was needed to greet M. Joly, an intense man with the air of a 1960s intellectual. Rapidly, and in impeccable English, he told me about his theories. It was as if he was used to being questioned about them incredulously, and wanted to get his explanation in first.

Having tasted a range of his wines in London, I needed no convincing that, whatever the theories that lay behind his wines, in practice he was doing everything right. Essentially, he has a strong belief in the principles of the *appellation contrôlée* system: for him, it is not just a geographical term but should cover the way the land is farmed – which means going back to what the soil was like before modern chemical farming arrived. He feels that, in adding standardized nutrients, chemicals take away the character of a plot of land, destroying the individuality of the wines produced on it.

Organic farming restores them, bringing back a situation where it is the land which is feeding the vines, not the chemicals.

The rules of biodynamics were devised by Rudolf Steiner during the early years of this century, and have been applied at Coulée de Serrant since 1982. Today there are fifty biodynamic growers in France, permitted to use the symbol of Demeter, the Greek goddess of the earth, after three years of using biodynamic practices. We have already met one, the Domaine Huët, in Vouvray. The theory concerns itself with the basic elements of earth, water, air and fire or heat. The skill of the wine-producer lies in balancing the critical poverty that his soil must possess by enriching it with the two lighter elements of air and fire. Excessively rich soil, in which earth and water dominate, will produce high-yielding vines with consequently mediocre wine.

So far, so good. Accepting a natural way of balancing the needs of the vine and the soil is now becoming widely understood throughout the wine world. It is perhaps when you go further, as M. Joly does, and talk about the effect of the solar system on wine production that eyebrows become raised. With a slightly rueful air, however, he plunges on with his explanations: how heat and light are stronger at certain times of the month and should be harnessed. That is why he ploughs at certain times of the month, why he likes to bottle at other times, why he touches the wine hardly at all during its vinification, and filters as lightly as possible.

The tasting is of course the final test of theories. And these wines are magnificent. Coulée de Serrant is one of the three *appellations contrôlées* in France under single ownership – the others are Romanée Conti in Burgundy and Château Grillet on the Rhône. To my mind, Coulée de Serrant is today the greatest of the three. M. Joly makes other white wines on the estate. There is an *appellation* Savennières called Becherelle; I tasted the 1992 with him – it was young, with the taste of greengages but a delicious weight of fruit. Then there is *appellation* Savennières Roche-aux-Moines, Clos de la Bergerie, of which M. Joly has four hectares. The 1991 had the flavour of currants and dusty perfumes, very intense, very rich, but bone-dry. And then there was the top of the bill: Coulée de Serrant 1991, with just a hint of botrytis, but always dry, with flavours of summer gardens and hints of minerals. With age, such a wine will develop classic Chenin Blanc flavours, with hints of petrol and nuts;

it could age twenty years or more, but even eighteen months after the harvest this wine had, as M. Joly put it, 'a song in it'.

Savennières: a love of the land

Just over the top of the hill and down the other side you will find the cellars of Pierre et Yves Soulez at Château de Chamboureau. Theirs is an old-fashioned cellar, comfortably rustic, with barrels and stainless-steel tanks juxtaposed. It is on one side of a courtyard, and the others are occupied by the château, which like La Roche-aux-Moines has magnificent views from a terrace facing east over the Loire, .

With Pierre Soulez – whose brother Yves is now making wine on their other estate in the Quarts de Chaume – I discussed these two mini-*appellations*. In his own way he is just as intense about their special character as M. Joly is. Coulée de Serrant, M. Joly's property, faces due west, while La Roche-aux-Moines, of which the Soulez family has 7 out of the total of 17 hectares, faces south-west. Both are on deep, almost sheer slopes running down to the Loire; the extra degrees of warmth from the wide waters of the river give the ripeness of the grapes, even on this northern bank. The soil is poor and schistous, while the other vineyards of Savennières, such as Clos du Papillon and La Bigolière, are sandier, producing comparatively lighter wines. Behuard, another Savennières vineyard, is on volcanic soil – there is a chapel on top of the hill – and the outflow of lava went to make up part of Roche-aux-Moines.

The Soulez family has been at Chamboureau since 1959. Although bought by their father, the property is now owned by his eleven sons, of whom three are directly involved in the work. In their time they have developed a deep love for the land: 'It's family, it's land and it's *savoir-faire* – knowing how to work the land,' says M. Soulez. He believes their vineyards are among the best in Savennières – who would disagree? – and his aim in the cellar is to bring out the taste of the land in his wines. Low yields – from clones of the Chenin Blanc which themselves give low yields – minimal treatment in the vineyard, several passes through the vineyard at harvest-time to get the ripest grapes (the system also used for making the sweet wines of the Coteaux du Layon): all this allows them to touch the wine as little as possible during vinification, where getting air to the wine and allowing it to rest on its lees are all parts of obtaining the maximum flavour. It is almost biodynamism without the theory.

The estate totals 28 hectares: 7 in Roche-aux-Moines, 2.5 in Quarts de Chaume across the river, 1.5 making red Anjou Rouge, and the remainder making Savennières. We started tasting with a 1990 Savennières, Domaine de la Bigolière: rich, honeyed, but dry, a wine that develops relatively quickly. Next came a 1990 Château de Chamboureau, more powerful from a big year, almost minty to taste, needing many more years to mature than the Bigolière.

We passed on to two vintages of Roche-aux-Moines. A 1990 had the honey and botrytis flavours on dryness which seem characteristic of the year, and which I had already met with M. Joly; this was a gloriously powerful wine, with hints of pepper from high alcohol – not typical perhaps, but nevertheless remarkable. The 1988 was more in the classic mould, slightly woody, earthy, somewhat austere at this stage in its development, power coupled with high acids, from a year that M. Soulez says is *tout droit*, 'straight down the line'.

Finally there was a *demi-sec* wine, harking back to an older tradition of Savennières when sweet wines were made. This came from the Clos du Papillon, a vineyard so called because it is shaped like a butterfly with wings outstretched. M. Soulez's 1990 Demi-Sec was lighter, softer than the other Savennières I had been tasting, becoming honeyed in the mouth: ideal, I was told, with *coquilles Saint-Jacques*, with *charcuterie*, or with the local *beurre blanc* sauce.

Quarts de Chaume: concentrating on sweetness

The little hamlet of Chaume is half-way down the slope above the river Layon. It is merely a collection of four or five houses on a country lane that appears to lead nowhere. That impression is wrong, since after another half-kilometre it turns into the private drive of M. Lalanne, owner of Château Bellerive and possessor of 18 out of the 34 hectares in Quarts de Chaume. The other large owner is Château de l'Écharderie, while Domaines Baumard, based in Rochefort-sur-Loire, has 6 hectares.

The château – more a large country house – is set in the middle of a very English wooded park. To one side, terraced vineyards on schist soil, looking more like the Douro Valley in Portugal than the

Loire, drop down the slopes of the ridges that make up the Quarts de Chaume. The *chai* is set to one side of the house, a small building with a tasting room in front and the working part of the cellar behind. I stayed in the tasting room while M. Lalanne, an energetic fifty-year-old with a ready smile who made his first wine in 1971, rushes to the back to get bottles.

He told me about making Quarts de Chaume. As with any botry-tized wine, he needs to make a number of *tries*, or passes, through the vineyard to pick the individual berries which have the right degree of boytrytis. It is skilled, back-breaking, time-consuming work, and at the end of the day it is a wonder how these wines can be so relatively inexpensive. After a gentle pressing the grapes are fermented slowly in small wooden barrels, which allows M. Lal-anne to keep each *trie* separate and to arrive at the end of fermen-tation with a number of different lots which can be blended together later. He only makes one wine from the best of his barrels, selling the rest to *négociants*. The style of wine he aims at is *moel-leux* – honeyed and liquorous – but not excessively so: 'I also want raciness, finesse, elegance. The wine shouldn't be too heavy, even though it should be full.'

We talked about the two great years of 1989 and 1990, when botrytis was rampant in the vineyards. For him, 1989 was the better year, 'wines with power, but also lightness'; 1990, by con-trast, 'was almost too ripe, too much weight, like a Sauternes – but this isn't Sauternes'. But in both years, some of the grapes had so much sugar that it was almost impossible to get the fermentation going.

We tasted the most recent vintages. The 1990 came first, because it is a lesser wine than the 1989. It was moving into a stage which all sweet Chenin wines enter, something already described under Vouvray. They are like children: after an initial year or two of attractiveness, they develop a hardness, an awkward adolescence which closes them up for several years before they emerge again with completely different flavours, balanced and maturing. The 1989 was a contrast, still fruity and open, very rich but beautifully balanced; 'I believe this is the greatest wine I have ever made,' said M. Lalanne. This 1989, he felt, will age for a minimum of twenty-five to thirty years, possibly fifty, and it is certainly not to be drunk for fifteen years.

Finally we tasted the 1992, the new wine, only just bottled when

I visited him in June 1993. This was attractively floral, balancing sweetness and dryness, delicate and quite light, a complete contrast to the blockbusters of 1990 and 1989. It is, said M. Lalanne, more of a food-orientated wine than the 1989, going well with fish, with white meat or with *sauce Roquefort*, blue cheese sauce. Like all French producers of sweet wines, he is always astonished by the Anglo-Saxon habit of drinking sweet wines with dessert; they are to accompany certain savoury dishes, or to be drunk as aperitif wines.

Bonnezeaux: the pink house of the *patissier*

Château de Fesles is the big name in Bonnezeaux, not just because it is the largest property, but also because it makes the best wines. For four generations it was the home of the Boivin family until, in 1991, Jacques Boivin sold the château – a nineteenth-century hunting lodge – to Gaston Lenôtre, a master *patissier*, who has painted it a pretty pink, and whose creations in chocolate dominate one end of the tasting room, casting a curious bouquet on the wines. M. Lenôtre owns another estate nearby, Château de la Roulerie, where he produces Anjou *appellation* and Coteaux du Layon wines.

M. Boivin, though, remains very much in charge of the vineyard and the cellars, and it was with him that I visited both. First, as the light began to fade on a cool June evening, we went out to see the vines. Just behind the château the land begins its slope down towards the Layon. It is here that the vines for Bonnezeaux are grown. In the other direction, on the plateau, the *appellation* is Anjou Blanc or Anjou Villages. To the right, as we looked over the Layon, was the windmill in the La Montagne vineyard, and just beyond was the collection of houses which makes up the smaller of the two hamlets both called Bonnezeaux (the other is on the plateau). The soil beneath our feet was a curious combination, slightly red in colour with blue-grey rocks, sandstone and schist.

Of the 32 hectares in the Château de Fesles estate, 12 are in the Bonnezeaux *appellation*, the rest producing a mix of *vin de pays* from Chardonnay, Anjou Blanc Sec, Anjou Rouge and Anjou Villages. The *chai*, to one side of the château, was completely renovated for the 1992 vintage and now looks more like a Bordeaux château, with the barrels laid out in rows and the discreet flood-lighting. Modern pressing equipment allows M. Boivin to handle the botrytized grapes for Bonnezeaux very delicately. After this pressing the must is put into wood for fermentation. It is not new wood, but two or three years old; he says he does not want the taste of wood, just the richness and roundness it can give.

We tasted, starting with Chardonnay Vin de Pays du Jardin de la France. Having spent the whole day with Chenin Blanc, it was something of a shock to the system to encounter the rich, soft, fruit and comparatively low acidity of the Chardonnay. There is no wood used for this fresh, clean, flavoursome wine, which is the least expensive made on the estate. An Anjou Blanc brought me back to Chenin, a delicious rich wine from the meagre 1991 vintage, with a hint of wood and herbs to give it flavour.

Red wines brought a good contrast between Anjou Rouge and Anjou Villages: the herbaceous, slightly vegetal flavours, compensated for by hints of figs, of the 1991 Anjou Rouge Vieilles Vignes contrasting with the much bigger, ripe tannins of the Anjou Villages 1991 – a justification, if one were needed, for the existence of separate *appellations*.

Then it was on to Bonnezeaux. They make two styles of this wine, one called Boisé because it has wood elements in the taste, having been aged in newer casks. Both come from the La Chapelle vineyard just behind the château, where we had walked earlier. The 1990 La Chapelle, from that great year, was sweet and rich enough, with tastes of apricots vying with honey and rose-water. But the 1990 Boisé was bigger again: here was where the roundness given by the wood came in, making this a stupendously rich wine, darker, more golden in colour than the other 1990 – botrytis and honey and quinces were all there. Even though this is a style that matures relatively fast, M. Boivin felt that it should not be drunk for ten years at least. Despite that comment, I could not spit out such unctuous nectar, as it almost involuntarily slid down my throat.

Coteaux du Layon: the wines from the beautiful place

The village of Beaulieu-sur-Layon consists of a narrow street that passes an attractive museum of local crafts before reaching the main N160 road which cuts across the Layon valley between Beaulieu and Rochefort-sur-Loire. On the other side of the main road, but still in the *commune* of Beaulieu, is the elegant, upright Château du Breuil, an early nineteenth-century structure with high roofs of grey slate and long, slim windows.

It has been the home of the Morgat family since 1961, when Marc Morgat's father bought the property from the original owners. Today, with 50 hectares of vines, they grow a whole range of grape varieties, thanks to their link to the École Supérieure d'Agriculture et Viticulture at Angers, which uses their land for experimental plantings. That is why there are Pinot Noir, Pinot Blanc, Chardonnay, Sauvignon Blanc, Cabernet Franc and Grolleau. Even with this range of grapes and consequent range of wines, it is still obvious from tasting with M. Morgat that what he really wants to make is sweet Coteaux du Layon – which, because he is in Beaulieu, he can call Coteaux du Layon Villages Beaulieu.

We discussed the problems of growing Chenin Blanc, especially its tendency to develop grey rot in wetter years – something to be avoided, unlike the welcome noble rot. To avoid this he has, with the encouragement of the École, planted his Chenin vines in rows which are 1.5 metres apart rather than the normal one metre. It brings the yield down, of course, but he says it does cut down the risk of grey rot.

M. Morgat is a computer man by training, and only got into wines when his cellar master left in 1980. He felt he ought to learn about noble rot – botrytis – and how it developed, so he went to Sauternes to find out. He discovered that, as the rot develops, the sugar in the grapes apparently falls, only increasing again when the rot is fully developed. Evaporation of the grapes occurs from inside, and you need three weeks between the grapes being simply super-ripe and them being perfectly rotten.

Then we discussed the various layers of *appellation* in Coteaux du Layon. While simple Coteaux du Layon is a basic wine, he sees the village wines, such as his Beaulieu, as the *cru* of Layon, and Quarts de Chaume and Bonnezeaux as the *grands crus*.

All this time, we were also tasting. Bottle after bottle from the huge range of wines made at Château du Breuil were being opened and poured out by Mme Morgat while her husband did the talking. We started, as seems the norm with a big range of wines in this part of the world, with a *vin de pays*; like Château de Fesles, this was a Chardonnay, perfumed, light, fresh, made in a mix of stainless-steel and cement tanks, the 1992 ready to drink nine months after harvest. A similar 1992 Sauvignon Blanc, which here is also *vin de pays*, had a light, clean, herbaceous character, fresh and dry.

Then it was on to *appellation* wines, starting with Anjou Blanc

Sec. M. Morgat said that, if it was not for the fact that he needed cash-flow, he would love to make a wine in the style of Savennières, but he needed to make one which sold quickly – hence this pleasantly soft 1992, honeyed, with some residual sugar and good fruit, to be drunk now. More medium sweetness followed, in the form of a rosé Cabernet d'Anjou with its 25 grams of sugar, well-made, certainly better than many. The style, said M. Morgat, is hard to make because of the difficulty of knowing when to stop the fermentation in order to get the right balance of sweetness and acidity with, as here, just enough tannin to give it shape.

Two reds followed, both Anjou Villages. M. Morgat finds the new *appellation* strange: 'The wines should either be good Anjou Rouge or nothing at all. I don't understand the point of this extra *appellation*.' Despite these reservations, he does make young Anjou Villages, more like the early-drinking Anjou Rouge and at the opposite extreme from some of the serious Anjou Villages made by other producers.

If you want longevity in a wine from Château du Breuil, you go to Coteaux du Layon Villages Beaulieu. I tasted the Château du Breuil 1990, 1991 and 1992: the 1990 is weighty, enormous, now entering its closed Chenin phase; the 1991 lightly honeyed, attractively balanced, light and elegant; the 1992 has hints of greenness, but with attractive sweet fruit. Then, to finish the tasting, M. Morgat produced a bottle of 1972, made, as he put it 'before I discovered the secrets of botrytis'. That may be, but he had still made a wine which has aged into rich, developed Chenin flavours, old golds and greens and balance.

Coteaux de l'Aubance: the wines of the windmill

Hervé Papin lives in a house with a windmill in the grounds. Not that it could benefit much from the wind these days, since the sails have long gone and the tower of the mill has been reduced to a stump. But its presence is enough to give the estate its name, Moulin des Besneries, just outside the village of Mozé-sur-Louet.

I first tasted M. Papin's wines at the Salon des Vins de Loire in Angers, and my first impressions were good enough for me to want to see where the wines were made. What I liked was the fact that, although he makes wine using eight different *appellations*, he manages to preserve the typicity of each. But I also wanted to go to the Moulin des Besneries for the Coteaux de l'Aubance.

Unless you know it is coming, you can pass the Aubance valley on the N160 without noticing it. There is only a slight dip in the road as it drops into the valley and only a slight rise as it comes out again. Only a row of trees indicates water. It is the shallowness of the valley which means that the conditions for good botrytis are much rarer than in the Layon, and therefore the incidence of good Coteaux de l'Aubance is that much lower.

Most of M. Papin's vineyard of 20 hectares is around his house, which stands on the plateau above the Aubance. Much was replanted ten or fifteen years ago, but there are patches of land to make the sweet Coteaux de l'Aubance on the slope down to the river. There is little to see on the rather flat, featureless plateau, and we concentrated our attentions on the cellar – with its newly-purchased stainless-steel tanks – and the wines, despite the power-cut caused by the stormy weather outside.

Although my prime purpose was to taste the sweet wines, I went through other wines as a prelude. First were two rosés: a pretty, currant-fruit flavoured Rosé d'Anjou and a fuller, sweeter Cabernet d'Anjou. Anjou Rouge 1992 was fresh and fruity, almost all Cabernet Franc, giving ripe tobacco flavours; while Anjou Villages 1990, big and round, made the usual contrast between the two *appellations* with its firm fruit and obvious ability to age.

Finally the lights came on again and M. Papin was able to find bottles of Coteaux de l'Aubance in what had until then been a very dark corner. He explained about the *appellation*, which was created in 1950 but had always been relatively obscure compared with the greater names on the Layon valley ten kilometres to the south. The area of the *appellation* covers ten *communes*. As with the sweet wines of the Layon, picking is done laboriously by *tries*, gathering the shrivelled, botrytized berries.

M. Papin goes one stage further in selecting grapes in the vineyard. In June he will carry out what is called a 'green' harvest, thinning out the bunches so that what remains can gain extra nutrients from the vine. We tasted first a 1992 Coteaux de l'Aubance; according to M. Papin, picking was very critical in that year, but the results suggest it will be very fine for sweet wines. Certainly, the wine was promising well: never as intense as the Layon wines, Aubance wines nevertheless have all the right orange marmalade and honey flavours of true botrytized wines, but with an extra streak of acidity that makes them very poised, elegant, light.

The 1990 which followed – from the second *trie* in the vineyard – was much heavier, simply because of the year. It was certainly rich, already developing the hardness of Chenin Blanc when maturing, and with a fascinating smoky character. Underneath, though, there was plenty of rich, sweet fruit. I found myself enjoying this less concentrated style of *moelleux* wine, and hoping that its relative scarcity and neglect will not mean it disappears.

Rosés and reds: Brissac's co-operative

The Caves de la Loire is big. Its production of 12 million litres of wine a year represents 12 per cent of all the *appellation contrôlée* wine made in Anjou and Saumur. It makes a quarter of all the rosé in Anjou plus quantities of all other styles, from dry white to sweet white, from red to sparkling. It has four cellars: at Brissac, Tigné, Beaulieu-sur-Layon and Thouarcé.

So many statistics and so much wine could be daunting or dispiriting. But the Caves de la Loire is neither. In its wine-making it may be highly professional, but in its sales presentation it is charmingly amateur, with an eager desire to welcome and explain that many equally large organizations would never understand.

Thus it was that I found myself at the wrong cellar – at Thouarcé rather than Brissac – and talking to Michel Renou, the sales director, on the telephone rather than face-to-face. Since he has two offices, there's always a chance that directions can be confusing. It meant, however, that I arrived at Brissac half an hour late, and with my next appointment an hour and a half later. Looking at the range of wines they wanted me to taste, I reckoned that speed would be required. But first I had to see the cellars.

Wine is made at the other three cellars as well as at Brissac (where they have just installed some modern Vinimatic rotating fermenters for red wines), but Brissac is where all the bottling and dispatch is done. Hence the all-pervading sound of bottling lines, the clank of bottles and the noise of fork-lift trucks moving them around which punctuated our tasting.

We first looked at rosés, beginning with Rosé de Loire. Having tasted a good number of sweeter Rosé d'Anjou and Cabernet d'Anjou, this dry Rosé de Loire was something of a relief, and the

1992 Les Terriades with its fresh fruity, slight appley edge and clean, raspberry after-taste was attractive and refreshing. The name Les Terriades, I was told by M. Renou, is being used on a range of wines launched with the 1992 vintage that are designed to reflect the land from which they come. To do this, they choose grapes which come from the most typical soil for the style of wine they are making. They selected 250 plots of land through geological testing.

So I next tasted Les Terriades Rosé d'Anjou, which comes from gravel and deep schistous soil, and has 20 grams of residual sugar; for someone who is no fan of these sweet rosés, it was attractively rich and flavoursome, well-balanced and with some acidity to counter the sweetness. Good summer quaffing wine, I thought. It certainly showed well against the Cabernet d'Anjou from schist soil, which I found just too heavy and certainly not refreshing, although probably true to type.

More interesting was an Anjou Blanc 1992 from chosen sites on quartz-siliceous clays, with lovely honeyed fruit which hinted at a malolactic fermentation to reduce the amount of acidity, but still very fresh and with heightened flavours – not a wine for ageing. This was followed by an Anjou red Les Terriades from slate schist soil, a soft wine with plenty of dusty, perfumed fruit and a round, easy finish.

Then we moved on to Anjou Villages. M. Renou and the oenologist of the Caves de la Loire, Patrice Rondeau, explained to me that the Anjou Villages vineyards are on much more rolling countryside than basic Anjou, which is on the flat plateau to the south. Comparing the Villages wines with the standard Anjou red I had just tasted, I found the same differences as I had already encountered: much greater depth of flavour, better tannins, richness and chunky fruit. This was true of the Anjou Villages 1991 Les Marzelles from a single vineyard site, and even more so for the 1990 which had huge, chewy tannins and big, flavoursome fruit, with hints of tobacco – certainly a wine for ageing.

By the time I had finished tasting, my hour and a half was more than up. But I am pleased I stayed, because this visit to the largest producer in Anjou encouraged me to believe that the quality of Anjou wines is getting better and better. While the great sweet wines and the dry Savennières remain the stars, it is to the lesser wines that we must also look. If they are doing well, then Anjou is on the right road.

14

The wines of Muscadet and the Pays Nantais

━━━━━

The terrace of Champtoceaux is a popular place for a Sunday stroll. The old village is perched on top of a cliff, its long, narrow main street backing on to a small public park with swings and a tourist office. Then comes the terrace and a sheer drop down to the Loire. Away to the right, towards the east, the cliffs disappear, the river is wider and flows around sandy islands. Beyond, the flatter land of Anjou is spread out. To the left, the west, there is already a whiff of salt in the air.

This view shows one of the great divisions of France. Here, the Loire is much more than a broad river on its way to the sea. It is the boundary between the north and the south. Across the river from Champtoceaux the roofs of the houses are grey slate; here on the south bank they are red tiles. To the north, the main drink is based on apples; to the south is one of the most concentrated vine-yard areas of France – Muscadet.

If you travelled a little further south, to the windmill of La Divatte with its huge stone cross, and made the unsteady climb up some badly-worn and dangerous steps, you would look down over a sea of vines. In every direction, west to Nantes, south towards Cholet, east to Anjou, north to the Loire, there are vineyards. Here is a monocultural region with a vengeance; this is Sèvre-et-Maine, the heart of Muscadet.

It is the heartland of an area that stretches from the marshes of the Lac du Grand Lieu in the west to the town of Ancenis and Saint-Florent-le-Vieil on the Loire, on the way to Angers. It covers surprisingly varied countryside. The western sector is flat, almost at sea-level, and imbued with the feel of the ocean. South and east of the city of Nantes, the land is more undulating, with gentle hills

The vineyards of the Pays Nanta

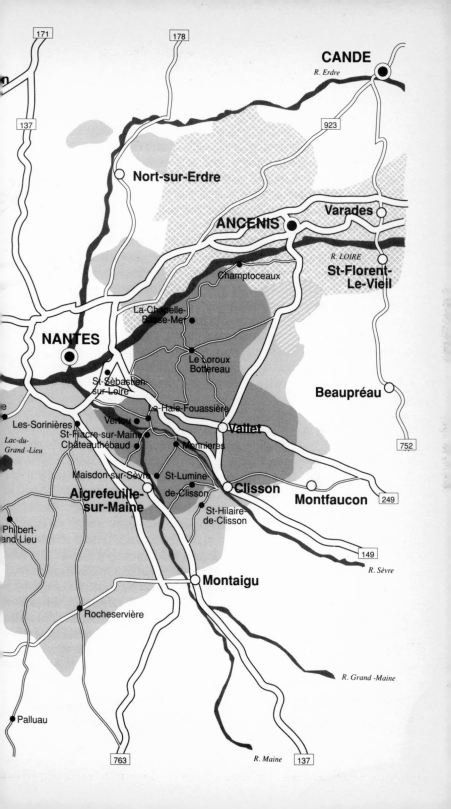

never more than about 70 metres high – but enough to give views of the land around. The twin rivers of the Sèvre Nantaise and the Maine flow south-east from the Loire, forming a V-shaped area of land. Both rivers have cut narrow, wooded valleys in the plateaux of vines, full of secret beauties such as the Maine at Gorges, where steep cliffs tower over the fast-flowing river.

The main towns of the Sèvre-et-Maine region each lend themselves to a different style of Muscadet – although it needs a local expert to detect the differences. They would argue that wines from the south-western side of Sèvre-et-Maine, from the towns of Saint-Fiacre, La Haie-Fouassière, Monnières, Gorges, Vertou and Haute Goulaine, are light, delicate and better drunk early. By contrast, they suggest that wines from the north-eastern half, from Vallet, Le Pallet (the last 't' is pronounced in Pallet but not in Vallet – nobody has been able to explain why) and La Chapelle-Heulin, develop more slowly and require some ageing in bottle.

While 80 per cent of wines from the Pays Nantais, the *département* of Loire-Atlantique, come from the 8,500 hectares of Sèvre-et-Maine, there are other *appellations*. There is simple Muscadet, much of which comes from the area around the Grand-Lieu lake. There is Muscadet des Coteaux de la Loire, a somewhat heavier style of wine that comes from the stretch of the Loire between Nantes and Ancenis and further east. There is the 3,000-hectare VDQS zone of Gros Plant du Pays Nantais which covers much of the Muscadet region, producing high-acid wines from the Gros Plant grape. And there is the VDQS area of Coteaux d'Ancenis, a curiosity in a region dominated by the two white grapes of Muscadet and Gros Plant in that it produces red wines from the Gamay, some white from Chenin Blanc and some sweet whites from the Malvoisie.

This is therefore an area dedicated to the vine. There are 1,540 growers in the Pays Nantais, having an average of 8 to 10 hectares. Muscadet is the second largest *appellation* in France after Bordeaux Rouge. The *commune* of Saint-Fiacre is reputed to have a higher percentage of land planted with vines than any other in France. Apart from parts of Bordeaux and Champagne, you are unlikely to see such a concentration of vines anywhere.

In the early summer it is normally a sea of green, as the vines move into their flowering cycle. But when I was there in May 1991 things were different: the vines that should have been sprouting prodigiously were still almost black, with just a faint haze of green. That was the year of the great frost, when in parts of Muscadet 90 per cent of the vineyard's first budding was destroyed. More importantly – because the ravages of the frost were already a thing of the past by the time of the 1992 harvest – that was the year when the growers finally began to take the upper hand in a region which has been heavily dominated by *négociants*. And it was the year in which the image of Muscadet as a cheap, quaffable white wine finally disappeared.

Muscadet production has been growing steadily. In 1987 the total output of Muscadet (most of it Sèvre-et-Maine) was 772,000 hectolitres of average wine, making it by far the highest production of any *appellation* on the Loire. In 1989 it was down to 732,000 hectolitres of high-quality wine, while in 1990, because of the dry summer, it was 592,897 hectolitres. Although the frost year of 1991 reduced the production drastically to 212,661 hectolitres, the 1992 harvest produced the largest crop ever: 795,019 hectolitres.

Sales have paralleled the harvests, with a high point in 1987–8 of 670,907 hectolitres, a dip in 1990–1 to 511,078 hectolitres, a crash in 1991–2 to 460,066 hectolitres and a recovery in 1992–3 to 618,784 hectolitres. What these figures hide, though, is that average sales of 605,696 hectolitres over a seven-year period seem to have outstripped average production over the same period of 546,285 hectolitres. Where, I wonder, has the extra wine come from?

The first great Muscadet frost

It is perhaps ironic that the foundations for the modern-day success of Muscadet were laid by a previous frost, back in 1709. This region at the western end of wine production along the Loire, cooled continually by winds from the Atlantic, was known before that time as a producer of thin red and white wines of little more than immediately local interest – except for one thing. Its situation around the major port of Nantes meant that its wines could easily be exported. And exported they were, to the Netherlands for distillation into brandy.

The Dutch demand was for thin, acid wines, something the region is climatically quite good at producing. It was they who encouraged the introduction of the Melon grape from Burgundy where at that time it was widely planted, if regarded as inferior. Come the great frost of 1709 and it was discovered that the Melon was relatively frost-resistant. Leases between landowners and tenant farmers dating from 1735 show that a general stipulation was the replanting of the vineyard with this Melon de Bourgogne. By the end of the century a third of the vineyard was planted with Melon, which by this time had also been named the Muscadet, possibly from the slightly musky (*musqué*) smell which is noticeable in some of the wines of the region.

The other two-thirds of the vineyard were planted with a completely different grape variety, whose origins lie in the opposite direction from Burgundy. This was the Folle Blanche, known locally as the Gros Plant because of the large size of the grapes it produces, and whose other home is in Cognac and Armagnac. The link with the Dutch and distillation is obvious, not only from the other areas where the Gros Plant is planted but also from its defiantly acidic taste.

Over the past two centuries the balance between Gros Plant and Muscadet has shifted, and now two-thirds of the Pays Nantais are planted with Muscadet, one-third with Gros Plant.

The present century saw a remarkable transformation of Muscadet from a genuinely local wine, with scant appeal further afield, into a resounding export success. The name came to epitomize light, uncomplicated and fresh white wine, the sort the world wants by the bucketful. And in fact right up to the end of the 1980s Muscadet, with its simple, homogeneous image, lack of confusing names, and generally wide distribution at inexpensive prices, seemed set to go for ever onwards and upwards.

If the poor 1991 harvest finally upset the apple-cart, cracks were already showing in the monolithic front presented by the wine: Muscadet is just Muscadet, *n'est ce pas*? But of course it is not. As in any wine area, there is good, there is bad and there is awful. A good part of the problem of Muscadet stems from the fact that too much of it falls into the last two categories, too little into the first. And like any commodity whose overall quality is sometimes dubious, once the price starts to rise (which is what happened to Muscadet) so demand inexorably starts to disappear.

The organic farmer

The increase in growers' *domaine* wines is one way of reversing this trend. One such grower is Guy Bossard. His vineyard, Domaine de l'Écu, is near Le Landreau in the heart of Sèvre-et-Maine. He is a serious man, whose wines have travelled far to great critical acclaim. Yet he has seen no need to indulge in any fancy visitors' reception area – just a small, low-ceilinged room next to the tractor park. One wall is lined with racks from which he selects bottles for tasting, the other has dusty labels and diplomas from wine exhibitions. A small counter at one end is used to dispense the wines.

We talked first about M. Bossard's second claim to fame after his wines. He works organically, one of only two growers in the region to do so. What is particularly surprising is that this is not some smart new idea, but something started by his father in 1975. He found that one parcel of land was suffering from too many chemical sprayings and was advised to try natural fertilizers and only simple Bordeaux mixture (copper sulphate) sprays.

Organic farming means maintaining your own source of fertilizer, as I saw when we walked over to M. Bossard's brand-new cellars in the middle of his 17 hectares of vineyard. There was a pile of rotting matter, maturing gently in the warm sun of a May morning. It did not look unpleasant, nor did it smell – in fact, I would have happily taken a load back for my garden.

Organic farming not only makes ecological sense, it also seems to be good for business. In marketing terms, it is a brilliant 'unique selling proposition', as his success in exporting proves: 75 per cent of his production goes abroad. Success finds its most concrete expression not in his house – which looked to me, peering in at a window, like any small farmhouse in provincial France – but in the *chai*, the cellars. Gleaming stainless steel, a brand-new pneumatic press, piles of space for expansion: that is where the money has gone.

M. Bossard is typical of the new generation of growers in Muscadet. They perceive the poor image much Muscadet conveys to the outside world. They have seen the rapid increase in price at the end of the 1980s, and have realized that this needs to be matched by an increase in quality. And since this is Muscadet, an essentially uncomplicated white wine, the way to achieve quality is through good vineyard management and through technology in the *chai*.

Tasting M. Bossard's wines proves the point, and introduces another aspect of the debate – whether Muscadet can age well. Tasting his 1988 Domaine de l'Écu in 1991 showed that there is potential there: it had lost its freshness, but had gained a roundness and a delicious apples and custard taste, and a good balance between tartaric and malic acids.

Before this we tasted his Gros Plant. It is an underrated grape variety, we both agreed, condemned to be seen as second fiddle to Muscadet, but in its way making wines which combine superbly with the shellfish of Brittany, of which Nantes was traditionally the capital. This 1990 Gros Plant was crisp, but with ripe fruit to balance the strong acidity: because of the acidity it is not so attractive to drink on its own as Muscadet, but would certainly come into its own with food.

Sur lie or not *sur lie*?

Both these wines are bottled *sur lie*. It is a term that appears on the label of many Muscadet and Gros Plant wines. It is also the source of much confusion, argument and downright chicanery in the region. The practice of bottling wines *sur lie* – literally, taking the wine directly off its lees and putting it in the bottle rather than filtering it first – is simply how things were done traditionally. The wine was left in old barrels during the winter, and then bottled or drawn off, just as it was, in the spring. It was found that this method gave the new wine an extra zing, a little sparkle, that made it particularly attractive.

So far, so good. Here is a simple way of producing ultra-fresh wine. It has even been enshrined in the *appellation contrôlée* laws for Muscadet and the VDQS laws for Gros Plant. They state that a Muscadet or Gros Plant may be labelled *sur lie* if it has been bottled before 1 July after the harvest. The wine must be bottled either in the grower's estate or in the cellars of a *négociant* (and it must arrive there before 13 February, still on its lees).

That is the theory. But as so often happens in wine, practice is not quite the same thing. Bottling at a grower's premises is fine – the wine does not need to be moved from its tank or barrel. But when it has to be taken to a *négociant*'s cellar, many things can happen to it. It will be racked off its lees for travelling; after all, you cannot transport the stainless-steel tank. It will then be racked and filtered again before bottling, by which time no trace of the original lees is present. So a faint trace of carbon dioxide will be added to reproduce the prickle on the tongue of *sur lie* bottling.

Grouping together

Muscadets treated in this way are hardly *sur lie,* according to many in the region. Muscadet yes, *sur lie* no. It is the view of one of the most outspoken campaigners of the area, Louis Metaireau. His latest campaign is against the spread of Chardonnay in the Pays Nantais – to make Vin de Pays du Jardin de la France, which can sell for more than Muscadet. He is not a *négociant* – indeed, he hates the word – but he does sell and promote the wines of other growers.

Over thirty years ago he thought up an idea which was revolutionary for the time. He brought together three growers who did not want to sell their wines through *négociants* but needed more muscle to make an impression on the market. This small group, called Les Vignerons d'Art, now numbers nine, with 100 hectares between them. They act as a committee, involving themselves all the way with the vinification of their wines, and tasting the finished wines blind before allowing them to be marketed under the Metaireau label. I suppose the nearest equivalent is a co-operative, but this is a private *marketing* co-operative, since all the wines are made on the individual growers' estates and bottled there – *sur lie,* of course.

Louis Metaireau's views have been echoed more recently by the Sauvion family. I first met their spokesman, Jean-Ernest Sauvion, a bearded ambassador for Muscadet, in Beaujolais. I had been visiting the cellars of Georges Duboeuf and returned to my hotel fully intending to relegate wine-tasting to the back of my mind. But there on a table in a large *salon* were rows of bottles of white wine. I looked with admiration and curiosity at this interloper in an almost exclusively red wine region. And behind the table was Jean Sauvion, showing off his range of *Découvertes* for the year. To a palate reluctant even to consider Muscadet, they were a revelation: crisp, clean (not a whiff of the sulphur that then seemed endemic in Muscadet) and above all, full of fruit and flavour.

More recently, I met Jean Sauvion again over lunch in Clisson, the pretty Italianate town built in the last century in homage to the Italian Riviera. He explained to me how his family's approach worked. Unlike other *négociant* firms, they do not have contracts with growers. Each year they select the best of the wines sent in by *vignerons* to become part of their *Découvertes*, their Discoveries series. The wines will be bottled separately – *sur lie* – at the growers' premises, and although the label will be of a standard design, there is a space which will be overprinted with the name of the grower. In order to get good wines, Sauvion offer high prices, as well as the chance to participate in annual tastings. Thus, by using a different approach to Louis Metaireau, Sauvion wines achieve the same ends: promoting wines from small vineyards under a larger marketing and sales umbrella.

The wines from both these firms show how good Muscadet can be. The Metaireau approach emphasizes elegance and delicacy, while those from Sauvion show greater power and firmness. And they epitomize new trends in Muscadet: a move away from bland *négociant* blends towards varied, individual *cuvées*, and a move back towards treating *sur lie* wines in a traditional way.

Négociants are in some ways an easy target. What is often forgotten is that, while about 80 per cent of Muscadet is sold through forty *négociant* firms, many of these firms are not based in the Pays Nantais at all, but in other parts of the Loire. They buy Muscadet to complete a range of Loire wines, and are generally more concerned with the wines of their area than distant Muscadet.

In the Pays Nantais itself there are a number of *négociants* who take the question of *sur lie* as seriously as Louis Metaireau and Sauvion. Take Donatien Bahuaud, whose cellars at La Chapelle Heulin are some of the largest in the region. Their top wine comes from their own estate of Château de Cassmichère, which they claim is where the Muscadet vine was first planted in the Pays Nantais. A highly-polished presentation greets the visitor, but the wines can live up to the image. The most recent innovation is Le Master de Donatien, a special *cuvée* in a glazed, flowered bottle, which represents the best wines chosen by an international selection panel.

The place of wood in Muscadet

Chéreau-Carré is, by contrast, the largest grower in the region. Their home vineyard of Château de Chasseloir, near Saint-Fiacre in

Sèvre-et-Maine, is a showplace of the region, the centre of 300 hectares of vines, enormous by local standards. Bernard Chéreau Junior – so called to distinguish him from his father, also Bernard – is a trained viticulturalist, typical of the rising generation which is keen to improve quality and image.

He is also a showman in a gentle sort of way. We walked around the estate, admiring the gardens, avoiding the automatic sprinklers that kept the lawns green, and peering into the medieval tower which looms over the narrow gorge of the Maine. Higher up the slope, the vineyard stretches into the distance. We passed into the cellars, admiring the obligatory rows of stainless-steel tanks. Then M. Chéreau threw open the doors of a long, ancient room, sandy-floored and cool. Along the walls stood rows of brand new *barriques*: 'And this is where we age the wine in wood,' he said, confident of the effect of his words.

I must admit I did know by then that Muscadet is being aged in new wood. But the sight is still a little unnerving. After all, wood implies a wine that ages, and that is the last thing one would expect in most Muscadet. Chéreau-Carré was the first to experiment with wood maturation of Muscadet, and here was my chance to find out why.

M. Chéreau is quick with his explanations – he has obviously been asked this question plenty of times already: 'We remembered that the Melon grape came originally from Burgundy, and thought that it could be treated as a grape that makes wine for ageing. It can certainly make light, fresh, early-drinking wines, but it can also make wines that have some of the greatness of a Chardonnay.'

Whether he is right about the potential greatness of the Melon, the grape of Muscadet, is yet another subject of hot debate in the Pays Nantais. I tasted the Château de Chasseloir de Saint-Fiacre, the new wood-aged *cuvée* of Chéreau-Carré. The 1988 had much more colour than a typical Muscadet, nearer to pale gold than straw. The bouquet mixes spicy fruit with new wood, while as regards the taste, the wood – although present – does not kill the fruit, as has been suggested, but simply adds a layer of complexity to a straightforward wine.

So yes, it works. Just as, when I was with Guy Bossard, it seemed to work when I tasted his Cuvée Finement Boisée 1990, 30 per cent of which was aged in wood for three months. He has used *barriques* from Burgundy which were used for Chardonnay there, and the general effect, compared with his non-wooded *cuvée*, is one of richness and weight rather than too much wood.

Other exponents of wooded Muscadet are the Luneau brothers, Pierre and Rémy, whose Manoir La Grange is aged in wood for a short period, which once again gives point to the fruit rather than layers of oak on top of the wine. Pierre Luneau is one of the region's great experimenters: he has something of the look of the crazed scientist, although his dress sense is much more in the style of Lord of the Manor. He makes separate *cuvées* to suit every parameter possible: soil type, area of cultivation, different yeasts. He has land in three areas – Le Landreau, La Chapelle-Heulin and Vallet – which means he can mix a whole range of different wines to make up his final blends.

These include a top *cuvée*, Le L d'Or, which shows yet another aspect of the changes in Muscadet in recent years: the proliferation of prestige *cuvées*. Le L d'Or is special in its concentration, its ripeness of flavour and fruit – and its suitability for ageing for a considerable period. Pierre Luneau keeps the wines in tank under a blanket of nitrogen to preserve their freshness, and may not bottle them for ten years. During that time they take on a taste which turns them, by some strange permutation, into something closely akin to Chablis – indeed, there is a local saying that old Muscadet will become '*Chablisé*'.

I tasted more old Muscadet with Bruno Cormerais, whose cellars at Saint-Lumine-de-Clisson are at the end of narrow lanes bounded by high hedges. He is one of those who is determined that you will taste everything he has made – no chore when the wines are as good as his – and is eager to put over the message that Muscadet can age. Every few minutes he would disappear into a distant cellar to retrieve more bottles, while his wife would warn me that the tasting could be a long-winded affair when he really got going.

The Bruno Cormerais 1985 Muscadet had not quite the Chardonnay character of the Luneau wines, more of the asparagus taste of mature Sauvignon, with an overlay of dusty maturity and richness rather than acidity to the fore. It was certainly not too old, tasted at the end of a succession of wines beginning with the 1990 – one of the series of superb vintages that started with the 1986 and ran, with the exception of 1987, until the abrupt break of 1991.

Bruno Cormerais also has his own Cuvée Prestige, fermented in old barrels to add an oxidative element to the taste, to round it, concentrate it and exaggerate the taste of the lees from which it was bottled. That barrel fermentation did improve this wine was amply proved when I tasted the same blend in tank: much thinner, lighter, altogether meaner.

I discovered the same quality in the prestige *cuvée* of another grower, Claude Branger. He has 14.5 hectares in La Haut Fèvrie, on the Sèvre near La Haie Fouassière, a football team's-worth of children, and like many smaller producers in the area, sells most of his wine at the cellar door. Again like many other growers, he has subterranean tanks, the tops of which form the floor of his *chai*. They are ideal, he told me, because they keep the wine at a pretty constant temperature throughout the year.

While I certainly enjoyed his Muscadet de Sèvre-et-Maine from both 1989 (quite full, certainly creamy, but with overlying crisp flavours) and 1990 (softer and more rounded than the 1989, less initially aggressive and with less acidity), it was his Cuvée Excellence which really stood out; still with an earthy taste from the lees, this is a wine that will last for a good few years.

The other Muscadets

There is an enormous contrast between the essentially intimate countryside of Sèvre-et-Maine and the flat, open spaces of Le Lac de Grand-Lieu, which is in the heart of the basic Muscadet region. Contrary to popular misconceptions, the AC of Muscadet was not created at the same time as Muscadet de Sèvre-et-Maine in 1936, but one year later. It covers a different area which, although geographically much larger, has a much smaller proportion of vineyards: 2,000 hectares. Here, permitted yields are higher, and nearly all the average annual production of 140,000 hectolitres is sold to *négociants*.

It would not be too unfair to basic Muscadet to say that it is not as good as Muscadet de Sèvre-et-Maine. But it would also be fair to say that the best Muscadet is better than less-than-average Sèvre-et-Maine. And it is this fact which has led to two complementary demands from producers. One is for a separate *appellation* for the best basic Muscadet from Le Lac de Grand-Lieu region. The other is for a recognition that some *communes* in Sèvre-et-Maine deserve a separate *appellation*. Whether this means an *appellation* Muscadet Villages for the best *communes*, or some sort of Premier and

Grand Cru (as in Chablis) for the best vineyards is a debate which looks like running for a good while before any decisions are made.

And creating separate *appellations* doesn't necessarily help a particular area. When Muscadet de Sèvre-et-Maine was created, another *appellation* was also delineated: Muscadet des Coteaux de la Loire. This covers both banks of the Loire: on the south Champtoceaux, Liré and Saint-Florent-le-Vieil, and on the north bank Oudon, Saint-Géréon, Ancenis and Saint-Herblon. The existence of this distinct *appellation* has simply led to consumer confusion and its gradual disappearance, leaving only about 350 hectares and an average of 25,000 hectolitres of production today.

The wine itself – to judge from the few examples I have tasted – tends to be somewhat heavier, more rustic and less zingy, although often more acidic, than Muscadet de Sèvre-et-Maine. The soil here is mainly chalk, compared with the sandy soil of Sèvre-et-Maine, although Saint-Herblon is granite and makes wines with a distinctly flinty style.

In Ancenis, as well as Muscadet des Coteaux de la Loire, we find the small VDQS area of Coteaux d'Ancenis. It is a comparatively recent creation, dating from 1954, and was a response to the increasing popularity of the local rosé wines. For such a small production – from 26,000 hectolitres in 1987 down to 10,300 hectolitres in 1992 from at most 220 hectares – it's a pretty complicated *appellation*: red and rosé from the Gamay with a little Cabernet Franc, dry white from Chenin Blanc, sweet white from Malvoisie. In a curious way, the star turn is the sweet wine – it is really sweet in good years, and has a delicious honeyed scent. At the end of a meal in a local restaurant where the wine list has been dominated by dry Muscadet, it is a relief and a pleasure to drink a glass of this rare sweet wine.

Ancenis is also home to Cana, the largest food processors in France, a testimony to the big production of vegetables (especially *primeurs*, or baby vegetables) in the Pays Nantais. As part of their activities, they run the only co-operative in the whole of the Pays Nantais, the 300-member Les Vignerons de la Noëlle, which has 2 per cent of Muscadet production. Its range is certainly as good as that of an average *négociant*, and its uniqueness in a region of small growers underlines why *négociants* are so important to the local economy. There is, I was told, something of the individualist about the Pays Nantais farmer which makes him reluctant to join co-operatives – although I would have thought that this applied to any farmer anywhere in France.

15

The wines of Poitou and the Vendée, *and* vins de pays

———

Vins du Thouarsais

Of all the tiny outposts of viticulture in the Loire region, this is the tiniest. All of 17 hectares come under the VDQS area of Vins du Thouarsais, south and east of the town of Thouars in the *département* of Deux-Sèvres, and in 1992 twelve *vignerons* produced a total of 1,436 hectolitres. In theory, the vineyard covers a wide area, all of fifteen *communes*, but in practice vines are only found in the *commune* of Oiron-Bilazais, south-east of Thouars.

Given the size of the *appellation*, it is usefully uncomplicated. White wines can be made from Chenin Blanc and Chardonnay (up to 20 per cent in a blend), reds and rosés from Gamay, Cabernet Franc and Cabernet Sauvignon. Vineyards are on chalky soil, facing south and south-east.

It is uncomplicated countryside as well, slightly undulating but never offering anything dramatic. The château of Oiron, former home of the Marquise de Montespan, with its charming, if somewhat run-down park, is the only notable local landmark

The style of the wine is light, with the most successful being made using carbonic maceration and the Gamay grape. That style lends itself to early drinking, and these wines are definitely not for keeping. A somewhat weightier style comes from red wines vinified in a traditional style with mainly Cabernet Franc grapes. The whites, mainly in a fairly acidic Chenin style, are really only satisfactory in warm years, when in addition to dry wines, a few *demi-sec* wines can be produced which have some keeping qualities.

The only producer of any consequence I have come across is Michel Gigon, who makes the most of the *appellation*. He produces dry white and *demi-sec* in most years in his well-tended vineyards and in his neat cellar, lined with large wooden barrels. His Cabernet Franc red is generally pleasantly fruity, although the 1990 I tasted had, like so many wines from that extraordinary year, surprising depth and flavour.

Vins du Haut-Poitou

A much more significant stretch of Poitevin vineyard is to be found in the *département* of Vienne, west of Châtellerault in a triangle of land formed by the rivers Vienne, Auxances and Dive. This VDQS *appellation* covers forty-seven *communes*, with vineyards scattered widely in tiny plots, many of them only fractions of a hectare. Today there are 484 hectares of land under vine, which in 1992 produced 19,684 hectolitres of white wine and 18,087 hectolitres of red and rosé.

With such a scattering of land, it is not surprising that the power of a co-operative has been needed to get the region moving. Prior to the creation of the Cave du Haut-Poitou at Neuville-de-Poitou in 1948, the area was heading for the sort of terminal decline experienced by so many peripheral vineyards in the centre of France. Today, with 95 per cent of Haut-Poitou production and 450 members, it virtually is the *appellation*. Thanks to its influence, the co-operative has been able to mechanize the harvesting of grapes in the vineyards of this relatively flat region, and has installed in the cellars a battery of modern equipment which ensures that what the wines lack in individuality they make up for in reliability and drinkability.

It is good that this region has regained some of its place in the vinous scheme of things. Its history is long and, like Muscadet and other western Loire *appellations*, has traditionally been orientated towards exports. From vineyards inevitably founded by monastic institutions, particularly the abbey of Neuville, wines were regularly exported through the port of La Rochelle to England and the Low Countries. In the eighteenth century the vineyard covered the enormous area of 4,000 hectares. At that time it was planted mainly with Folle Blanche, the white grape of Cognac, and one must assume that much of the wine ended in the distillery. Today, tiny quantities of Folle Blanche remain, and are made into a thin table wine. Phylloxera and oidium took their usual toll, and the area declined until the establishment of the co-operative.

Reds, rosés and whites are produced under the VDQS rules.

Reds come from Gamay, Pinot Noir, Cabernet Franc, Cabernet Sauvignon, Cot, Merlot and Groslot; wines from Gamay and the Cabernets are the most significant. Whites are made from Sauvignon Blanc, Chardonnay, Pinot Blanc and Chenin Blanc. Again, two grape varieties – Sauvignon and Chardonnay – are the most significant in production terms.

This is one of the few regions of the Loire, apart from Touraine, where it is still possible to find varietally-labelled wines; 100 per cent Sauvignon Blanc, Chardonnay, Gamay and Cabernet Franc represent the vast majority of production, from both the co-operative and the handful of private growers. This has been an enormous sales advantage for the co-operative among today's varietally-conscious consumers, and is certainly part of the reason for the success of these wines not just in France but in export markets.

The size of the co-operative and the sophistication of its equipment are impressive. Pneumatic presses are on hand to care for the white grapes; low-temperature fermentation is in epoxy and stainless-steel tanks, some containing as much as 1,500 hectolitres, others smaller to cope with the grapes from individual *domaines*. Vinimatic fermenters are used, especially for the Gamay, to extract colour while leaving the wines soft and fruity. The top red *cuvée* – Héritage, made from Cabernet Franc – spends four months in large wooden barrels. Sparkling wine – Diane de Poitiers is the brand – is made for the Cave du Haut-Poitou at the co-operative of Saint-Cyr-en-Bourg in Saumur.

While the bulk of the production here is of the simple varietal wines, a few *domaine* wines are also made. Château de Brizay is a Sauvignon Blanc wine, Château Le Logis is Chardonnay, and Château Le Fuye is a Cabernet Franc which spends seven months in wood.

The only private producer in Haut-Poitou whose wines I have tasted is Christophe Croux, who owns Domaine de la Tour-Signy at Marigny-Dizay between Poitiers and Châtellerault. His Sauvignon Blanc is more earthy, less obviously crisp and fruity than the wine from the co-operative, perhaps more a style that goes with food.

Fiefs Vendéens

The Atlantic littoral south of the mouth of the Loire is a region of flatlands, of marshes and bird sanctuaries. It is also the home of the

Vendéens, whose reputation as a tough, individualistic people reached its apogee in the uprising which took place during the French Revolution. Brutally suppressed by the revolutionary government, the Vendée has never recovered economically.

Not the least to suffer were the vineyards which, until then, had been an important export business for many farmers. Like those of the Haut-Poitou, the wines passed through La Rochelle on their way to Britain, Flanders and the Netherlands – a trade that had developed during the Middle Ages, when this coast was controlled by the Plantagenet kings of England.

Today, as in so many minor areas, the wines of the Vendée are but a shadow of their former selves. The creation of a VDQS area in 1984 has done something to create a market, at least among the thousands of tourists who come to the area in the summer. Called Fiefs Vendéens – *fief* is a term for ecclesiastical land – the *appellation* in 1990 covered 355 hectares of vineyard producing 24,822 hectolitres (28,982 in 1992) in nineteen *communes*.

The area is divided into four zones. The largest is centred on Mareuil-sur-Lay, twenty kilometres south-east of La Roche-sur-Yon, and covers ten *communes*. The second and third, north and south of Fontenay-le-Comte, cover the *communes* of Pissotte and Vix, standing right on the edge of the marshlands of the Marais. The last section is right on the coast, north of Les Sables d'Olonne.

Each section of the Fiefs Vendéens has its own speciality or style. In the area around Mareuil, for instance, the style is for red wines, with some rosés, made from a blend of Cabernet Franc, Cabernet Sauvignon and at least 50 per cent of either Gamay or – curiously, this far west – Pinot Noir. The vineyards of Pissotte and Vix go in more for whites, made from Sauvignon Blanc, Chardonnay, Chenin Blanc and Melon de Bourgogne (the grape of nearby Muscadet). A few light reds and rosés are made from Gamay and Cabernet Franc.

In the fourth zone, that of the coast, it is white wines all the way, made from Chenin Blanc, Grolleau Gris and Sauvignon Blanc. To say that the wines have a whiff of the sea may be fanciful, but they are certainly light, very fresh, and delicious with local shellfish delicacies. A few reds and rosés are made, but amount to little.

Vins de pays

Since the creation of the concept of *vins de pays* in the 1970s, the Loire has had very little to do with them. Only one *vin de pays* zone, the Vin de Pays du Jardin de la France, covering the whole of the valley from Sancerre to the ocean, has seen any significant production. Other, more local *vins de pays* do exist, but production is generally in insignificant quantities.

The regional Vin de Pays du Jardin de la France is an omnibus *appellation*, created in 1981 and covering the *départements* of Cher, Loiret, Indre, Loir-et-Cher, Indre-et-Loire, Vienne, Maine-et-Loire, Deux-Sèvres, Loire-Atlantique and Vendée. It is partly used for wines from vineyards outside the main *appellation* areas, but like the similar Vin de Pays d'Oc in the south of France, is more likely to be used for wines which, although grown in *appellation* vineyards, do not fit into the strait-jacket of AC rules, often because they are made from non-traditional grapes.

Thus you will find 100 per cent single varietal wines labelled as such, which is only occasionally found among AC wines of the Loire. These varietal wines are often developed for the export market – where varietal-consciousness is more acute than in France – and are sold in supermarkets and other large retail shops. The main grape varieties appearing under their own names are Sauvignon Blanc and Chardonnay in whites, and Gamay in reds. Groslot and Pineau d'Aunis are used in rosés. Other grape varieties – Cabernet Sauvignon, Chenin Blanc – are found, but are much less common.

While much of the annual average production of 4,500 hectolitres a year comes from co-operatives, who are making special *cuvées* for particular customers, individual *domaines* have increasingly realized the advantage of having an extra, inexpensive wine in their range and are making a *vin de pays*, particularly from the white varietals. However, the style of all these wines is in the modern idiom, emphasizing technology as much as origin, international wine-making rather than local tradition.

Other *vin de pays* zones

All thirteen Loire wine *départements*, from Puy-de-Dôme to Vendée, have their own *vins de pays*. But such has been the popularity of Vin de Pays du Jardin de la France (the name obviously helps a lot) that many of them are virtually ignored. The most important of these departmental *vins de pays* are in Cher, mainly wines from Gamay and Sauvignon; in Indre-et-Loire, with wines from Sauvignon Blanc, Chenin Blanc and Chardonnay, following very much the style of white Touraine; in Loir-et-Cher, from the east of the *département* outside the Touraine AC area, come whites from Chenin and Sauvignon, reds and rosés from Cot, Gamay and Cabernet Franc; in Maine-et-Loire, production is mainly of reds from Cabernet Franc and Gamay; and in Loire-Atlantique, of light, tart reds, whites and rosés.

There is also a handful of local *vins de pays*. The most significant are in Loire-Atlantique. From the south of the *département* comes Vin de Pays des Marches de Bretagne: whites are from Muscadet and Folle Blanche, Sauvignon Blanc, Chenin Blanc and Chardonnay; reds, the majority, come from Gamay and Cot. Further to the west of the *département*, is the Vin de Pays de Retz (named after Gilles de Retz, the original Bluebeard). These are mainly red and rosé wines from Gamay, Groslot and Cot: the few whites come from Folle Blanche, Sauvignon Blanc and Chenin Blanc.

Right at the other end of the river, in the *département* of Loire, near the Côtes du Forez, reds and rosés under the Vin de Pays d'Urfé are made from Gamay and Pinot Noir in a sub-Beaujolais style.

16

The food of the Loire

The food of the Loire region is as varied as its wines. Between the meat-based cuisine of the upper reaches of the river and its tributaries in the Massif Central, and the seafood and fish of the Pays Nantais, there is little obvious connection. But put together, the profusion of fresh produce – the fruit and vegetables, the river fish like sander, eel, pike and crayfish, the pork and beef – goes to produce a cuisine that is the most archetypically French in France.

This is the land where modern French cooking began. It was in Touraine in the sixteenth century that Catherine de Medici brought Italian food to the French court. By doing so, she laid the groundwork for French cooking as it is today. The cooking of the south of France, with its emphasis on olive oil and herbs, may now be seen as more healthy, but if people think about French cooking, they still think in terms of rich sauces, of recipes dominated by cream and butter – the cooking of the Loire Valley and the north of France.

There are two main influences on the cooking of the Loire. One is water: the sea and the rivers. The other is the rich pasture-land. The former produces the rich variety of seafood and fish, the latter produces the excellent meat and the fruit and vegetables. The two come together most obviously in the Pays Nantais. To the west, the Atlantic Ocean gives a tang to the air of the marshes at the mouth of the Loire, to the salt-pans of Guérande on the promontory of Le Croisic west of Saint-Nazaire. From here too come the *fruits de mer*, the crabs, langoustines, oysters, clams and lobsters which make such excellent partners to Muscadet or Gros Plant wines. Sea fish, such as sea bass, are equally part of the local cuisine, invariably accompanied by a sauce which can be found right along the Loire: *beurre blanc*, a combination of local butter, shallots and white wine, rich, piquant from the shallots, and ladled profusely over any fish dish.

To the other side, in the countryside to the south and east of the city of Nantes, on the rich soil close to the river-banks, are huge market gardens which produce, under glass, many of the *primeurs*, or baby vegetables, which are exported round the world as well as eaten at local tables. Tiny carrots, potatoes, mange-tout, leeks, turnips, radishes, cucumbers and sweet corn all make their way from here to the big MIN market in Nantes, or go up the *autoroute* to the Paris markets at Rungis.

There are other local delicacies in Nantes: *mascarons Nantais*, chocolate-covered biscuits which have been produced by the local chocolate industry since the seventeenth century. Chocolate and sugar are important industries in the city, a reminder that Nantes is still the major port for imported sugar and cocoa from the West Indies and the Americas.

Further upstream, in Touraine and Anjou, the influence of the sea diminishes and is replaced by that of the rivers. Freshwater fish include shad, carp and tench, but above all it is the *sandre* (or pike perch), a firm, richly-flavoured, white-fleshed fish that is classically accompanied by the ubiquitous *beurre blanc* sauce. Dry white wines – those of Savennières are the supreme example – are standard and delicious partners.

The *anguille*, or river eel, makes regular appearances at the table in these middle reaches of the Loire. *Matelote d'anguille,* a rich stew of eel with young, tannic red wine (Chinon or Bourgueil are best), small onions, garlic and herbs, and topped at the last minute with croutons, is to be found all over Touraine. At Saint-Germain-sur-Vienne there is even a restaurant named after the fish, the Anguille Vagabonde.

Meat also makes a strong showing, especially in Touraine. The richness of the land in Touraine – vegetables grown beside the river, vines on the cliff-tops away from flooding, cereals grown in bright golden swathes in the valleys behind – has meant that there are few dishes which have remained exclusively local. Pork, beef and game – rabbit and venison – are all on the menus. The locals, the Tourangelles, claim that *coq au vin* and what is now called *boeuf Bourguignon* were actually invented in Touraine. Certainly those two dishes, with their rich, wine-based sauces, are typical of the approach here to cooking meat. Just upriver in the Orléanais a local dish is called *pot-au-feu du braconnier*, poacher's stew, in recognition of the place of rabbit as the prime meat in the dish.

Touraine was also the home of Rabelais, born just outside Chinon. The little valley of Lerné, just to the west, was the scene of the famous battle between Gargantua and the locals over *fouaces*, saffron-flavoured unleavened loaves, which thanks to an enterprising baker are still a speciality of the village.

Charcuterie is Touraine's other claim to fame: *andouillettes* (sausages made with chitterlings), *boudins* (black and white puddings), stuffed pigs' trotters, *rillons de veau* (savoury pork nuggets), *rillettes* (terrine of pork, carrots and shallots), meat in a wine jelly, *foie de veau* (the local version of foie gras). Any visitor to Vouvray must on no account miss the *charcuterie* of the Hardouin family whose two shops in the village are famous the length and breadth of the Loire. And no tasting of their produce is complete, they reckon, without a glass or two of medium-sweet Vouvray or Montlouis.

Local cheeses can be divided neatly into two styles. There are those from the upper reaches of the river, from the pastures of the mountains. The Massif Central produces cows'-milk cheese such as Forme de Montbrison, which comes from the slopes of the Côtes du Forez. Further downriver, Pithiviers in the Orléanais produces the mild cows'-milk Caillebotte and the stronger-tasting Bondaroy au Foin. From nearby in the Loir Valley is the blue Vendôme Bleu, while from the mouth of the river comes soft, creamy Crémet Nantais.

Goats'-milk cheeses are equally profuse. The most famous is the Crottin de Chavignol, produced in the Sancerrois and renowned as a perfect partner for white Sancerre. Equally local is Chabichou, a cone-shaped cheese with a blue rind. Touraine produces the pyramid-shaped cheeses of Saint-Maure and Valençay.

For dessert, the Loire can offer a mouth-watering range of pastries. They are found particularly in Anjou and Touraine. *Gâteau Pithiviers* is puff pastry filled with frangipane, while another delicacy from this town dedicated to gourmets is *tarte aux abricots à la crème de Pithiviers*, a sauce which combines almonds and rum. *Tarte Tatin*, perhaps the most celebrated tart in France, comes from the Sologne region of eastern Touraine: an upside-down, caramelized fruit tart normally made of apples, it was named after the Tatin sisters who created it in the nineteenth century.

Fruits soaked in Cointreau could also be considered a local dish in Anjou, since Angers is the home of this famous liqueur.

Any gourmet faced with this huge variety of foods need have no worries about the choice of wines to accompany them. If the Loire region is rich in food, its equally rich range of wines – from dry white with fish, through rosés with *charcuterie* and red wines with meat and stews, to sweet wines with *foie de veau*, blue cheeses or pastries, topped off with a glass of sparkling wine – is more than a match.

APPENDIX I

The appellations *of the Loire*

APPELLATIONS CONTRÔLÉES

Anjou
Date created: 31 December 1957
Hectares*: 1,995 for red; 1,289 for white
Yield*: 68 for red; 67 for white
Communes: 170 in Maine-et-Loire, 17 in Deux-Sèvres, 8 in Vienne.
Grape varieties permitted: Reds – Gamay, Cabernet Sauvignon, Cabernet Franc. White – Chenin Blanc, Chardonnay, Sauvignon Blanc. For rosés, see under Rosé d'Anjou.

Anjou Coteaux de la Loire
Date created: 26 August 1946
Hectares: 45
Yield: 35
Communes: Montjean, La Pomeraye, Chalonnes-sur-Loire, Ingrandes-sur-Loire, Champtocé, Saint-Georges-sur-Loire, La Possonnière, Savennières, Bouchemaine, Saint-Barthélemy, Brain-sur-Authion.
Grape varieties permitted: Chenin Blanc.

Anjou Gamay
Date created: 31 December 1957
Hectares: 376
Yield: 65
Communes: 170 in Maine-et Loire, 17 in Deux-Sèvres, 8 in Vienne.
Grape varieties permitted: Gamay.

Anjou Pétillant
Date created: 31 December 1957
Hectares: None

* *Hectares* actually planted in 1990; *Permitted Yield* in 1990 (hl/ha).

Yield: 72
Communes: 170 in Maine-et-Loire, 17 in Deux-Sèvres, 8 in Vienne.
Grape varieties permitted: Chenin Blanc, Cabernet Franc, Gamay.

Anjou Mousseux
Date created: 31 December 1957
Hectares: 110
Yield: 72
Communes: 170 in Maine-et-Loire, 17 in Deux-Sèvres, 8 in Vienne.
Grape varieties permitted: Chenin Blanc, Cabernet Franc, Gamay.

Anjou Villages
Date created: 14 November 1991
Hectares: 330
Yield: 62
Communes: 46 in Maine-et-Loire.
Grape varieties permitted: Cabernet Franc, Cabernet Sauvignon.

Bourgueil
Date created: 31 July 1937
Hectares: 1,136
Yield: 62
Communes: Bourgueil, Benais, Chouzé-sur-Loire, Ingrandes-de-Touraine, La Chapelle-sur-Loire, Restigné, Saint-Patrice, Saint-Nicolas-de-Bourgueil.
Grape varieties permitted: Cabernet Franc, Cabernet Sauvignon.

Bonnezeaux
Date created: 6 November 1951
Hectares: 85
Yield: 35
Communes: Thouarcé.
Grape varieties permitted: Chenin Blanc.

Cabernet d'Anjou
Date created: 9 May 1964
Hectares: 2,060
Yield: 70
Communes: As for Anjou.
Grape varieties permitted: Cabernet Franc, Cabernet Sauvignon.

Cabernet de Saumur
Date created: 9 May 1964
Hectares: 60
Yield: 62
Communes: 28 in Maine-et-Loire, 10 in Vienne, 1 in Deux-Sèvres.
Grape varieties permitted: Cabernet Franc, Cabernet Sauvignon.

Cheverny
Date created: 1992
Hectares (VDQS): 337
Yield (VDQS): 70
Communes: Cande-sur-Beuvron, Cellettes, Cheverny, Chitenay,
Cormeray, Cour-Cheverny, Feings, Fougères-sur-Bièvre, Fresnes,
Huisseau-sur-Cosson, Les Montils, Maslives, Mont-près-Chambord,
Montlivault, Muides-sur-Loire, Nouan-sur-Loire, Ouchamps, Sambin,
Saint-Claude-di-Diray, Saint-Dye-sur-Loire, Seur, Tour-en-Sologne,
Vineuil.
Grape varieties permitted: Red – Gamay, Pinot Noir, Cabernet Franc,
Cabernet Sauvignon, Cot. Rosé – as for red, plus Pineau d'Aunis, Pinot
Gris. White – Romorantin, Chenin Blanc, Menu Pineau, Chardonnay,
Sauvignon Blanc.

Chinon
Date created: 31 July 1937
Hectares: 1,765
Yield: 58
Communes: Anché, Avoine, Avon-les-Roches, Beaumont-en-Véron,
Chinon, Cravant-les-Coteaux, Crouzilles, Huisnes, L'Île Bouchard, Ligré,
Marçay, Panzoult, La-Roche-Clermault, Rivière, Saint-Benoît-la-Forêt,
Savigny-en-Véron, Sazilly, Tavant, Theneuil.
Grape varieties permitted: Red and rosé – Cabernet Franc, Cabernet
Sauvignon. White – Chenin Blanc.

Coteaux de l'Aubance
Date created: 18 February 1950
Hectares: 65
Yield: 45
Communes: Brissac-Quincé, Denée, Juigné-sur-Loire, Mozé-sur-Louet,
Murs-Erigné, Saint-Jean-des-Mauvrets, Saint-Melaine-sur-Aubance, Saint-
Saturnin-sur-Loire, Soulaines-sur-Aubance, Vauchrétien.
Grape varieties permitted: Chenin Blanc.

Coteaux du Layon
Date created: 18 February 1950
Hectares: 1,011
Yield: 38
Communes: 24 in Maine-et-Loire.
Grape varieties permitted: Chenin Blanc.

Coteaux du Layon Villages (followed by village name)
Date created: 18 February 1950
Hectares: 285
Yield: 32
Communes: Beaulieu-sur-Layon, Faye d'Anjou, Rablay-sur-Layon, Rochefort-sur-Loire, Saint-Lambert-du-Lattay.
Grape varieties permitted: Chenin Blanc.

Coteaux du Layon Chaume
Date created: 18 February 1950
Hectares: 78
Yield: 34
Communes: Chaume.
Grape varieties permitted: Chenin Blanc.

Coteaux du Loir
Date created: 12 May 1948
Hectares: 37
Yield: 50
Communes: 16 in Sarthe, 7 in Indre-et-Loire.
Grape varieties permitted: Red – Cabernet Franc, Pineau d'Aunis, Cot. Rosé – as for red, plus Grolleau. White – Chenin Blanc.

Coteaux de Saumur
Date created: 21 April 1962
Hectares: 20
Yield: 49
Communes: Brézé, Chacé, Dampierre-sur-Loire, Epieds, Fontevrault, Montsoreau, Parnay, Saint-Cyr-en-Bourg, Saint-Hilaire-Saint-Florent, Saiz, Saumur, Souzay-Champigny, Turquant.
Grape varieties permitted: Chenin Blanc.

Cour-Cheverny
Date created: 1992
Hectares: included with Cheverny
Yield: included with Cheverny

Communes: Cour-Cheverny.
Grape varieties permitted: Romorantin.

Crémant de Loire
Date created: 17 October 1975
Hectares: 434
Yield: 81
Communes: production areas of Anjou, Saumur and Touraine.
Grape varieties permitted: White and rosé – Chenin Blanc, Chardonnay, Menu Pineau, Pineau d'Aunis, Pinot Noir, Cabernet Franc, Cabernet Sauvignon, Grolleau Noir, Grolleau Gris.

Jasnières
Date created: 31 July 1937
Hectares: 31
Yield: 42
Communes: Lhomme, Ruille-sur-Loir.
Grape varieties permitted: Chenin Blanc.

Menetou-Salon
Date created: 23 January 1959
Hectares: 196
Yield: 68
Communes: Aubinges, Humbligny, Menetou-Salon, Morogues, Parassy, Pigny, Quantilly, Saint-Céols, Soulangis, Vignoux-sous-les-Aix.
Grape varieties permitted: Red and rosé – Pinot Noir. White – Sauvignon Blanc.

Montlouis
Date created: 6 December 1938
Hectares: 247
Yield: 53
Communes: Lissault, Montlouis-sur-Loire, Saint-Martin-le-Beau.
Grape varieties permitted: Chenin Blanc.

Montlouis Pétillant
Date created: 6 December 1938
Hectares: see Montlouis Mousseux
Yield: see Montlouis Mousseux
Communes: Lissault, Montlouis-sur-Loire, Saint-Martin-le-Beau.
Grape varieties permitted: Chenin Blanc.

Montlouis Mousseux
Date created: 6 December 1938
Hectares: 111 (incl. Pétillant)
Yield: 72
Communes: Lissault, Montlouis-sur-Loire, Saint-Martin-le-Beau.
Grape varieties permitted: Chenin Blanc.

Muscadet
Date created: 23 September 1938
Hectares: 1,110
Yield: 60
Communes: 46 in Loire-Atlantique, 4 in Vendée, 3 in Maine-et-Loire.
Grape varieties permitted: Muscadet (also known as Melon de Bourgogne).

Muscadet des Coteaux de la Loire
Date created: 14 November 1936
Hectares: 453
Yield: 57
Communes: 24 in Loire-Atlantique and Maine-et-Loire.
Grape varieties permitted: Muscadet (also known as Melon de Bourgogne).

Muscadet de Sèvre-et-Maine
Date created: 14 November 1936
Hectares: 9,717
Yield: 53
Communes: 23 in Loire-Atlantique.
Grape varieties permitted: Muscadet (also known as Melon de Bourgogne).

Pouilly-sur-Loire
Date created: 31 July 1937
Hectares: 56
Yield: 68
Communes: Garchy, Mesves-sur-Loire, Pouilly-sur-Loire, Saint-Andelain, Saint-Laurent, Saint-Martin-sur-Nohain, Tracy-sur-Loire.
Grape varieties permitted: Chasselas.

Pouilly Fumé (also called **Blanc Fumé de Pouilly**)
Date created: 31 July 1937
Hectares: 745
Yield: 74

Communes: Garchy, Mesves-sur-Loire, Pouilly-sur-Loire, Saint-Andelain, Saint-Laurent, Saint-Martin-sur-Nohain, Tracy-sur-Loire.
Grape varieties permitted: Sauvignon Blanc.

Quarts-de-Chaume
Date created: 10 August 1954
Hectares: 28
Yield: 25
Communes: Rochefort-sur-Loire.
Grape varieties permitted: Chenin Blanc.

Quincy
Date created: 6 August 1936
Hectares: 119
Yield: 56
Communes: Brinay, Quincy.
Grape varieties permitted: Sauvignon Blanc.

Reuilly
Date created: 24 August 1961
Hectares: 74
Yield: 51
Communes: Cerbois, Chery, Diou, Lazenay, Lury-sur-Arnon, Preuilly, Reuilly.
Grape varieties permitted: Red and rosé – Pinot Noir, Pinot Gris. White – Sauvignon Blanc.

Rosé d'Anjou
Date created: 31 December 1957
Hectares: 1,961
Yield: 72
Communes: 170 in Maine-et-Loire, 17 in Deux-Sèvres, 8 in Vienne.
Grape varieties permitted: Cabernet Franc, Cabernet Sauvignon, Pineau d'Aunis, Grolleau, Gamay, Cot.

Rosé d'Anjou Pétillant
Date created: 31 December 1957
Hectares: included with Rosé d'Anjou
Yield: included with Rosé d'Anjou
Communes: 170 in Maine-et-Loire, 17 in Deux-Sèvres, 8 in Vienne.
Grape varieties permitted: as for Rosé d'Anjou.

Rosé de Loire
Date created: 4 September 1974
Hectares: 701
Yield: 72
Communes: production areas of Anjou, Saumur and Touraine.
Grape varieties permitted: Cabernet Franc, Cabernet Sauvignon, Pineau d'Aunis, Pinot Noir, Gamay, Grolleau.

Sancerre
Date created: 23 January 1959
Hectares: 1,958
Yield: 70
Communes: Bannay, Bué, Crézancy, Menetou-Ratel, Ménétréol-sous-Sancerre, Montigny, Sainte-Gemme-en-Sancerrois, Sanit-Satur, Sancerre (incl. Chavignol), Sury-en-Vaux, Thauvenay, Veaugues, Verdigny, Vinon.
Grape varieties permitted: Red and rosé – Pinot Noir. White – Sauvignon Blanc.

Saint-Nicolas-de-Bourgueil
Date created: 31 July 1937
Hectares: 788
Yield: 60
Communes: Saint-Nicolas-de-Bourgueil.
Grape varieties permitted: Cabernet Franc, Cabernet Sauvignon.

Saumur
Date created: 31 December 1957
Hectares: 509 for white, 688 for red
Yield: 74 for white, 72 for red
Communes: production areas of 28 in Maine-et-Loire, 10 in Vienne, 1 in Deux-Sèvres.
Grape varieties permitted: Red – Cabernet Franc, Cabernet Sauvignon, Pineau d'Aunis. White – Chenin Blanc, Chardonnay, Sauvignon Blanc.

Saumur-Champigny
Date created: 31 December 1957
Hectares: 1,075
Yield: 72
Communes: Chacé, Dampierre-sur-Loire, Montsoreau, Parnay, Saint-Cyr-en-Bourg, Saumur, Souzay-Champigny, Torquant, Varrains.
Grape varieties permitted: Cabernet Franc, Cabernet Sauvignon, Pineau d'Aunis.

Saumur Pétillant
Date created: 31 December 1957
Hectares: see Saumur Mousseux
Yield: see Saumur Mousseux
Communes: 55 in Maine-et-Loire, Vienne and Deux-Sèvres.
Grape varieties permitted: Rosé – Cabernet Franc, Cabernet Sauvignon, Gamay, Pinot Noir, Grolleau, Pineau d'Aunis. White – Chenin Blanc, Chardonnay, Sauvignon Blanc and the red varieties above.

Saumur Mousseux
Date created: 26 August 1976
Hectares: 1,571
Yield: 75
Communes: 55 in Maine-et-Loire, Vienne and Deux-Sèvres.
Grape varieties permitted: Rosé – Cabernet Franc, Cabernet Sauvignon, Gamay, Pinot Noir, Grolleau, Pineau d'Aunis. White – Chenin Blanc, Chardonnay, Sauvignon Blanc and the red varieties above.

Savennières
Date created: 8 December 1952
Hectares: 69
Yield: 47
Communes: Bouchemaine, La Possonnière, Savennières.
Grape varieties permitted: Chenin Blanc.

Savennières Coulée-de-Serrant
Date created: 8 December 1952
Hectares: 7
Yield: 47
Communes: Savennières.
Grape varieties permitted: Chenin Blanc.

Savennières Roche-aux-Moines
Date created: 8 December 1952
Hectares: 17
Yield: 47
Communes: Savennières.
Grape varieties permitted: Chenin Blanc.

Touraine
Date created: 24 December 1939
Hectares: 2,610 for white, 3,090 for reds
Yield: 66 for whites, 63 for reds

Communes: production areas of 113 in Indre-et-Loire, 42 in Loir-et-Cher, 1 in Indre.
Grape varieties permitted: Red – Gamay, Cabernet Franc, Cabernet Sauvignon, Cot, Pinot Noir, Pinot Gris, Pineau d'Aunis. Rosé – the same, plus Grolleau. White – Sauvignon Blanc, Chenin Blanc, Menu Pineau, Chardonnay.

Touraine Azay-le-Rideau
Date created: 24 December 1939
Hectares: 43
Yield: 50
Communes: Artannes-sur-Indre, Azay-le-Rideau, Cheillé, Lignières-de-Touraine, Rivarennes, Sache, Thilouze, Vallères.
Grape varieties permitted: Rosé – Grolleau, Cot, Cabernet Franc, Cabernet Sauvignon, Gamay. White – Chenin Blanc.

Touraine Amboise
Date created: 24 December 1939
Hectares: 216
Yield: 64
Communes: Amboise, Cangey, Chargé, Limeray, Mosnes, Nazelles, Pocé-sur-Cissé, Saint-Ouen-les-Vignes.
Grape varieties permitted: Red and rosé – Gamay, Cabernet Franc, Cabernet Sauvignon, Cot. White – Chenin Blanc.

Touraine Mesland
Date created: 24 December 1939
Hectares: 209
Yield: 53
Communes: Chambon-sur-Cissé, Chouzy-sur-Cissé, Mesland, Molineuf, Monteaux, Onzain.
Grape varieties permitted: Red and rosé – Gamay, Cabernet Franc, Cabernet Sauvignon, Cot. White – Chenin Blanc, Sauvignon Blanc.

Touraine Pétillant
Date created: 24 December 1939
Hectares: very rarely found.
Communes: 113 in Indre-et-Loire, 42 in Loir-et-Cher, 1 in Indre.
Grape varieties permitted: Rosé – Cabernet Franc, Cabernet Sauvignon, Cot, Pinot Meunier, Grolleau. White – the rosé varieties, plus Chenin Blanc, Menu Pineau, Chardonnay.

Touraine Mousseux
Date created: 16 October 1946
Hectares: 135
Yield: 75
Communes: 113 in Indre-et-Loire, 42 in Loir-et-Cher, 1 in Indre.
Grape varieties permitted: Rosé – Cabernet Franc, Cabernet Sauvignon, Cot, Pinot Meunier, Grolleau. White – the rosé varieties, plus Chenin Blanc, Menu Pineau, Chardonnay.

Vouvray
Date created: 8 December 1936
Hectares: 1,134
Yield: 57
Communes: Chançay, Noizay, Parçay-Meslay, Reugny, Rochecorbon, Sainte-Radegonde, Vernou-sur-Brenne, Vouvray.
Grape varieties permitted: Chenin Blanc.

Vouvray Pétillant
Date created: 8 December 1936
Hectares: included with Vouvray Mousseux
Yield: included with Vouvray Mousseux
Communes: Chançay, Noizay, Parçay-Meslay, Reugny, Rochecorbon, Sainte-Radegonde, Vernou-sur-Brenne, Vouvray.
Grape varieties permitted: Chenin Blanc.

Vouvray Mousseux
Date created: 8 December 1936
Hectares: 612
Yield: 75
Communes: Chançay, Noizay, Parçay-Meslay, Reugny, Rochecorbon, Sainte-Radegonde, Vernou-sur-Brenne, Vouvray.
Grape varieties permitted: Chenin Blanc

VINS DÉLIMITÉS DE QUALITÉ SUPÉRIEURE

Châteaumeillant
Date created: 18 February 1965
Hectares: 57
Yield: 51
Communes: 4 in Cher, 4 in Indre.
Grape varieties permitted: Gamay, Pinot Gris, Pinot Noir.

Coteaux d'Ancenis
Date created: 27 August 1973
Hectares: 273
Yield: 70
Communes: 16 in Loire-Atlantique, 11 in Maine-et-Loire.
Grape varieties permitted: Red and rosé – Gamay, Cabernet Franc,
Cabernet Sauvignon. White – Chenin Blanc, Pinot Gris (Malvoisie).

Coteaux du Giennois
Date created: 26 November 1954
Hectares: 95
Yield: 59
Communes: Aligny-Cosne, Beaulieu, Bonny-sur-Loire, Briare, La Celle-
sur-Loire, Châtillon-sur-Loire, Cours-les-Cosne, Cosne-sur-Loire, Gien,
Myennes, Neuvy-sur-Loire, Ousson-sur-Loire, Pougny, Saint-Loup, Saint-
Père, Thou.
Grape varieties permitted: Red and rosé – Gamay, Pinot Noir. White –
Sauvignon Blanc, Chenin Blanc.

Coteaux du Giennois Cosne-sur-Loire
Date created: 26 November 1954
Hectares: included with Coteaux du Giennois
Yield: 59
Communes: Cosne-sur-Loire.
Grape varieties permitted: Red and rosé – Gamay, Pinot Noir. White –
Sauvignon Blanc, Chenin Blanc.

Coteaux du Vendômois
Date created: 21 June 1968
Hectares: 94
Yield: 64
Communes: 34 in Loir-et-Cher.
Grape varieties permitted: Red – Pinot Noir, Cabernet Franc, Cabernet
Sauvignon. Rosé – red varieties, plus Pineau d'Aunis, Gamay. White –
Chenin Blanc, Chardonnay.

Côtes d'Auvergne
Date created: 14 March 1977
Hectares: 414
Yield: 50
Communes: Boudes, Chanturge, Châteaugay, Corent, Madargues (all
permitted on the label).
Grape varieties permitted: Gamay, Pinot Noir, Chardonnay.

Côtes du Forez
Date created: 1962
Hectares: 163
Yield: 56
Communes: 21 between Boën and Montbrison.
Grape varieties permitted: Gamay.

Côte Roannaise
Date created: 1955
Hectares: 100
Yield: 66
Communes: 25 between La Picaudière and Bully in the region of Renaison and Roanne.
Grape varieties permitted: Gamay.

Fiefs Vendéens
Date created: 1984
Hectares: 355
Yield: 70
Communes: 19 in Loire-Atlantique.
Grape varieties permitted: Red and rosé – Gamay, Pinot Noir, Cabernet Franc, Cabernet Sauvignon, Negrette, Grolleau Gris. White – Chenin Blanc, Sauvignon Blanc, Chardonnay, Muscadet, Grolleau Gris.

Gros Plant du Pays Nantais
Date created: 1954
Hectares: 2,976
Yield: 71
Communes: 72 in Loire-Atlantique, 16 in Maine-et-Loire, 6 in Vendée.
Grape varieties permitted: Gros Plant.

Saint-Pourçain-sur-Sioule
Date created: 1951
Hectares: 515
Yield: 49
Communes: 19 between Moulins and Chantelle.
Grape varieties permitted: White – Chardonnay, Tressalier, Sauvignon, Aligoté, Saint-Pierre-Doré. Red – Pinot Noir, Gamay.

Valençay
Date created: 1970
Hectares: 113
Yield: 64

Communes: 14 around the town of Valençay.
Grape varieties permitted: White – Menu-Pineau (Arbois), Chenin Blanc, Sauvignon Blanc, Chardonnay. Red – Cabernet Sauvignon, Cabernet Franc, Cot, Gamay, Pineau d'Aunis.

Vins du Haut-Poitou
Date created: 1970
Hectares: 484
Yield: 65
Communes: 45 in Vienne, 2 in Deux-Sèvres.
Grape varieties permitted: Red and rosé – Gamay, Pinot Noir, Cabernet Franc, Cot, Merlot, Grolleau. White – Sauvignon Blanc, Chardonnay, Pinot Blanc, Chenin Blanc.

Vins de l'Orléanais
Date created: 1951
Hectares: 152
Yield: 55
Communes: Cléry-Saint-André, Mareau-aux-Prés, Mézières-les-Cléry, Olivet, Saint-Hilaire-Saint-Mesmin (all on the left bank of the river), plus 19 *communes* on the right bank of the river.
Grape varieties permitted: Red and rosé – Pinot Meunier, Pinot Noir, Cabernet Franc. White – Chardonnay.

Vins du Thouarsais
Date created: 1966
Hectares: 17
Yield: 53
Communes: Coulonges-Thouarsais, Luche-Thouarsais, Luzay, Massais, Maulais, Misse, Oiron-Bilazais, Pas-de-Jeu, Pierrefitte, Rigne, Saint-Jacques-de-Thouars, Saint-Jean-de-Thouars, Sainte-Gemme, Saint-Varent, Taize.
Grape varieties permitted: Red and rosé – Gamay, Cabernet Franc, Cabernet Sauvignon. White – Chenin Blanc, Chardonnay.

APPENDIX 2

Production figures by appellation *(in hectolitres)*

━━━

APPELLATIONS CONTRÔLÉES	1985	1988	1990	1992
Anjou Blanc	105,792	66,206	62,542	84,634
Anjou Rouge	115,729	101,016	119,420	96,000
Anjou Coteaux de la Loire	1,029	1,195	1,894	1,621
Anjou Gamay	23,144	18,572	22,506	22,702
Anjou Pétillant/Anjou Mousseux	6,112	3,627	4,311	4,905
Anjou Villages		14,083	18,362	12,960
Bourgueil	55,154	61,001	70,534	78,464
Bonnezeaux	1,215	1,788	2,623	2,278
Cabernet d'Anjou	145,568	122,581	135,010	154,344
Cabernet de Saumur	2,066	2,674	4,009	4,386
Cheverny	16,880	13,017	23,577	22,278
Chinon	69,039	86,059	103,889	125,501
Coteaux de l'Aubance	2,364	1,749	4,046	2,579
Coteaux du Layon	50,151	45,782	50,666	45,151
Coteaux du Loir	1,485	1,237	1,859	2,392
Coteaux du Saumur	423	422	982	57
Cour-Cheverny	[Not AC until 1993; figures included in Cheverny]			
Crémant de Loire	10,089	9,804	35,141	48,651
Jasnières	926	786	1,292	1,791
Menetou-Salon	5,958	9,841	13,231	16,909
Montlouis still	10,594	7,928	12,974	7,804
Montlouis Pétillant/ Montlouis Mousseux	3,105	4,667	8,043	10,303
Muscadet	205,370	131,579	66,974	88,543
Muscadet des Coteaux de la Loire	17,929	17,203	26,037	28,580

APPELLATIONS CONTRÔLÉES	1985	1988	1990	1992
Muscadet de Sèvre-et-Maine	491,335	540,398	513,327	675,418
Pouilly-sur-Loire	3,421	3,441	3,785	3,306
Pouilly Fumé	34,347	44,702	55,316	60,759
Quarts-de-Chaume	837	559	703	1,250
Quincy	2,825	4,591	6,729	8,643
Reuilly	1,083	2,506	3,766	5,570
Rosé d'Anjou	194,753	158,782	141,020	166,169
Rosé de Loire	29,365	23,486	50,194	50,274
Sancerre	104,296	125,082	136,914	140,554
Saint-Nicolas-de-Bourgueil	38,908	42,105	47,276	55,359
Saumur Blanc	40,523	30,522	37,707	35,854
Saumur Rouge	27,055	39,952	49,489	48,606
Saumur-Champigny	51,204	58,773	77,421	75,505
Saumur Pétillant/Saumur Mousseux	56,442	69,243	117,852	144,277
Savennières	2,198	2,408	2,536	3,769
Touraine Blanc	130,081	148,545	172,396	187,304
Touraine Rouge	156,340	166,138	195,304	214,599
Touraine Azay-le-Rideau	1,381	2,414	2,164	2,072
Touraine Amboise	11,002	10,413	13,876	9,573
Touraine Mesland	11,290	9,996	11,052	8,666
Touraine Pétillant/Touraine Mousseux	2,098	5,900	10,064	13,189
Vouvray	86,608	48,840	64,482	40,035
Vouvray Pétillant/Vouvray Mousseux	21,090	69,197	46,184	83,547
Total AC	2,348,604	2,330,810	2,549,479	2,897,131
VDQS AREAS				
Châteaumeillant	2,435	4,280	2,929	4,200
Coteaux d'Ancenis	19,958	21,445	19,205	25,956
Coteaux du Giennois	3,490	5,400	5,589	7,482
Coteaux du Vendômois	5,854	3,571	6,049	14,312
Côtes d'Auvergne	18,983	20,073	20,841	21,851
Côtes du Forez	6,230	8,551	9,141	10,518
Côte Roannaise	3,137	4,823	4,989	7,815
Fiefs Vendéens	21,439	19,433	24,822	28,982

PRODUCTION FIGURES BY *APPELLATION*

VDQS AREAS	1985	1988	1990	1992
Gros Plant du Pays Nantais	279,082	222,604	212,466	224,993
Saint-Pourçain-sur-Sioule	20,511	29,162	25,157	29,538
Valençay	6,556	5,956	7,253	6,173
Vins du Haut-Poitou	35,659	31,415	31,488	37,771
Vins de l'Orléanais	6,015	6,205	8,394	9,953
Vins du Thouarsais	1,548	1,824	893	1,436
Total VDQS	430,897	384,742	379,216	430,980

APPENDIX 3

Loire vintages as at autumn 1993

━━━━━

(I am indebted to Charles Sydney, Courtier en Vins de Loire, for much of this vintage information.)

Pre-war vintages still to be found in some cellars. The wines that would still be drinkable are the sweet wines of Vouvray and the Coteaux du Layon (including Quarts-de-Chaume and Bonnezeaux), the dry whites of Vouvray and Savennières, and the reds of Chinon and Bourgueil.

1893: One of the earliest harvests on record – started at the end of August in many *appellations*.

1900: The quality of wines made throughout France that year was reflected on the Loire.

1921: Like 1893, a particularly hot year.

1928: Some delicious sweet white wines from Anjou are still very drinkable. This was the best vintage between 1921 and 1937.

1933: Wines still have another ten years of life.

1937: Regarded by Michael Broadbent in *The Great Vintage Wine Book* as 'one of the most successful white wine vintages of the century'.

Post-war vintages

1947: Exceptional vintage on a par with 1989 and 1990, with some hugely-rich reds and (still-youthful) Chenins from the Layon and Vouvray.

1959: One of the great vintages of the century, with even some Sancerres staying the course and developing a butteriness often associated with good Meursault.

1964: A great vintage for reds and for Vouvray, less so in the Layon.

1969: Excellent, with some reds still showing well and with plenty of exquisite (now mature) Layons and Vouvrays. Even some Muscadets have held up well, maturing into deep dry wines which could be mistaken for Chardonnay or Chenin Blanc.

More recent vintages

1976: Superb vintage, certainly the best of the decade, with fine wines along the river. Particularly good keeping wines, with delicious *moelleux* (sweet) from Vouvray and the Layon, and rich, well-balanced reds that have taken on a deep 'Burgundian' gaminess.

1977: Could be the second-worst of the century (1991 was the worst). Spring frosts with up to 50 per cent crop loss, followed by a damp, cool summer.

1978: Good year for white wines from Sancerre/Pouilly and Savennières from Anjou.

1979: A good to average year which produced a fine crop of early-maturing wines.

1980: Average vintage across the Loire, though some good reds produced, now fully mature.

1981: Now a great rarity, as production was very low following a poor flowering. Some fine reds and Vouvrays, though less successful in Anjou.

1982: Good to excellent vintage following a fine summer; wines with great fruit, though perhaps lacking a little concentration as yields tended to be high.

1983: Good vintage, with particularly fine, savoury reds. Production in Vouvray perhaps a little too high to make really fine wines.

1984: Very much an average vintage, though low acidity levels made for plenty of easy-drinking reds.

1985: Excellent vintage across the Loire, with particularly fine Chenin Blancs (some fine *moelleux* Vouvrays) and Cabernet Francs. The wines from Chinon and Bourgueil are particularly fine, though marked with a clear 'green pepper' character.

1986: Good vintage, though perhaps a touch severe, with the reds and the Chenins making wines with good structure and fruit that needed time to open. Many of the finest reds are only now really opening up.

1987

Muscadet: good, plenty of fruit with good balanced acidity producing crisp wines that have held well.

Anjou and the Coteaux du Layon: soft, fruity, well-balanced wines – a particularly easy-drinking and highly commercial vintage for all the styles produced in this region, from dry to sweet whites through to the reds. Although not a great vintage for keeping wines, the best Coteaux du Layon and Savennières are now maturing nicely. Drink 1998–2008.

Saumur: Good average vintage producing wines with comparatively low acidity, giving easily-approachable dry whites and supple reds with plenty of ripe fruit for early drinking. Now maturing. Drink now to 1998.

Chinon, Bourgueil and Saint-Nicolas-de-Bourgueil: A fine classic vintage for these red *appellations*, producing fresh, attractive wines with plenty of fruit. Good for early drinking, the finer examples are now beginning to attain a rich, gamey maturity. Drink now to 1998.

Vouvray and Montlouis: A reasonably average vintage, though certainly not one for producing *moelleux*. Some fine *demi-secs* and *secs* for easy drinking.

Sancerre, Pouilly and the Centre: A good vintage, perfectly suited to the production of crisp, aromatic Sauvignon Blanc.

1988

Muscadet: Similar to 1987 with perhaps less poise.

Anjou and the Coteaux du Layon: A dry summer led to wines with some structure. The Coteaux du Layon produced wonderfully aromatic wines that were a delight to drink in their youth, but which will continue to improve.

Saumur: A good summer led to firm wines with structure, better than 1987 in the long term, though perhaps less attractive for early drinking. A good vintage for dry whites and sparkling.

Chinon, Bourgueil and Saint-Nicolas-de-Bourgueil: Some firmness will help these wines mature slowly. Most commentators prefer the 1988s to the 1987s, but Charles Sydney comments: 'I like the suppler fruit of the earlier vintage and find some of the 1988s a little green.'

Vouvray and Montlouis: Richer than 1987, with altogether firmer and riper wines (and some fine *moelleux*) with a better balance of acidity to fruit. Excellent young (and particularly aromatic), these are now beginning to open into a more complex maturity and should continue to improve.

Sancerre, Pouilly and the Centre: Marginally firmer and more complex than 1987, these are wines with a natural acidity sufficient to ensure that they can hold and improve over a number of years.

1989

Muscadet: A marvellous summer and dry growing season led to wines with a high natural ripeness and low acidity, making rounded, almost exotic wines for early drinking.

Anjou and the Coteaux du Layon: Exceptional weather throughout the growing season led to wines – red and white – of greater power. The drought and heat particularly concentrated the sweet Coteaux du Layon, producing wines of a natural ripeness not seen since 1947, though this concentration came more from *passerillage*, a drying-out of the grapes on the vines, than through noble rot. Currently as closed as only Chenin can be, both these and dry Savennières should be left until at least 1995, when they will start to open up. The best will keep fifty years.

Saumur: Clearly the finest vintage for several decades, certainly equalling 1959, 1947 and perhaps even the legendary 1893. Perfect conditions throughout the growing season led to unprecedentedly ripe grapes that were harvested in ideal conditions, though the fine weather at harvest led to some producers having problems in keeping fermentations under control. The best reds are rich and ripe with exceptional balance of fruit and tannins, giving wines that are already drinking well and should last twenty years or more. An excellent vintage for whites too (leading to some scarcity of base wines for sparkling Saumur) with deep, complex dry whites and – exceptionally – the production of some fine *moelleux* Coteaux de Saumur.

Chinon, Bourgueil and Saint-Nicolas-de-Bourgueil: Certainly the vintage of the generation, and arguably the vintage of the century. Flowering took place in perfect conditions, and was followed by a long, hot and dry summer that produced grapes being harvested at optimum ripeness. A vintage for rich, well-structured wines with plenty of weight and tannin; the lighter wines from sand and gravel vineyards are drinking well now, while the richer *cuvées* from old vines or from limestone vineyards are only just beginning to open and will continue to mature for twenty-five years or more.

Vouvray and Montlouis: A vintage of such grandeur as to take many producers by surprise, as very few had had the opportunity of working with grapes with such high natural ripeness, with some *cuvées* made from grapes harvested at around 20 degrees potential alcohol. As in the Coteaux du Layon, this ripeness was more the result of concentration of the grapes than of a noble rot, so the *moelleux* and *liquoreux* tend to a particularly firm structure that will only soften with age, a trait shared to a lesser degree by the richer *demi-secs* which are only now beginning to open. A vintage to drink in the twenty-first century.

Sancerre, Pouilly and the Centre: The exceptional conditions of the summer led to particularly ripe wines with rich, complex fruit flavours (all those exotic fruits the New World seems so fond of), wines that were superb for early drinking. However, this ripeness meant that acidity levels were lower than normal, making wines that on the whole were unable to keep; these should now be drunk up. Exceptionally – perhaps for the first time ever – conditions allowed a dozen or so producers of Sancerre to make late-harvest wines of great power. Only time will tell their full potential, but the signs are that these will prove spectacular.

1990

Muscadet: Smilar to 1989, though higher yields led to wines with subtler character and a more classic Muscadet finesse.

Anjou and the Coteaux du Layon: The miracle vintage, the second 'year of the century' in two years. In the short term this surpasses the 1989, as a less severe drought has led to wines with equal ripeness but more fruit. The reds are particularly rewarding for drinking over the next five years (when the 1989s will come into their own), while the Layons are exceptionally rich and seem not to be closing up as severely as the 1989s.

Saumur: Perhaps finer for *moelleux* wines even than 1989 (with some Coteaux de Saumur capable of lasting 100 years). The reds tend to more fruit and less complex structure – fine, super-ripe wines that are unparalleled for drinking from now to 1999, but which will probably take second place to 1989 in the long term. One unexpected problem is that the fine conditions led some growers to reduce the use of sulphur to levels that have proved insufficient, and these wines are already showing signs of oxidation.

Chinon, Bourgueil and Saint-Nicolas-de-Bourgueil: Weather conditions very similar to 1989, with the exception of a little rain in late summer (helping the grapes to ripen more easily), led to wines of equal ripeness to the 1989s but with a softer structure that makes them more easily approachable now – though the best 1990s are undoubtedly finer than the lighter 1989s. The vintage to enjoy while waiting for the 1989s to mature.

Vouvray and Montlouis: Certainly of equal quality to the 1989; opinion is divided as to whether the 1990 or the 1989 is the greater vintage. More classic growing conditions certainly helped the onset of noble rot and the production of particularly powerful and elegant *moelleux*, producing wines with equal ripeness and more immediately attractive fruit than 1989. A vintage that will keep as well as 1989, but which will be more attractive to drink before maturity.

Sancerre, Pouilly and the Centre: Similar to 1989, with wines of great natural ripeness, though a more normal summer produced a more classic balance of acidity and wines with perhaps more elegance. Again, a vintage to be drunk young, though some of the finer reds should keep and improve over the next five years.

1991

Muscadet: Heavily affected by spring frosts, yields were down by as much as 70 per cent. This led to the production of particularly fine Muscadets (a truly lovely vintage) from the leading growers, but also to a number of very indifferent blends being released on to the market in an effort to satisfy demand.

Anjou and the Coteaux du Layon: As with the rest of the Loire, Anjou suffered from the spring frosts, though damage was not as universal (Savennières was hardly touched, while the Quarts-de-Chaume was down to 2 hectolitres per hectare), and the overall crop loss was less (around 50 per cent). Qualitatively, this was a pretty average year, with some of the better growers producing fine Layon wines with depth and richness (natural ripeness up to 17 degrees or even 18), though lacking the weight of the 1990s. Savennières made some particularly attractive wines.

Saumur: Frost damage again severely restricted production, bringing 70 per cent crop loss of reds and at least 50 per cent of whites. Those wines that were produced are split between the hopelessly green *cuvées* made with too high a proportion of under-ripe grapes, and riper, more classic wines (and particularly interesting dry whites) that are good for easy drinking – quite a blessing after two vintages of wines that need keeping.

Chinon, Bourgueil and Saint-Nicolas-de-Bourgueil: What 1991? With yields down to 5 hl/ha or less, this is as rare a vintage as can be found. It is easy to understand those growers who harvested anything that even looked like a grape, but it is worth hunting out the wines made by growers with the courage to reject any rotten or unripe grapes, as these have good soft fruit and plenty of character.

Vouvray and Montlouis: Frost damage led to a 90 per cent crop loss, and the vast majority of the grapes harvested went to the production of base wines for the sparkling Vouvrays (stocks were at a low level following 1989 and 1990). The few still wines (*secs* and *demi-secs*) produced show good fruit and are balanced with reasonable acidity, making delicious wines for early drinking.

Sancerre, Pouilly and the Centre: Less universally affected by the spring frosts than other areas of the Loire (an overall 35 per cent crop loss in Sancerre, compared with 90 per cent in Pouilly, Quincy and Menetou-Salon) this was a more classic Sauvignon vintage than 1989 or 1990, producing many wines of great fruit and finesse, wines that can genuinely claim to be elegant.

1992

Muscadet: As elsewhere on the Loire, vineyards rested after the 1991 frosts had a tendency to over-compensate, producing high yields. Growers who had been hit financially by the previous lack of wine tended to resist calls to prune short, so in general wines were made with perhaps excessive quantities per hectare, leading to a lack of depth and concentration. Better growers had foreseen this eventuality and produced exceedingly attractive wines with plenty of ripe fruit and low acidity, particularly fine in their youth.

Anjou and the Coteaux du Layon: Not a great year for Anjou as quantities were up, effectively diluting many wines. The better producers had foreseen this and had pruned short accordingly, and even in some cases carried out a 'green' harvest in the summer to reduce yields further. These producers made many fine, supple reds and dry whites and the occasional *cuvée* of rich *moelleux*, with the quantities of Layons depending on the care of the growers harvesting in successive *tries* and in their rejection of grapes affected by grey rot.

Saumur: Plenty of good, easy-drinking reds and dry whites, with those from the top producers showing greater depth and complexity, the result of keeping yields as low as possible. The best wines are on a par with some softer 1990s, giving a good drinking vintage and good quantities. The year also provided a major relief for producers of sparkling Saumur, as the ripeness of the 1989 and 1990 vintages had already led to a scarcity of stock before the 1991 frosts.

Chinon, Bourgueil and Saint-Nicolas-de-Bourgueil: A good vintage, producing wines with great fruit for early drinking. Although quantities were higher than average, yields were not excessive and wines are generally most attractive.

Vouvray and Montlouis: Yields were sufficiently high fully to replenish stocks of base wines for sparkling Vouvray. However, 'serious' havesting by the better growers (either in successive *tries* or with severe selective picking) who had already done everything to reduce yields, has produced a number of delicious still wines in a vintage particularly suited to the off-dry *sec-tendre* style.

Sancerre, Pouilly and the Centre: A good vintage, with many wines comparable to the excellent 1991s as yields, although higher than average, were generally reasonable. In the Sancerre villages of Bué and Crezancy, spring hail damage kept yields low and produced wines of great concentration.

1993

Muscadet: In contrast to other regions of France, the Loire escaped the worst excesses of the summer. It was, instead, marked with good, dry weather in July and August, the latter being practically rain-free.

Conditions were spoilt in the Pays Nantais just before harvest by a heavy storm, which downgraded the quality slightly but did not affect quantity.

After the high yields of 1992, 1993 saw a more normal crop, and little or no rot. The wines are attractively aromatic with good fruit and concentration. They have more structure than 1992 and more long-term potential. The best wines will benefit from not being released until after Easter, and will arguably give wines of a more classic balance than has been seen since 1988.

Anjou and Saumur: A dry end to winter and warm temperatures in March led to an early budding for all the different varieties of the region. A bad storm slowed flowering and caused the onset of mildew. However, a dry July and August with above average temperatures helped stop the attack, and good conditions continued through September.

1993 will thus see plenty of fine, aromatic dry whites, marked with freshness, *nervosité* and concentration. The reds are notable for the depth of colour and for the softness of their tannins. Although not superior to 1989 and 1990, these are obviously better than 1991, 1992 or even 1988.

Coteaux du Layon: It all depends on the number of *tries* and when the growers harvested. Those who harvested late picked at high sugar levels up to mid-November, with a high percentage of noble rot. With those growers, the wines will have great class, on a par with 1986 and 1988.

Touraine: Throughout the Touraine, despite cloudy weather and rain in the eastern half during the harvest, the vintage has produced exceptional wines. Touraine Sauvignons are crisp and invitingly aromatic, the best with a freshness and balance. To the west of the region, the reds of Chinon, Bourgueil and St-Nicolas-de-Bourgueil have tremendous fruit and colour, and 1993 promises a wealth of supple, well-balanced wines with notably more depth than the early-drinking 1992s.

Vouvray and Montlouis: Although great *moelleux* will be something of a rarity, these *appellations* have produced fine *secs* and *demi-secs*.

Sancerre and Pouilly Fumé: Hail storms in early May affected sectors of these vineyards and Menetou-Salon, cutting production down to 30 hl/ ha or less. Rain in the harvest caused an onset of rot in the Sauvignon Blanc, although Pinot Noir was picked in good condition.

Despite the weather, those who vinified carefully have made successful 1993s. The whites are aromatic with good fruit and reasonable acidity. The reds are rich and well-rounded with deep colour and excellent fruit.

APPENDIX 4

Major producers and their addresses

In the following list, producers are arranged alphabetically within the *appellation* in which their cellars are located. Many producers make wines under more than one *appellation*. For those unfamiliar with French addresses, the first two numbers in the postal code indicate the *département* in which the address is located. Relevant *départements* for this book are: 03, Allier; 18, Cher; 36, Indre; 37, Indre-et-Loire; 41, Loir-et-Cher; 42, Loire; 44, Loire-Atlantique; 45, Loiret; 49, Maine-et-Loire; 58, Nièvre; 63, Puy-de-Dôme; 69, Rhône; 72, Sarthe; 79, Deux-Sèvres; 85, Vendée; 86, Vienne.

Côtes d'Auvergne
M & R Rougeyron, 27 Rue de la Crouzette, 63119 Châteaugay.
Cave Saint-Verny, Route d'Issoire, 63960 Veyre-Monton.

Côtes du Forez
Les Vignerons Foreziens, Trelins, 42130 Boën-sur-Lignon.

Côte Roannaise
Pierre Gaume, Les Gillets, 42155 Lentigny.
Maurice Lutz, Domaine de Pavillon, 42820 Ambierle.

Saint-Pourçain
Guy et Serge Nebout, Route de Montluçon, 03500 Saint-Pourçain-sur-Sioule.
Ray Père et Fils, 03600 Saint-Pourçain-sur-Sioule.
Union des Vignerons, 03500 Saint-Pourçain-sur-Sioule.

Châteaumeillant
Jean-Pierre Bourdeau, Domaine du Parc, 18370 Châteaumeillant.
Maurice Landoix, Domaine de Feuillat, Beaumerle, 18370 Châteaumeillant.

P. Raffinat et Fils, Domaine des Tanneries, Rue des Tanneries, 18370
Châteaumeillant.

Cave des Vins de Châteaumeillant, Route du Culan, 18370
Châteaumeillant.

Sancerre

Bailly-Reverdy, Bué, 18300 Sancerre.

Bernard Balland, Bué, 18300 Sancerre.

Domaine Henri Bourgeois, Chavignol, 18300 Sancerre.

Lucien Crochet, Place de l'Église, Bué, 18300 Sancerre.

Vincent Delaporte, Chavignol, 18300 Sancerre.

Fouassier Père et Fils, Avenue de Verdun, 18300 Sancerre.

Gitton Père et Fils, Chemin de Lavaud, Ménétréol, 18300 Sancerre.

Pascal Jolivet, Les Franches, Route de Chavignol, 18300 Sancerre.

Domaine Laporte, Cave de la Cresle, Saint-Satur, 18300 Sancerre.

Alphonse Mellot, 18300 Sancerre.

Joseph Mellot, 18 Rue Saint-Martin, 18300 Sancerre.

Paul Millerioux, Champtin, 18300 Crézancy-en-Sancerre.

Domaine de la Poussie, Bué, 18300 Sancerre.

Jean Reverdy et Fils, Verdigny, 18300 Sancerre.

Jean-Max Roger, Bué, 18300 Sancerre.

Domaine Thomas, Verdigny, 18300 Sancerre.

Domaine Vacheron, 1 Rue du Puits Poulton, 18300 Sancerre.

Pouilly Fumé and Pouilly-sur-Loire

Michel Bailly, Les Loges, 58150 Pouilly-sur-Loire.

Patrick Coulbois, Les Berthiers, 58150 Pouilly-sur-Loire.

Didier Dagueneau, Saint-Andelain, 58150 Pouilly-sur-Loire.

Jean-Claude Dagueneau, Domaine des Berthiers, Les Berthiers, 58150
Pouilly-sur-Loire.

Paul Figeat, Les Loges, 58150 Pouilly-sur-Loire.

Jean-Michel Masson, Domaine Masson-Blondelet, 1 Rue de Paris, 58150
Pouilly-sur-Loire.

Patrick de Ladoucette, Château de Nozet, 58150 Pouilly-sur-Loire.

Les Caves de Pouilly-sur-Loire, Les Moulins à Vent, 58150 Pouilly-sur-
Loire.

Michel Redde et Fils, La Moynerie, 58150 Pouilly-sur-Loire.

Guy Saget, Route de Nevers, 58150 Pouilly-sur-Loire.

Château de Tracy, Tracy-sur-Loire, 58150 Pouilly-sur-Loire.

Menetou-Salon

Bernard Clement et Fils, Château de Chatenoy, 18510 Menetou-Salon.

Les Vignerons Jacques Coeur, Le Pré Babiau, 18510 Menetou-Salon.

Georges Chavet et Fils, GAEC des Brangers, 18510 Menetou-Salon.
Domaine Henri Pelle, Morogues, 18220 Les Aix-d'Auguillon.

Quincy
Claude Houssier, Domaine du Pressoir, 18120 Quincy.
René Marchais, 18120 Quincy.
Jean Mardon, Route de Reuilly, 18120 Quincy.
Domaine de la Maison Blanche, 18120 Quincy.
Domaine Meunier, 18120 Quincy.
Jean-Michel Sorbe, 18120 Quincy.

Reuilly
Bernard Aujard et Alain Mabillot, 36260 Reuilly.
Domaine Henri Beurdin, Le Carroir, 18120 Preuilly.
Gerard Bignonneau, La Chagnat, 18120 Brinay.
André et Pascal Desroches, Le Bourg, 18120 Lazenay.
Claude Lafond, Bois Saint-Denis, 36260 Reuilly.
Jacques Vincent, Les Chaumes, 18120 Lazenay.

Vins de l'Orléanais
Arnold Javoy et Fils, Mézières-les-Cléry, 45370 Cléry-Saint-André.
Clos Saint-Fiacre, 560 Rue de Saint-Fiacre, Mareau-aux-Prés, 45370
    Cléry-Saint-André.
Les Vignerons de la Grand'Maison, 550 Route des Muids, Mareau-aux-
    Prés, 45370 Cléry-Saint-André.

Coteaux du Giennois
INRA Station Vinicole, Cours-les-Cosne, 58201 Cosne-sur-Loire.
Domaine des Ormousseaux, Saint-Père, 58201 Cosne-sur-Loire.
Alain Paulat, Villemoison, Saint-Père, 58201 Cosne-sur-Loire.

Touraine
Jacky et Philippe Augis, Le Musa, Meusnes, 41130 Selles-sur-Cher.
Bougrier, 1 Rue des Vignes, 41400 Saint-Georges-sur-Cher.
Paul Buisse, 69 Route de Vierzon, 41400 Montrichard.
Pierre Chainier, La Boitardière, 37400 Amboise.
Château de Chenonceaux, 37150 Chenonceaux.
Jacques Delaunay, Domaine des Sablons, 40 Rue de la Liberté, 41110
    Pouillé.
Clos de la Dorée, Le Vau, 37320 Esvres-sur-Indre.
Héritiers Dubois, BP15, 41400 Saint-Georges-sur-Cher.
Domaine Dutertre, 20/21 Rue d'Enfer, 37530 Limeray.
Domaine de la Gabillière, 13 Route de Bléré, 37400 Amboise.

Château Gaillard, 41150 Mesland.
Lucien Launay, Angé, 41400 Montrichard.
Henry Marionnet, Domaine de la Charmoise, 41230 Soings.
Jacky Marteau, La Tesnières, 41110 Pouillé.
J-M Monmousseau, 71 Route de Vierzon, 41400 Montrichard.
Domaine Octavie, Oisly, 41700 Contres.
Gaston Pavy, La Basse-Chevrière, Saché, 37190 Azay-le-Rideau.
Jacky Preys, Le Bois Pontois, Meusnes, 41130 Selles-sur-Cher.
Gustave Rabier et Fils, 41500 Menars-le-Château.
Jean-Jacques Sard, La Chambrière, 37320 Esvres-sur-Indre.
Hubert Sinson, Le Musa, Meusnes, 41130 Selles-sur-Cher.
Les Vignerons des Coteaux Romanais, 41140 Saint-Romain-sur-Cher.
Confrérie des Vignerons de Oisly et Thésée, Oisly, 41700 Contres.

Valençay
Jean-François Roy, Lye, 36600 Valençay.
Les Vignerons de Fontguenand, Fontguenand, 36600 Valençay.

Cheverny
Michel Gendrier, Les Huards, 41700 Cour-Cheverny.
Patrice Hahusseau, Rue de la Chaumette, 41500 Muides-sur-Loire.
Maison Père et Fils, La Roche, 41120 Sambin.
Domaine du Salvard, Le Salvar, 41120 Fougères-sur-Bièvre.
Domaine Sauger Père et Fils, Les Touches, 41700 Fresnes.
Philippe Tessier, La Rue Colin, 41700 Cheverny.

Coteaux du Vendômois
Colin et Fils, La Gaudetterie, 41100 Thoré-la-Rochette.
Claude Norguet, Berger, 41100 Thoré-la-Rochette.
Cave Coopérative du Vendômois, 60 Avenue Petit Thouars, 41100 Villiers-sur-Loir.

Jasnières and Coteaux du Loir
André Fresneau, La Potence, Marçon, 72340 Chartre-sur-Loir.
Aubert de Rycke, Coteaux de la Pointe, Marçon, 72340 Chartre-sur-Loir.
Joël Gigou, 4 Rue des Caves, 72340 Chartre-sur-Loir.
Martial Boutard, La Varenne, Lhomme, 72340 Chartre-sur-Loir.

Vouvray
Domaine des Aubuisières, 32 Rue Gambetta, 37210 Vouvray.
Benoît-Gauthier, Domaine de la Racauderie, 37210 Parçay-Meslay.
Domaine Bourillon d'Orléans, 4 Rue du Chalateau, 37210 Rochecorbon.
Marc Brédif, 87 Quai de la Loire, 37210 Rochecorbon.

Philippe Brisebarre, Vallée Chartier, 37210 Vouvray.

Catherine et Didier Champalou, 7 Rue du Grand Ormeau, 37210
Vouvray.

Philippe Foreau, Le Clos Naudin, 14 Rue de la Croix Buisée, 37210
Vouvray.

Domaine Freslier, La Caillerie, 37210 Vouvray.

Château Gaudrelle, 87 Route de Monnaie, 37210 Vouvray.

Gaston Huët, Le Haut Lieu, 37210 Vouvray.

Jean-Pierre Laisement, 15 Rue de la Vallée Coquette, 37210 Vouvray.

Château de Moncontour, Rue de Moncontour, 37210 Rochecorbon.

Prince Philippe Poniatowski, Le Clos Baudin, 37210 Vouvray.

Cave des Producteurs, 38 Rue de la Vallée Coquette, 37210 Vouvray.

Domaine la Saboterie, 37210 Rochecorbon.

Vignerons du Val de Loire, 11 Rue du Commerce, 37210 Vouvray.

Cave des Viticulteurs du Vouvray, Château de Vaudenuits, 37210
Vouvray.

Domaine Viking, Melotin, 37380 Reugny.

Montlouis

Patrice Benoît, Nouy, 37270 Saint-Martin-le-Beau.

Berger Frères, Domaine et Caves des Liards, 136 Rue de Chenonceaux,
37370 Saint-Martin-le-Beau.

François Chidaine, 5 Grande Rue, Husseau, 37270 Montlouis-sur-Loire.

Deletang et Fils, 37320 Saint-Martin-le-Beau.

Cave Coopérative de Montlouis, 2 Route de Saint-Aignan, 37270
Montlouis-sur-Loire.

Domaine de la Taille aux Loups, 3 Rue du Serpent Volant, 37000 Tours.

Chinon

Bernard Baudry, 13 Coteau de Sonnay, 37500 Cravant-les-Coteaux.

Domaine Dozon, Le Rouilly, Ligré, 37500 Chinon.

Couly-Dutheil, 12 Rue Diderot, 37500 Chinon.

Château de la Grille, 37500 Chinon.

Charles Joguet, 37220 Sazilly.

Château de Ligré, Route de Champigny-sur-Veude, 37500 Chinon.

Cave des Vins de Rabelais, Les Aubuis, Saint-Louans, 37500 Chinon.

Jean-Maurice Raffault, La Croix, Savigny-en-Véron, 37420 Avoine.

Olga Raffault, Savigny-en-Véron, 37500 Chinon.

Domaine du Roncée, Panzoult, 37220 L'Île-Bouchard.

Gerard Spelty, 17 Rue Principale, 37500 Cravant-les-Coteaux.

Bourgueil and Saint-Nicolas-de-Bourgueil

Audebert et Fils, 20 Avenue Jean Causeret, 37140 Bourgueil.

Pierre et Catherine Bonhomme, Les Galichets, 37140 Restigné.

Caslot-Galbrun, La Hurolaie, 37140 Benais.

Christophe Chasle, 37130 Saint-Patrice.

Pierre-Jacques Druët, Le Pied Fourrier, 37140 Benais.

Domaine des Forges, 37140 Restigné.

Pierre Gauthier, La Motte, 37140 Benais.

Cave des Grands Vins de Bourgueil, Les Chevaliers, 37140 Restigné.

Pierre et Jean-Jacques Jamet, Le Fondis, 37140 Saint-Nicholas-de-Bourgueil.

Lamé-Delille-Boucard, Domaine des Chesnaies, 37140 Ingrandes-de-Touraine.

Pascal Lorieux, Le Bourg, 37140 Saint-Nicolas-de-Bourgueil.

Jacques Mabileau, La Gardière, 37140 Saint-Nicolas-de-Bourgueil.

Jean-Paul Mabileau, Domaine du Bourg, 37140 Saint-Nicolas-de-Bourgueil.

Bernard et Patrick Olivier, La Forcine, 37140 Saint-Nicolas-de-Bourgueil.

Joël Taluau, Chevrette, 37140 Saint-Nicolas-de-Bourgueil.

Saumur d'Origine and Crémant de Loire

Ackerman-Laurance, BP45, Saint-Hilaire-Saint-Florent, 49426 Saumur.

Bouvet-Ladubay, 1 Rue de l'Abbaye, Saint-Hilaire-Saint-Florent, 49400 Saumur.

Gratien et Meyer, Château Gratien, BP22, 49401 Saumur.

Domaine Langlois-Chateau, 3 Rue Léopold Palustre, BP 57, Saint-Hilaire-Saint-Florent, 49426 Saumur.

Caves de Moc et Baril, 24 Rue Jules Amiot, BP125, 49404 Saumur.

De Neuville, 31 Rue Jean Ackerman, BP8, Saint-Hilaire-Saint-Florent, 49426 Saumur.

Rémy-Pannier, Rue Léopold Palustre, Saint-Hilaire-Saint-Florent, 49426 Saumur.

Veuve Amiot, Compagnie Française des Grands Vins, 74 Rue d'Orléans, 49401 Saumur.

Saumur

Château de Beauregard, 2 Rue Saint-Julien, 49260 Le-Pûy-Notre-Dame.

Château de Brézé, 49260 Brézé.

Marc et Luc Delhumeau, Domaine de Brizé, 49540 Martigné-Briand.

Yves Lambert, Le Bourg, 49260 Saint-Just-sur-Dive.

Château de Montreuil-Bellay, 49260 Montreuil-Bellay.

Domaine de la Renière, 49260 Le-Pûy-Notre-Dame.

Régis Neaux, Domaine de Nerleux, 4 Rue de la Paleine, Saint-Cyr-en-
Bourg, 49260 Montreuil-Bellay.
Caves de Vignerons de Saumur, Saint-Cyr-en-Bourg, 49260 Montreuil-
Bellay.
Union Vinicole du Val de Loire, 54 Rue des Isles, 49400 Saumur.

Saumur-Champigny

Jean-Pierre et Eric Charruau, Domaine du Valbrun, 74 Rue Valbrun,
49730 Parnay.
Claude et Laurent Daheuiller, Domaine des Varinelles, 28 Rue du Ruau,
49400 Varrains.
Domaine Filliatreau, Chaintres, 49400 Dampierre-sur-Loire.
Château de Hureau, Le Hureau, 49400 Dampierre-sur-Loire.
Edouard Pisani-Ferry, Château de Targé, 49730 Parnay.
Rattron Frères, Clos de Cordeliers, Champigny, 49400 Saumur.

Anjou

Amy Frères, 41 Rue du Comte de Champagny, 49310 Vihiers.
Aubert Frères, Route d'Anjou, La Varenne, 49270 Saint-Laurent-des-
Autels.
Domaine de Bablut, Moulin de Bablut, 49320 Brissac-Quincé.
Les Caves de la Loire, 49320 Brissac-Quincé.
Collégiale des Domaines de Loire, 37 Rue Bourgonnier, 49000 Angers.
Vins Mottron, 49540 Martigné-Briand.
Christian Papin, Domaine de Haute-Perche, 9 Chemin de la Godelière,
49610 Saint-Melaine-sur-Aubance.
Maxime et Hervé Papin, Moulin des Besneries, 49610 Mozé-sur-Louet.
Château de Passavant, 49560 Passavant-sur-Layon.
Domaine Richou, Chauvigné, 49190 Mozé-sur-Louet.
Les Vins Touchais, Avenue Général Leclerc, 49700 Doué-la-Fontaine.

Savennières

Domaine du Closel, 1 Place du Mail, 49170 Savennières.
Clos de la Coulée de Serrant, 49170 Savennières.
Château d'Epiré, 49170 Savennières.
Mme Laroche, La Roche-aux-Moines, 49170 Savennières.
Pierre et Yves Soulez, Château de Chamboureau, 49170 Savennières.

Quarts-de-Chaume, Bonnezeaux and Coteaux du Layon

Château Bellerive, Chaume, 49190 Rochefort-sur-Loire.
Domaine des Baumard, Logis de la Giraudière, 8 Rue de l'Abbaye, 49190
Rochefort-sur-Loire.
Château du Breuil, Le Breuil, 49750 Beaulieu-sur-Layon.

Delaunay Père et Fils, Daudet, 49570 Montjean-sur-Loire.

Château de Fesles, 49380 Thouarcé.

Domaine des Forges, Les Barres, 49190 Saint-Aubin-de-Luigne.

Château de Fresnes, Le Fresne, 49380 Faye d'Anjou.

Laffourcade, Suronde, 49190 Rochefort-sur-Loire.

Vincent Lecointre, Château la Tomaze, 49380 Champ-sur-Layon.

Domaine de la Motte, 31 Avenue d'Angers, 49190 Rochefort-sur-Loire.

Vincent Ogereau, 44 Rue de la Belle Angevine, 49750 Saint-Lambert-du-Lattay.

Château de Plaisance, 49190 Rochefort-sur-Loire.

Château de la Roche, Rablay-sur-Layon, 49190 Rochefort-sur-Loire.

Domaine de Terrebrune, Place du Champ de Foire, 49380 Thouarcé.

Pierre-Yves Tijou, Château Soucherie, 49750 Beaulieu-sur-Layon.

Haut-Poitou

Cave Coopérative de Haut-Poitou, 32 Rue Alphonse Plauit, 86170 Neuville-de-Poitou.

Vins du Thouarsais

Michel Gigon, Route du Château, Oiron, 79100 Thouars.

Muscadet, Gros Plant and Coteaux d'Ancenis

Barre Frères, Beau-Soleil, 44190 Gorges.

Auguste Bonhomme, 1 Rue de la Roche, Gorges, 44190 Clisson.

Guy Bossard, Domaine de l'Écu, La Bretonnière, 44430 Le Landreau.

Claude Branger, Domaine de la Haute Fèvrie, La Fèvrie, 44690 Maisdon-sur-Sèvre.

Le Cellier des Ducs, Rue de Sèvre-et-Maine, 44450 La Chapelle-Basse-Mer.

Chéreau-Carré, Chasseloir, 44690 Saint-Fiacre-sur-Maine.

Bruno et Marie-Françoise Cormerais, La Chambaudière, 44190 Saint-Lumine-de-Clisson.

Donatien Bahuaud, La Loge, La Chapelle-Heulin, 44330 Vallet.

Drouet Frères, 8 Boulevard du Luxembourg, 44330 Vallet.

Gabare de Sèvre, Le Pé de Sèvre, Le Pallet, 44330 Vallet.

Gautier Audas, La Laize, 44115 Haute-Goulaine.

Château de la Galissonière, Le Pallet, 44330 Vallet.

Château de Goulaine, Haute-Goulaine, 44115 Basse-Goulaine.

Guilbaud Frères, Les Lilas, BP1, 44330 Mouzillon.

Jacques Guindon, La Couleuverdière, 44150 Saint-Géréon.

Hardy-Luneau, La Grange, 44330 Mouzillon.

Louis Metaireau, La Fèvrie Près Saint Fiacre, 44690 Maisdon-sur-Sèvre.

Château La Ragotière, 44330 Regrippière.

Beauquin Sautejeau, Domaine de l'Hyvernière, 44330 Le Pallet.
Sauvion et Fils, Château de Cleray, 44330 Vallet.
Les Vignerons de la Noëlle, Boulevard des Alliés, BP155, 44154 Ancenis.

Fiefs Vendéens
Vignobles Mercier, La Chaignée, 85770 Vix.
Patrice Michon et Fils, 11 Rue des Vallées, 85470 Brem-sur-Mer.

APPENDIX 5
Useful addresses in the Loire Valley

―――――

This is a list of professional wine organizations and promotional bodies who can supply information and literature about the wines of their area. For those telephoning the numbers given below, the number in brackets is the area code. If phoning from outside France, the country code is 33. *Addresses of producers and co-operatives will be found in Appendix 4, and addresses of hotels and restaurants in Appendix 6.*

Chapter 4: Sancerre
Union Viticole Sancerrois, 9 Route de Chavignol, 18300 Sancerre.
  Tel (48) 54 00 10.

Chapter 5: Pouilly
Commission de Promotion des Vins de Pouilly, 1 Rue de Paris, 58150
  Pouilly-sur-Loire. Tel (86) 39 00 34.

Chapter 6: Reuilly, Quincy and the lesser *appellations*
Claude Lafond, Bois Saint-Denis, 36260 Reuilly. Tel (54) 49 22 17.
Syndicat d'Initiative de Reuilly, 5 Rue Rabelais, 36260 Reuilly.
  Tel (54) 49 29 94.
Jean Mardon, Route de Reuilly, 18120 Quincy.
Hubert Veneau, Ormousseau Saint-Père. Tel (86) 28 01 17. (For Coteaux
  du Giennois.)

Chapter 7: Touraine and the Loir
Comité Interprofessionel des Vins de la Touraine et du Coeur Val de
  Loire, 19 Square Prosper Mérimée, 37000 Tours. Tel (47) 05 40 01.
Marcel Gendrier, Le Portail, 41700 Cheverny. Tel (54) 79 91 19.
André Fresneau, La Potence, 72340 Marçon. Tel (43) 44 13 70 (for
  Coteaux du Loir and Jasnières).
Maison des Vins de Blois, 84 Avenue de Verdun, 41000 Blois.

Chapter 8: Vouvray
Comité Interprofessionel des Vins de la Touraine et du Coeur Val de
Loire, 19 Square Prosper Mérimée, 37000 Tours. Tel (47) 05 40 01.
Office du Tourisme, RN152, 37210 Vouvray. Tel (47) 52 68 73.
L'Espace de la Vigne et du Vin, 37210 Vouvray. Tel (47) 52 76 00.
(Museum of viticulture and wine.)

Chapter 9: Montlouis
Comité Interprofessionel des Vins de la Touraine et du Coeur Val de
Loire, 19 Square Prosper Mérimée, 37000 Tours. Tel (47) 05 40 01.
Union Syndicale des Vins de Montlouis, 2 Grande Rue, 37270 Montlouis.
Tel (47) 50 83 72.

Chapter 10: The red wines of Touraine
Comité Interprofessional des Vins de la Touraine et du Coeur Val de
Loire, 19 Square Prosper Mérimée, 37000 Tours. Tel (47) 05 40 01.
Cave Touristique de la Dive Bouteille, 37140 Bourgueil.
Tel (47) 97 72 01. (For a display of Bourgeuil wines and wine tasting.)

Chapter 11: Saumur and Loire sparkling wines
Conseil Interprofessionel des Vins d'Anjou et de Saumur, 73 Rue
Plantagenet, 49023 Angers. Tel (41) 87 62 57.
Office du Tourisme, Place de la Bilange, 49400 Saumur.
Tel (41) 51 03 06.
Maison du Vin de Saumur, 25 Rue Beaurepaire, 49400 Saumur.
Tel (41) 51 16 40.
Association des Producteurs de Saumur, Lycée Viticole de Montreuil-
Bellay, 49260 Montreuil-Bellay. Tel (41) 52 31 96.

Chapter 12: Still Saumur and Saumur-Champigny
Conseil Interprofessionel des Vins d'Anjou et de Saumur, 73 Rue
Plantagenet, 49023 Angers. Tel (41) 87 62 57.
Office du Tourisme, Place de la Bilange, 49400 Saumur.
Tel (41) 51 03 06.
Maison du Vin, 25 Rue Beaurepaire, 49400 Saumur. Tel (41) 51 16 40.

Chapter 13: Anjou
Office du Tourisme, 71 Rue Plantagenet, 49024 Angers.
Tel (41) 88 69 93.
Conseil Interprofessionel des Vins d'Anjou et de Saumur, 73 Rue
Plantagenet, 49023 Angers. Tel (41) 87 62 57.

Chapter 14: Muscadet and the Pays Nantais

Comité Interprofessionel des Vins de Nantes, Maison des Vins, Bellevue,
44690 La Haye-Fouassière. Tel (40) 36 90 10.

Maison du Tourisme, Place du Commerce, 44000 Nantes.
Tel (40) 47 04 51.

APPENDIX 6

Where to eat and stay in the Loire

Here is a personal selection of hotels and restaurants which were good and worth the visit when I stayed or ate in them. Inevitably, standards and owners change, and some recommendations may not be as good as they were, while new ones will appear. I have chosen a range of hotels and restaurants from inexpensive to luxurious. When telephoning hotels to make bookings, always check on the room rate before confirming. Similarly, ask a restaurant the cost of *prix fixe* menus. That way, you won't be shocked by the size of the bill.

Chapter 3: The *appellations* of the mountains

HOTELS

Hôtel du Rhône, 8 Rue de Paris, 03200 Vichy. Tel (70) 98 28 01.
Pavillon Sevigné, 50–52 Boulevard Kennedy, 03200 Vichy.
   Tel (70) 32 16 22.
Le Chêne Vert, 35 Boulevard Ledru-Rollin, 03500 Saint-Pourçain-sur-
   Sioule. Tel (70) 45 40 65.

RESTAURANT

Le Vigosche, 2 Rue du Château, 63119 Châteaugay.
   Tel (73) 87 24 42.

Chapter 4: Sancerre and Menetou-Salon

HOTEL

Hôtel le Saint-Martin, 10 Rue Saint-Martin, 18300 Sancerre.
   Tel (48) 54 21 11.

RESTAURANTS

Le Caveau de Bué, 18300 Bué. Tel (48) 54 22 08.
Le Laurier, 29 Rue du Commerce, 18300 Saint-Satur. Tel (48) 54 17 20.
Restaurant de la Tour, 31 Place de la Halle, 18300 Sancerre.
    Tel (48) 54 00 81.
Auberge Joseph Mellot, 16 Nouvelle Place, 18300 Sancerre.
    Tel (48) 54 20 53.

Chapter 5: The wines of Pouilly

HOTEL

Le Relais Fleuri, 42 Avenue de la Tuilerie, 58150 Pouilly-sur-Loire.
    Tel (86) 39 12 99.

RESTAURANT

Le Coq Hardi, 42 Avenue de la Tuilerie, 58150 Pouilly-sur-Loire.
    Tel (86) 39 12 99.

Chapter 6: Reuilly, Quincy and the lesser *appellations* of the Centre

HOTELS

Hôtel d'Arc, 37 Rue de la République, 45000 Orléans.
    Tel (38) 53 10 94.
Le Sologne, Route de Châteauroux, 18100 Vierzon. Tel (48) 75 15 20.

RESTAURANT

Au Piet à Terre, Place de la Gendarmerie, 18370 Châteaumeillant.
    Tel (48) 61 41 74.

Chapter 7: Touraine and the Loir

HOTELS

Hôtel de l'Espace, Parc des Bretonnières, 37300 Joué-les-Tours.
    Tel (47) 67 54 34.
Domaine de Beauvois, 37230 Luynes. Tel (47) 55 50 11.
Le Choiseul, 36 Quai Charles Guinot, 37400 Amboise.
    Tel (47) 30 45 45.
Domaine de la Tortinière, 37250 Veigné-Montbazon. Tel (47) 26 00 19.
Relais des Landes, 41120 Les Montils. Tel (54) 44 03 53.
Hôtel l'Espagne, 9 Rue du Château, 36600 Valençay.
    Tel (54) 00 00 02.

Château du Breuil, Route de Fougères-sur-Bièvre, 41700 Cheverny.
 Tel (54) 44 20 20.

RESTAURANTS

Hôtel l'Espagne, 9 Rue du Château, 36600 Valençay.
 Tel (54) 00 00 02.
Les Trois Marchands, Place de l'Église, 41700 Cour-Cheverny.
 Tel (54) 79 96 44.
Le Saint-Romain, Saint-Romain-sur-Cher, 41140 Noyers-sur-Cher.
 Tel (54) 71 71 10.

Chapter 8: Vouvray

HOTELS

Auberge du Grand Vatel, 8 Rue Brulé, 37210 Vouvray.
 Tel (47) 52 70 32.
Les Hautes Roches, 86 Quai de la Loire, Rochecorbon.
 Tel (47) 52 88 88.

RESTAURANTS

Auberge du Grand Vatel, 8 Rue Brulé, 37210 Vouvray.
 Tel (47) 52 70 32.
Au Virage Gastronomique, 25 Rue Brulé, 37210 Vouvray.
 Tel (47) 52 70 02.

Chapter 9: Montlouis

HOTELS

Hôtel de la Ville, Place de la Mairie, 37270 Montlouis.
 Tel (47) 45 08 43.
Château de la Bourdaisière,25 Rue de la Bourdaisière, 37270 Montlouis.
 Tel (47) 45 16 31.

RESTAURANT

La Treille, 37270 Saint-Martin-le-Beau. Tel (47) 50 67 17.

Chapter 10: The great red wines of Touraine

HOTELS

Les Cèdres, Route du Château de Vilandry, 37510 Savonnières.
 Tel (47) 53 00 28.

Grand Hôtel de la Boule d'Or, 66 Quai Jeanne d'Arc, 37500 Chinon.
  Tel (47) 93 03 13.
L'Écu de France, Rue de Tours, 37140 Bourgueil. Tel (47) 97 70 18.
Le Chinon, Centre Saint-Jacques, 37500 Chinon. Tel (47) 98 48 48.
Château de Marçay, Marçay, 37500 Chinon. Tel (47) 93 03 47.

RESTAURANTS

Au Plaisir Gourmand, Quai Charles VII, 37500 Chinon.
  Tel (47) 93 20 48.
L'Anguille Vagabonde, Place de l'Église, 37500 Saint-Germain-sur-
  Vienne. Tel (47) 95 96 48.
Auberge de l'Île, 3 Place Bouchard, 37220 L'Île-Bouchard.
  Tel (47) 58 51 07.

Chapter 11: Saumur and Loire sparkling wines

HOTELS

Loire Hôtel, Rue du Vieux Pont, 49400 Saumur. Tel (41) 67 22 42.
Hôtel le Prieuré, 49350 Chenehutte-les-Tuffaux. Tel (41) 67 90 14.
Auberge du Thouet, 46 Place de la Mairie, 49400 Chacé.
  Tel (41) 52 97 02.

RESTAURANT

Les Délices du Château, Les Fouquières, Château de Saumur, 49400
  Saumur. Tel (41) 67 65 60.

Chapter 12: Still Saumur and Saumur-Champigny

HOTELS

See addresses under Chapter 11.

RESTAURANT

Champignonnière du Saut-aux-Loups, Avenue de Saumur, 49370
  Montsoreau. Tel (41) 51 70 30.

Chapter 13: Anjou

HOTELS

Hôtel d'Anjou, 1 Boulevard Maréchal Foch, 49100 Angers.
  Tel (41) 88 24 82.

Hôtel de France, 8 Place de la Gare, 49100 Angers. Tel (41) 88 49 42.

RESTAURANTS

Le Relais de Bonnezeaux, 49380 Thouarcé. Tel (41) 54 08 33.
Le Toussaint, 7 Rue Toussaint, 49000 Angers. Tel (41) 87 46 20.
Restaurant du Grand Pont, Behuard, 49190 Rochefort-sur-Loire.
   Tel (41) 72 21 64.

Chapter 14: Muscadet and the Pays Nantais

HOTELS

Hôtel le Jules Verne, 3 Rue du Couedic, 44000 Nantes.
   Tel (40) 35 74 50.
Abbaye de Villeneuve, Route des Sables-d'Olonne, 44840 Les Sorinières.
   Tel (40) 04 40 25.

RESTAURANTS

La Bonne Auberge, 1 Rue Olivier-de-Clisson, 44190 Clisson.
   Tel (40) 54 01 90.
Auberge Bel-Air, RN23 Direction Angers, 44150 Ancenis.
   Tel (40) 83 02 87.
Les Jardins de la Forge, Place Piliers, 49270 Champtoceaux.
   Tel (40) 83 56 23.
Villa Mon Rêve, 44115 Basse-Goulaine. Tel (40) 03 55 50.

APPENDIX 7

Areas under vine on the Loire

Département/region	1860	1956	1990
Loiret (Orléanais)	28,951	200	152
Cher (Sancerre and Menetou)	13,045	840	2,273
Eure-et-Loir (Coteaux du Loir etc.)	5,496	650	162
Touraine (Loir-et-Cher/Indre-et-Loire)	51,079	6,000	12,019
Indre (Reuilly and Valençay)	16,625	145	187
Maine-et-Loire (Anjou and Saumur)	26,401	16,000	18,925
Loire-Atlantique (Pays Nantais)	30,000	12,000	11,280

figures in hectares

Bibliography

General books

Broadbent, Michael, *The Great Vintage Wine Book II*, Mitchell Beazley, London, 1991

Chaptal, J. A., *Traité Théorique et Pratique sur la Culture de la Vigne*, Milan, 1801

Coates, Clive, *The Wines of France*, Century, London, 1990

De Serres, Olivier, *Le Théâtre d'Agriculture et le Mesnage des Champs*, Paris, 1804

Dion, R., *Histoire de la Vigne et du Vin en France*, Paris, 1959

Galet, Pierre, *Cépages et Vignobles de France*, Montpellier, 1958

George, Rosemary, *French Country Wines*, Faber and Faber, London, 1990

Hachette, *Guide Hachette des Vins de France*, Hachette, Paris, 1992

Johnson, Hugh, *The Story of Wine*, Mitchell Beazley, London, 1989

Johnson, Hugh, and Duijker, Hubrecht, *The Wine Atlas of France*, Mitchell Beazley, London, 1987

Jullien, A., *Topgraphie de Tous les Vignobles Connus*, Paris, 1816

Lachiver, M., *Vins, Vignes et Vignerons*, Paris, 1988

Redding, C., *A History and Description of Modern Wines*, London, 1833

Robinson, Jancis, *Vines, Grapes and Wines*, Mitchell Beazley, London, 1986

Spurrier, Steven, *Guide to French Wines*, Mitchell Beazley, London, 1991

Yapp, Robin and Judith, *Vineyards and Vignerons*, Blackmore Press, Shaftesbury, 1979

Books on the Loire

Blanchet, Suzanne, *Les Vins du Val de Loire*, Éditions Jema, Paris, 1982

Bréjoux, Pierre, *Les Vins de Loire*, Compagnie Parisienne d'Éditions Techniques, Paris, 1956

Duijker, Hubrecht, *The Loire, Alsace and Champagne*, Mitchell Beazley, London, 1983

BIBLIOGRAPHY

Dumay, Raymond *et al.*, *Les Vins de la Loire*, Paris, 1979

Girard, Monseigneur André, *Les Vignerons du Sancerrois*, Sancerre, 1962

Mastrojanni, Michel, *Le Grand Livre des Vins de Loire*, Éditions Solar, 1991

Raimbault, Henri, *Les Vins d'Anjou et de Saumur*, Angers, 1967

Seely, James, *The Loire Valley and its Wines*, Lennard Publishing, Oxford, 1989

Voss, Roger, *The Wines of the Loire, Alsace and the Rhône*, Mitchell Beazley, London, 1992

Index

Ackerman, Jean 137, 140
Ackerman-Laurance 137, 138, 140,
  145
  Cuvée Jean Baptiste 141
Alfred Gratien Champagne 138
Amboise 69, 77, 80, 82, 83, 110
Amigny 27, 39
andouillettes 202
Angers 158–9, 203
Angier, Philippe 73, 74
anguille 201
Anjou xi, 1, 4, 6, 7, 8, 10, 14, 68, 98,
  122, 136, 140, 144, 145, 158–78
Anjou Blanc ix, 10, 90, 159, 162, 167,
  172, 173, 174, 178
Anjou Coteaux de la Loire 162
Anjou Gamay 164–5
Anjou Rosé 72
Anjou Rouge 164, 165, 167, 170, 172,
  173, 175, 176
  Vieilles Vignes 173
Anjou Villages 162, 164, 165, 167,
  172, 173, 175, 176, 178
  Les Marzelles 178
Appellation Contrôlée (AC) 10, 14, 16
Appellation d'Origine Contrôlée (AC
  or AOC) 10
Arnaison 69
Aubance *see* Coteaux de l'Aubance
Aubinges 43
Aubois, Les 134–5
  Cuvée Jeanne d'Arc 135
Audebert et Fils 133
Augis, Jacky 87
Aujard, Bernard 61
Aupy, François 157
Auvergnat Blanc 67
Auvergnat Gris 67

Auvergnat Rouge 67
Azay-le-Rideau 6, 68, 83

Bahuaud, Donatien 188
Bailly, Jean-Louis 56
Balland-Chapuis, Joseph 65
Balzac, Honoré de 93, 95
Barbier, André 63
Baronnie d'Aignan 74
Batisses, Les 117
Baudry, Bernard 125, 126
Beaujolais 18, 19, 21, 22, 23
Beaujolais Nouveau 13, 22, 72
Beaujolais Primeur 165
Beaumont-en-Veron 124
Berger, Jean 114
Berger, Laurent 114
Berger, Michel 114
Berger, Philippe 114
Berger Frères 114
Berthiers, Les 48, 49, 50, 55
Besombes, Albert 63
beurre blanc 200–201
Bidon, Mlle 33
Bigolière, La 169
Bigonneau, Gerard 61
Billet, Jean-Yves 126–7
biodynamics 168
Blanc Foussy 145
Blanc Fumé de Pouilly 46
Bléré 69, 72
Blot, Jacky 117
boeuf Bourguignon 201
Bohier, Thomas 78
Bois-Gibault 47, 48, 53
Bois St-Denis 57, 60
Boisé 173
Boivin, Jacques 172, 173

Bondaroy 202
Bonnezeaux xi, 166, 172–3, 174
Bossard, Guy 185, 190
botrytis cinerea see noble rot
boudins 202
bouille Bordelaise 12
Bourdeau, Jean-Paul 64
Bourgeois, Arnaud 39, 40, 42
Bourgeois, Henri 39
Bourgeois, Jean-Marie 39
Bourgeois family 39, 41
Bourgeoise, La 41
Bourgueil xi, 4, 14, 68, 80, 119, 121–4, 126–9, 133, 201
Bourillon, Frédéric 98, 106
Bousset d'Or 21
Bouvet Cuvée Saphir 142
Bouvet Cuvée Trésor 142–3
Bouvet-Ladubay 137, 139–43, 145, 146
Branger, Claude 191
Brédif, Marc 52, 95
Brédut family 95, 107–8, 146
Bréjoux, Pierre 7, 42, 46, 89, 151
Breton, Le (Cabernet Franc) 69, 122
Brinay 62
Brissac 177
Brissac-Quincé 165
Brissebarre, Philippe 105, 108
Bué 25, 27, 28, 29, 30, 32, 33, 34
Buisse, Paul 80

Cabernet d'Anjou 163, 164, 175–8
Cabernet de Saumur 147, 149
Cabernet Franc 7, 67, 69, 72, 74, 75, 77, 78, 81, 82, 83, 85–8, 90, 117, 122, 123, 127, 128, 138, 139, 141, 144, 146, 151, 152, 154, 156, 157, 164, 165, 174, 176, 192, 194, 195, 196, 197, 199
Cabernet Sauvignon 7, 72, 83, 87, 90, 123, 138, 151, 152, 156, 164, 165, 194, 196, 197, 198
Caillebotte 202
Cave Co-operative, Chateaumeillant 64, 65
Cave Co-operative de Montlouis 115
Cave de le Bonne Dame 98, 106
Cave de la Cresle 41
Cave des Producteurs de Vouvray 108
Cave des Vignerons de Saint-Pourçain 24
Cave des Vignerons de Saumur 149

Cave des Viticulteurs de Vouvray 108
Cave du Haut-Poitou 195, 196
Cave Saint-Verny 19
Caves de la Loire, Les 145, 177
Caves de la Loire, Les 134, 135
Centre Pressurage du Val de Loire 141
Chabichou 202
Chablis 23, 27, 52, 190, 192
Chainier, François 80
Chainier, Pierre 80, 81
Chambray 79
Champagne 14, 27, 32, 60, 107, 136–41, 143
Champagne Berrichonne, La 60
Champagne Gosset 131
Champalou, Catherine 98, 99
Champalou, Didier 98, 99, 108
Champenois Pinot Meunier 79
Champigny 5
Champtin 25, 38, 39
Chançay 96
Chanturgue 19
Chapelle, La 173
Chapelle Heulin, La 188
chaptalization 51, 60, 103, 157
Charcuterie 202, 203
Chardonnay 10, 12, 19, 22, 23, 37, 67, 72, 74, 77, 84, 85, 87, 90, 91, 107, 138, 139, 141–6, 153, 156, 157, 172, 173, 174, 187, 189, 190, 194, 196–9
Charte de Qualite *cuvées*
Chasle, Christophe 129
Chasselas 7, 32, 46, 53, 54, 56
Château Bellerive 170
Ch de Brézé 157
Ch de Brizay 196
Ch de Cassmichère 188
Ch de Chaintres 152, 155
Ch de Chamboureau 169, 170
Ch de Chasseloir 189
Ch de Chenonceaux 77, 78
Ch de Fesles 172, 174
Ch de Fontaine-Audon 145
Ch de la Grille 131
Ch de la Roulerie 172
Ch de l'Aulée 83
Ch de l'Echarderie 170
Ch de Moncontour 95, 107
Ch de Montreuil-Bellay 157
Ch de Targé 151–2, 154
Ch de Tracy 52, 53
Ch du Breuil 173, 174, 175

Ch du Nozet 47, 48, 49, 50, 52
Ch du Nozet Baron de L 49, 52
Ch d'Yquem 118
Ch Gaillard 81
Ch Gaudrelle 99
  Reserve Spéciale 100
Ch Le Fuye 196
Ch Le Logis 196
Ch Moncontour 146
  Cuvée Brut Mosny 146
Châteaugay 18, 19–20
Châteaumeillant 64–5
Chaussard, Christian 100
Chavignal 27, 29, 30, 39, 42
cheeses 202
Chêne Marchand 29, 35
Chenin Blanc 7, 12, 66, 69, 72, 74, 77,
  78, 80, 81, 83, 85–91, 96, 98,
  99–100, 102, 105, 106, 107, 110,
  116, 117, 124, 135, 138, 139,
  141–6, 153, 154, 156, 157, 159,
  162, 165, 168, 169, 171, 173, 175,
  177, 182, 192, 194, 196–9
Chenonceaux 69, 77–8
Chéreau, Bernard Jr 189
Chéreau Carré 189
Cheverny 68, 74, 83–6
Chidaine, Yves 112–13, 114
Chinon ix, xi, 4, 6, 14, 68, 69, 72, 80,
  119, 121–5, 128–34, 141, 201
Choquet, Jacques 73
Chouze-sur-Loire 124
Cléry-Saint-André 67
Clos Chateau-Chevrier 100
Clos de Bourg 101, 102
Clos de Bourg Moelleux 102
Clos de Chailloux 33
Clos de Chêne Vert 130
Clos de l'Abbaye 157
Clos de la Comtesse 41
Clos de la Cure 130
Clos de la Dioterie 130
Clos de la Dorée 79
Clos de la Poussie 29, 32, 33, 34
Clos de l'Écho 133
Clos de l'Olive 134
Clos des Blanchais 44
Clos du Breuil 113
Clos du Papillon 169, 170
Clos du Pavillon 83
Clos le Vigneau 99
Clos Naudin 103, 104
Clos Saint-Fiacre 67

Clos Varennes de Grand Clos 130
Cointreau 203
Colbert family 157
Colin, Patrice 90
Colin et Fils 90–91
Comité Interprofessionel des Vins de
  Touraine 104
Compagnie Française des Grands Vins
  143
Confrérie des Vignerons de Oisly et
  Thésée 73, 74
coq au vin 201
Cordier company 33
Corent 19
Cormerais, Bruno 190, 191
Cosne 65, 66
Cot 72, 74, 76–9, 81–3, 85–8, 138,
  164, 196, 199
Côte Roannaise 18, 22–3
Coteaux Champenois 136
Coteaux d'Ancenis 182, 192
Coteaux de l'Aubance 166–7, 176–7
Coteaux de Saumur 147, 149, 154, 156
Coteaux de Touraine 69
Coteaux du Giennois 65–6
Coteaux du Giennois Cosne-sur-Loire
  65
Coteaux du Layon 10, 162, 166, 169,
  172, 173–5
  Chaume 166
  Villages 166
  Villages Beaulieu 174, 175
Coteaux du Loir 88, 90
Côtes d'Auvergne 18–21, 22
Côtes de Gien 65–6
Côtes du Forez xi, 21–22, 23
Coulbois, Patrick 55–6
Couly, Bertrand 133, 134
Couly-Dutheil 133, 134
Cour-Cheverny 68, 83–6
Couturaud, Patricia 19
Cravant-les-Coteaux 124, 125
Crémant Blanc Brut 77
Crémant de Loire 74, 77, 83, 107, 115,
  144–6, 163
Crémet Nantais 202
Crézancy 25, 27, 34, 35, 38, 42
Crochet, Lucien 34, 35
Crochet, Mme 34, 35
Crochet, Octave 32–33
Crottin de Chavignol 29–30, 39, 42,
  202
Croux, Christophe 196

Crus Classés ix
cuvée 14
Cuvée Finement Boisée 190
Cuvée François Ier 82, 83

Dagueneau, Didier 49, 50, 51, 52
Dagueneau, Jean-Claude 49, 50
Dagueneau, Serge 49
Dagueneau family 48–9
De Neuville 140
Delaille, Emmanuel 86
Delaille, Gilbert 86
Delaporte family 39
Deletang, Olivier 116, 117
Deletang et Fils 116, 117
Diane de Poitiers 196
Domaine Bourillon d'Orléans 98, 107
Domaine de Chatenoy 44
Domaine de Feuillat 64
Domaine de Grand'Maison 145
Domaine de la Bigolière 170
Domaine de la Chatoire 74
Domaine de la Croix 135
Domaine de la Gabillière 77
Domaine de la Poussie 33, 34
Domaine de la Renière 156
    Cuvée Prestige 157
    Cuvée Vieilles Vignes 157
Domaine de la Taille aux Loups 117
Domaine de la Tour-Signy 196
Domaine de Langlois-Chateau 145
Domaine de L'Écu 185, 186
Domaine de Maison Blanche 63
Domaine de Nerleux 150
Domaine de Salvard 86
Domaine Deletang 116–17
Domaine des Aubuisières 99
Domaine des Berthiers 49
Domaine des Forges 126
    Cuvée Les Bezards 127
    Cuvée Printemps 127
    Vieilles Vignes 127
Domaine des Liards 114
Domaine des Ormousseaux 66
Domaine du Grand Cerf 74
Domaine du Hureau 153, 154
Domaine du Parc 64
Domaine du Pressoir 63
Domaine du Rochoy 41
Domaine Filliatreau 155
Domaine Henri Beurdin 61
Domaine Huët 168
Domaine Jacques Mabileau 132

Domaine Jean Mardon 63
Domaine la Moussière 38
Domaine la Sabotière 100
Domaine Laporte 41
Domaine Masson-Blondelet 54
Domaine Paul Buisse 80
Domaine René Couly 134
Domaine Richou 145
Domaines Baumard 170
Domes de Chenonceaux, Les 78
Druet, Pierre-Jacques 127, 128, 129
Duboeuf, Georges 187
Dutertre, Gilles 82
Dutertre, Jacques 82, 83
Dutheil, Madeleine 133

Ecole Supérieure d'Agriculture et
    Viticulture 174
Estutt d'Assay, Alain 53
Estutt d'Assay, Henri 53
Estutt d'Assay family 52–3

Fié Gris 76
Fiefs Vendéens 196–7
Filliatreau, Mme 155
Filliatreau, Paul 155
fish 200, 201, 203
foie de veau 202, 203
Folle Blanche see Gros Plant
Foreau, André 103
Foreau, Philippe 102–3
Forme de Montbrison 202
fouaces 202
Fouquet, Bernard 99

Gadais, Christophe 41
Gamay xi, 7, 8, 13, 19, 22, 23, 24,
    27–8, 60, 62, 64, 66, 72–5, 77, 78,
    79, 81, 82, 83, 85–8, 90, 91, 123,
    138, 164, 182, 192, 194, 196–9
Gamay Côte Roannaise 22–3
Gamay Coteaux du Loir 89–90
Gamay d'Auvergne 19
Gamay de Touraine 74
Gamay Noir-Jus Blanc 22
Gamay Romain 22
Gateau Pithiviers 202
Gaudrelle, La 99
Gautier, Benoît 100
Gien 65, 66
Gigon, Michel 194–5
Gigou, Joël 88, 89, 90
Girard, André 31

Girault, Beatrice 81, 82
Girault, Vincent 81, 82
Grand Chermarin, Le 28, 29, 31
Grand Domaine 42
Grand Mont, Le 128
Grand Noir, Le 32
Gratien, Alfred 141
Gratien et Meyer 137, 138, 141, 149
    Cardinal 141
    Cuvée Flame 141
Gravières d'Amador, Les 134
Gravois, Les 129
Gravot vineyard 119
Grezeaux 126
Gris Meunier 67, 79
Grolleau 69, 72, 77, 83, 87, 88, 139,
    164, 174
Grolleau Gris 197
Gros Plant (Folle Blanche) 182, 184,
    186, 195, 199, 200
Groslot 146, 196, 198
Gues d'Amants 99
Guyot, 89

Haies Martels 126
Hardouin family 202
Haut Lieu, Le 101, 102
Haut-Poitou 195, 197
Houssier, Claude 63
Huët, Gaston 101–2
Hugues-Gay, René 156, 157
Humbligny 43

INAO 74
Institut National de la Recherche
    Agricole (INRA) 66
Isoles 27

Jasnières 88, 89, 90
Jasnières Cuvée de l'Aillerie 89
Joguet, Charles 129–31
Joly, Nicolas 167–9, 170
Joué 69
Joué-les-Tours 79
Jullien, A. 32, 46, 66, 67, 69, 89, 151

L d'Or, Le 190
La Ferté 57, 60
la Morandière, M. de 78
Ladoucette, de (family) 48
Ladoucette, Patrick de 52, 95
Lafond, Claude 60, 61, 62
Lafond, Comte 52

Lalanne, M. 170, 171, 172
Landois, Maurice 64
Langlois-Chateau 137, 138, 144, 145,
    157
Langlois Crémant 146
Larçay 79
Laurance, Emilie 137
Laurent, Joseph 24
Lenôtre, Gaston 172
Lerné 72
Loges, Les 47, 48, 49, 56
Loir river 88
Luneau, Pierre 190
Luneau, Remy 190

Mabileau, Jacques 132
Mabillot, Alain 61
Mace-Doux 69
Madargues 19
Maimbray 27
Malbec 72, 74, 77
Malvoisie 192
Manoir La Grange 190
Marchais, René 63
Marcilly 22
Mareau-aux-Prés 66, 67
Mareuil 197
Martini e Rossi 143
mascarons Nantais 201
Masson, Jean-Michel 48, 54
Masson, Michelle, née Blondelet 54
Masson-Blondelet family 53
Master de Donatien, Le 188
Matelote d'anguille 201
meat 201, 203
Melier 32
Mellot, Alphonse 37–8, 39
Melon de Bourgogne 7, 183–4, 189,
    197
Menetou-Ratel 27
Menetou-Salon 30, 31, 42–4
Ménétréal-sous-Sancerre 27
Menier family 78
Menu Pineau 72, 87
Merlot 196
Mesland 81, 82
Metaireau, Louis 187, 188
Méthode Traditionelle 105
Meyer, Jean 141
Mézières-lez-Cléry 66, 67
Millerioux, Paul 38, 39
Monmousseau 96, 107
Monmousseau, Armand 99, 100

Monmousseau, J.M. 146
Monmousseau, Patrice 140–43
Mont, Le 101
Montagne, La 172
Montgolfier, M. de 144, 145
Montigny 27
Montigny family 67
Montlouis 6, 14, 68, 80, 93, 110–18, 145, 146, 202
   Cuvée des Loups 118
   Cuvée Les Lys 113
   Moelleux 115
   Mousseux 115
   Mousseux Cuvée Prestige 115–16
   Sec 115
Montrichard 80, 146
Monts Damnés, Les 30, 40, 41
Morgat, Marc 174
Morgat, Mme 174
Morillon 69
Morogues 43
Moueix family 133
Moulin des Besneries 175, 176
Mousseau, Michel 79
Moyer, Dominique, 116
Mureau, Vincent 75
Muscadet ix, xi, 7, 8, 13, 15, 16, 17, 23, 80, 106, 133, 145, 179–93, 195, 199, 200
Muscadet des Coteaux de la Loire 182, 192
Muscadet Sèvre et Maine 15, 182, 191, 192

Neau, Marcel 150
Neau, Régis 150
négociants (main references) 11, 12, 15, 16, 17, 80–81, 133, 134
New World Sauvignon Blanc 47
Nicolay, Nicolas de
Noble Joué, Le 79–80
noble rot 14, 93, 98, 99, 100, 102, 105, 115, 116, 117, 165, 166, 168, 170–77
Noizay 96

oidium 69, 195
Oisly 73, 74, 75, 80
Olivet 67
Onzain 81
organic farming 185–6
Orléans 66–7

Panzoult 124
Papin, Hervé 175, 176
Parassy 43
Parçay-Meslay 96
Paul Raffinat et Fils 64
Paulat, Alain 66
Pelle, Eric 43
Pelle, Henri 43
Petits-Boulay 117
phylloxera xi, 7, 8, 18, 32, 53, 69, 129, 195
Pibaleau Père et Fils 83
Pic, Albert 52
Piet-Finet, M. et Mme 64
Pigny 43
Pineau, Le 32
Pineau d'Anjou 7
Pineau d'Aunis 7, 69, 72, 76, 87, 88, 90, 91, 123, 139, 156, 164, 198
Pineau de la Loire 7, 85, 96, 110
Pinguet, Noël 101
Pinot Blanc 66, 174, 196
Pinot Gris 32, 60, 62, 72, 79
Pinot Meunier 67, 69, 72, 146
Pinot Noir 7, 8, 19, 22, 23, 24, 27, 28, 31, 32, 39, 42, 44, 60, 61, 62, 64, 66, 67, 72, 76, 77, 79, 85, 86, 87, 90, 91, 107, 123, 138, 145, 164, 174, 196, 197, 199
Pisani-Ferry, Edouard 152–3
Pissotte 197
Plafond Limité de Classement (PLC) 16
pot-au-feu du broconnier 202
Pouilly Fumé ix, 30, 46, 47, 49, 51–6, 63, 65, 66, 162
   Cuvée d'Ève 49, 50
   Cuvée la Moynerie 54–5
   Cuvée Majorum 55
   Cuvée MB 56
   La Charnoie 56
   La Corneille 56
   Les Angelots 54
   Les Bascoins 54
   Les Loges 56
   Tradition Cullus 54
   Villa Paulus 54
Pouilly-sur-Loire xi, 4, 7, 8, 15, 27, 28, 32, 38, 42, 45–56, 65
Poupat, Jean 66
pourriture noble see noble rot
Preys, Jacky 75–7, 87
primeurs 201
Puy de Dôme 18, 19

Quantilly 43
Quarts de Chaume xi, 166, 169, 170–72, 174
Quincy 7, 42, 60–63, 86

Rabelais, François 72, 89, 119, 122, 202
Raffault, Jean-Maurice 121, 132, 135
Redde, Michel 54
Redde, Thierry 54, 55
Redding, Cyrus 69, 151
Rémy-Pannier 140
Renaison-de-la-Tache 22
rendement 16–17
Rendement Annuel 16
Renou, Michel 177, 178
Restigné 124
Reugny 96
Reuilly 6, 7, 42, 57, 60–62, 63, 86
Reverdy family 39
rillettes 202
rillons de veau 202
Robinson, Jancis 7
Roche-aux-Moines 101, 167, 169, 170
Rochecorbon 96, 100, 106, 111, 146
Rochecot 129
Roger, Jean-Max 28–31
Romorantin grape 84, 85, 87
Ronsard, Pierre de 69, 89
Rosé d'Anjou 163, 164, 176, 177, 178
Rosé de Loire 163, 164, 177
Rougeyron, Michel 19, 21
Rougeyron, Roland 19, 21

Sacy 23
Saint-Aignan 76
Saint-Andelain 47, 48, 49, 51, 54, 56
Saint-Avertin 79
Saint-Céols 43
Saint-Cyr-en-Bourg 139, 149–50, 151, 157, 196
Saint-Emilion 122
Saint-Hilaire-Saint-Florent 137, 140–43
Saint-Hilaire-Saint-Mesmin 67
Saint-Jacques Jasnières 89
Saint-Jean-de-Bray 66
Saint-Lumine-de-Clisson 190
Saint-Martin-le-Beau 112, 114, 116
Saint-Maure 202
Saint-Nicholas-de-Bourgueil 119, 122–5, 132
Saint-Patrice 124, 129

Saint-Pourçain-sur-Sioule 23–24
Saint-Roman-sur-Cher 74, 75
Saint-Satur 27
Sainte-Gemme-en-Sancerrois 27
Sainte-Marie clos 66
Sainte-Radegonde 96
Salon des Vins de Loire 158–9, 175
Sancerre xi, 4–8, 15, 16, 25–47, 50–54, 61, 63, 65, 106, 145, 162, 202
  Blanc 27
  Clos du Roy 35–6, 39
  Croix du Roy 35–6
  Cuvée Edmond 38
  Cuvée Etienne Henri 40, 41
  Cuvée GC 28, 29
  Cuvée Le Chêne 35
  Cuvée Prestige 35
  Grande Réserve 41
  Rouge 119
  Vieilles Vignes 40
sandre 201
sauces 200, 201
Saulcet 23
Saumur x, 1, 7, 15, 17, 63, 72, 136–46, 158
Saumur Blanc 147, 149, 153, 155, 156, 157
Saumur-Champigny 4, 5, 119, 147, 149–56
  Cuvée du President 150
  Cuvée Lena Filliatreau 155–6
  Vieilles Vignes 155
Saumur d'Origine 139, 144, 147
Saumur Rouge 147, 149, 156
  Cuvée du Conseil 150
Sauvignon 32, 34, 37, 46, 51, 61, 81, 85, 86, 87, 199
Sauvignon Blanc ix, 7, 12, 23, 27, 28, 29, 33, 42, 44, 45, 46, 50, 52, 57, 60, 62, 63, 66, 72–5, 77, 78, 84, 87, 117, 138, 146, 156, 174, 196, 197, 198, 199
Sauvignon de Touraine 74, 80
Sauvignon Rosé 76
Sauvion, Jean-Ernest 187, 188
Savary, Teddy 144, 145
Savennières 4, 6, 90, 101, 159, 162, 165, 167, 175, 178, 201
  Becherelle 168
  Couleé de Serrant 162, 167, 168, 169
Savennières-Roche-aux-Moines 162, 167, 168

Clos de la Bergerie 168
Savigny-en-Véron 124
Sazilly 129, 130
Scott, Sir Walter 101
Seely, James 155
Selection Chainier 80
Seydoux family 141
Sinson, Hübert 87
Sorbe, Jean-Michel 61, 63
Soulangis 43
Soulez, Pierre 169, 170
Soulez, Yves 169
Steiner, Rudolf 168
sur lie 186–7, 188
Sury-en-Vaux 27
Syndicat des Viticulteurs 28

Taitlinger Champagne 142
tarte aux abricots à la crème de
    Pithiviers 202
Tarte Tatin 202
Teinturier 67
Terriades, Les 178
Tessier, Philippe 85, 86
Thauvenay 27, 45
Thésée 73, 75, 80
Thoré-la-Rochette 90
Thouarcé 177
Tigny, de (family) 155
Touraine xi, 1, 4, 6, 7, 8, 10, 68–93,
    114, 119–35, 136, 140, 144, 145,
    146
Touraine-Amboise 72, 82
Touraine-Azay-le-Rideau 72
Touraine Blanc 76
Touraine-Mesland 72, 81
Touraine Mousseux 72
Touraine Pétillant 72
Touraine Primeur 13, 72
Touraine Rouge 72, 79, 83, 115
    Tradition 72
Touraine Sauvignon AC 86
Touraine Sauvignon Clos des
    Pillotières 76
Tracy-sur-Loire 47, 48, 53
Tresallier 23

Union Viticole 49

Vacheron, Denis 36, 37, 39
Vacheron, Jean-Loius 36, 37, 39
Valençay 68, 76, 86–7, 202
Vatan, Philippe 153, 154, 155
Vaumoreau 129
Veaugues 27
Vendée 197
Vendôme 90
Vendôme Bleu 202
Veneau, Hubert 66
Verdigny 27
Vernou-sur-Brenne 96
Veuve Amiot 137, 141, 143–4, 145
Veyre-Mouton 19
vignerons 11
Vignerons d'Art, Les 187
Vignerons de la Grand'Maison, Les 67
Vignerons de la Noëlle 192–3
Vignerons Foreziens, Les 22
Vignoux-sous-les-Aix 43
Vin de l'Orléanais 67
Vin de Pays de Retz 199
Vin de Pays des Marches de Bretagne
    199
Vin de Pays du Cher 62
Vin de Pays du Jardin de la France 10,
    62, 74, 173, 187, 198, 199
Vin de Pays d'Urfé 19, 22, 199
vin de table 9, 16
'Vin Noble' 63
Vincent, Jacques 62
Vinon 34
vins de cépages 80
vins de pays 9–10, 60, 198–9
Vins Délimités de Qualité Superieure
    (VDQS) 10, 19, 21, 22, 64, 65, 67,
    68, 76, 83, 84, 86, 87, 90, 182, 186,
    192, 194, 195, 197
Vins du Thouarsais 194–5
viticulteurs 10–11
Vix 197
Vouvray 6, 10, 14, 16, 52, 68, 80–109,
    110–13, 116, 145, 146, 165, 202
    Brut 102, 108
    Club Tradition 98
    Moelleux 99
    Mousseux 108
    Pétillant 95, 97
    Tendre 99